Counseling Women With Breast Cancer

Women's Mental Health and Development

Series Editor: Barbara F. Okun, *Northeastern University*

Women's Mental Health and Development covers therapeutic issues of current relevance to women. This book series offers up-to-date, practical, culture-sensitive, professional resources for counselors, social workers, psychologists, nurse practitioners, family therapists, and others in the helping professions. Volumes in this series are also of significant value to scholars in gender studies and women's studies.

This series is designed to deal particularly with those issues and populations underrepresented in the current professional literature. Particular attention is paid to the sociocultural contexts of these issues and populations. While some of the volumes of this series cover topics pertinent to all women, others focus on topics applicable to specific groups. The series integrates material from established models, emerging theoretical constructs, and solid empirical findings in a format designed to be applicable for clinical practice. Professionals and trainees in a variety of mental health fields will find these readable, user-friendly volumes immediately useful.

Authors of volumes in this series are selected on the basis of their scholarship and clinical expertise. The editorial board is composed of leading clinicians and scholars from psychology, counseling, and social work.

Editorial Board

Counseling
Women
With
Breast Cancer
A Guide for Professionals

Merle A. Keitel
Mary Kopala

Women's Mental Health & Development, Volume 5

SAGE Publications
International Educational and Professional Publisher
Thousand Oaks   London   New Delhi

For information:

Sage Publications, Inc.
2455 Teller Road
Thousand Oaks, California 91320
E-mail: order@sagepub.com

Sage Publications Ltd.
6 Bonhill Street
London EC2A 4PU
United Kingdom

Sage Publications India Pvt. Ltd.
M-32 Market
Greater Kailash I
New Delhi 110 048 India

Printed in the United States of America

Library of Congress Cataloging-in-Publication Data

Keitel, Merle A.
 Counseling women with breast cancer: A guide for professionals / by: Merle A. Keitel and Mary Kopala.
     p. cm. — (Women's mental health and development; v. 5)
 Includes bibliographical references and index.
  ISBN 0-7619-0833-1 (cloth: alk. paper)
  ISBN 0-7619-0834-X (pbk.: alk. paper)
  1. Breast—Cancer—Patients—Counseling of. I. Kopala, Mary. II.
Title. III. Series.
  RC280.B8 K44 2000
  616.99′449—dc21   00-009082

This book is printed on acid-free paper.

00 01 02 03 04 05 06 7 6 5 4 3 2 1

Acquiring Editor:	Nancy Hale
Editorial Assistant:	Heidi Van Middlesworth
Production Editor:	Sanford Robinson
Editorial Assistant:	Candice Crosetti
Typesetter:	Rebecca Evans
Indexer:	Molly Hall
Cover Designer:	Candice Harman

Contents

Series Editor's Introduction

Breast cancer is an issue for and concern of every woman. Primarily, breast cancer is a woman's issue. However, it is also a concern for men, both those rare men who contract this form of cancer and those men who experience a loved one's breast cancer. Some women, because of their personal experiences, are consciously attuned to breast cancer issues; others prefer to ignore these issues because of personal or cultural ignorance, denial, or other individual factors. The frank, open discussions of women such as Betty Ford and Nancy Reagan have contributed to reducing the social stigma and avoidance of acknowledging the incidence and effects of breast cancer. Today, the media report daily on emerging experimental treatments and possible cultural and geographical contributing factors to the incidence of breast cancer. There are also public campaigns by the American Cancer Society, health care, and women's groups to educate the public about the importance of early detection.

These educational efforts have led to one of the many controversies in health care economics today. The controversy is about the validity and accessibility of early screening procedures, such as mammograms, self-examinations, and physical examinations. Cost-effective health care administrators question the efficacy of these procedures. Health care providers differ in their views, influenced by gender, personal backgrounds, and professional contexts.

The Sage Women's Mental Health and Development series is proud of Merle Keitel and Mary Kopala's state-of-the-art, comprehensive volume *Counseling Women With Breast Cancer.* We believe this to be a unique book in its integration of the authors' personal experiences with family members' struggles with cancer; their extensive clinical experience with women who have had, who currently have, or who are coping with a family member or close friend's breast cancer; their scholarly synthesis of the significant current literature on breast cancer incidence, diagnoses, treatment, follow-up, and psychological and physical impact on the patient and her family. They also present us the most recent epidemiological data, cutting across race, ethnicity, and class.

This book fills the need for a scholarly, clinically relevant discussion about women's individualized and culture-based reactions and responses to breast cancer. It advocates a multidisciplinary treatment approach (which includes all health care providers, the patient, and her family) and focuses on the woman, her reactions and responses to this disease, and her quality of life as she struggles to balance competing demands from living with cancer with her personal, family, and work responsibilities and commitments. Obviously, a woman's views about her self, herself-in-relation, and the medical and larger worlds shift as her previous notions falter in the dramatic crisis of dealing with a potentially fatal illness.

One of the most significant features of this volume for clinicians and their patients is the authors' documented refutation of stereotypical myths. They present available documented knowledge about the incidence, diagnoses, treatments, prognoses, and available resources (both traditional and alternative) regarding breast cancer. The authors' emphasis on diversity and on the highly individualized responses of patients and their family members is an important part of this feature.

The authors are multipartial in their discussions of different perspectives. Their suggestions and guidelines for clinicians' thinking about, understanding of, and assessment and treatment for women coping with breast cancer are presented respectfully and helpfully rather than as dogmatic directives. Their writing is both scholarly and accessible and is an effective learning and teaching tool.

Because of these features, our Editorial Board has been enthusiastic about this project since its inception. As clinicians, we can all benefit from extended discussion of what reactions to expect from diagnosed women and their families and of what to look for, as well as detailed information about how to respond. We all need to continuously update our understanding of the nature, course, and treatment options for the various types of breast cancer.

This is the final volume of the Sage Women's Mental Health and Development series. Jim Nageotte, the Sage editor of this series, and I are grateful to our editors (female and male) and authors for their creative inputs and steadfast dedication to issues concerning diverse women's contemporary health (which includes mental health) and life quality across the life span.

Barbara F. Okun, Ph.D.
Series Editor

Preface

Counseling Women With Breast Cancer comprehensively reviews the medical, psychological, social, and political aspects of breast cancer and is intended primarily for mental health practitioners (e.g., social workers, counselors, psychologists, and psychiatrists) who work closely with breast cancer patients or their significant others and family members. It is also recommended for physicians, nurses, and other medical personnel who interact with women who have been diagnosed with breast cancer.

Mental health professionals have a vital role to play in improving the quality of life and even the survival time of breast cancer patients. They can, of course, directly provide psychological services, but they can also serve as advocates for breast cancer patients in the larger political sphere. Finally, they can train physicians, nurses, and other medical personnel in active listening skills and familiarize them with the psychosocial issues that women with breast cancer confront at various points in the disease and treatment process.

Mental health professionals can consult with medical personnel so that they can more effectively provide the type of support patients need. Learning that women with breast cancer have different coping styles and varying needs for information may help physicians to tailor their communications to patients. For example, crisis intervention literature suggests that people experience high distress for up to 6 weeks after being diagnosed with a life-threatening disease. After that period, coping responses and resources are engaged more effectively, and distress tends to decrease. Understanding the time frame for psychological morbidity can help medical personnel to refer women whose psychological distress remains elevated.

Counseling Women With Breast Cancer focuses primarily on how mental health professionals can intervene with women diagnosed with breast cancer. It also addresses issues relevant to women who are worried about developing breast cancer. Concerns of family members—especially partners and children—of women with breast cancer are discussed. This book presents integrated reviews of the literature and case studies drawn from different racial-ethnic and cultural groups that illustrate psychological issues and interventions. At all times, the development of a therapeutic relationship is emphasized.

Chapter 1 describes our rationale for writing this book. Our personal experiences with our mothers' illnesses, our clinical experiences with women with breast cancer, our recognition of the rapidly changing health care system in the United States, and the growing evidence for a mind-body connection (psychoneuroimmunology) were the driving forces for this project. Managed health care is affecting both medical and psychological treatment. Helping professionals must increasingly take on roles as advocates for all their clients, and particularly for low-income and racial minority women, who are more likely to be diagnosed at later stages of the disease and have higher rates of mortality.

Chapter 2 explains different types of breast cancer, medical and surgical treatments and their side effects, and alternatives to traditional medical treatments. Chapter 3 provides information about prevention of breast cancer, including mammography (and the controversies surrounding it), breast exams, and the impact of physicians on health promotion. We discuss psychological and emotional reactions of individuals who are at high risk for breast cancer, prophylactic treatment, and genetic testing for breast cancer susceptibility.

Chapter 4 explores the early, middle, later, and terminal stages of the cancer experience. What is it like to discover a lump, participate in diagnostic testing, receive a diagnosis, undergo surgical or medical treatment, and live with the uncertainty of the posttreatment period? The discussion includes psychological reactions, changes in identity and life patterns, and fears and concerns at each stage of the process.

Chapter 5 details the process of psychosocial assessment. It underscores the importance of exploring social variables, such as culture, religion, and socioeconomic status; biological and health considerations; and psychological variables such as coping styles, developmental stages, and personality. It also explicates how social, biological, and psychological factors can influence psychological adjustment, treatment and compliance issues, and prognosis.

Chapter 6 describes different individual interventions that are useful when counseling women with breast cancer. Chapter 7 describes group counseling. Chapter 8 focuses on the family members of women with breast cancer, including reactions of partners and children and their impact on the woman's own adjustment to breast cancer. Given the family history component of the disease, daughters of women with breast cancer are likely to have concerns about their own risks. These issues are also explored. Case illustrations are used in Chapters 5, 6, and 8 to demonstrate how counselors might work with individuals. All case examples are composites of clients, and all identifying information has been changed.

Chapter 9 explores potential obstacles to psychological treatment for women with breast cancer. Because these women are ill, traditional therapy boundaries may be inappropriate; for example, the frequency and location of sessions may need to change in order to accommodate changes in the client's physical status. Obstacles to effective treatment may also revolve around issues the therapist is experiencing. Working with women with breast cancer can evoke strong countertransferential feelings (e.g., mortality, fears about the disease, family issues). These feelings and how to manage them are discussed at length.

Finally, Appendix A provides resources for women with breast cancer. The names, phone numbers, addresses, and web sites of relevant organizations are included.

Acknowledgments

This book was the result of the efforts of many people. We wish to thank our families and friends, who have been most patient and understanding as we have engaged in this process of writing our first book. Without their support, it is clear that we could not have completed this project. We are especially indebted to our spouses, Dale Blumenthal and David William Adams, and to Sam and Emily Blumenthal, Merle's children, for their patience and good humor. We also wish to thank Drs. Leo Goldman and John Kennedy, and Jean Witmer, who graciously agreed to edit the book. Their editorial comments and insights were especially valuable. We are indebted to Barbara Okun, Series Editor, and Jim Nageotte of Sage Publications for believing in us and our ability to complete this project; thank you for this opportunity. Several doctoral students in counseling psychology at Fordham University also assisted in this project by doing library work, proofreading drafts of the book, and giving us substantive feedback. Thank you, Denise Gretchen, Netta Shaked, and Lisa Robin. At the early stages of writing, Carolyn Bromley tirelessly searched for and retrieved relevant sources and summarized information from research articles. An extra thank you to Lisa Robin and Connie Yeung for having meticulously checked the reference section for completeness and accuracy—a tedious task. Merle would like to thank Fordham University for granting her a faculty fellowship at the early stages of the project. A special thank you to Joe Ponterotto for taking over as Coordinator of the Counseling programs during Merle's sabbatical. Last but not least, a special thanks to Laurie Leibowitz, Erica Leon, Olga Prince, and Robin Rosenberg for assisting Merle with child care. Their willingness to pitch in and help allowed us blocks of time in which to work. Thank you one and all!

Merle A. Keitel and Mary Kopala

This book is dedicated to our mothers,
Shirley and Emma, with love.

1

Setting the Stage

When I entered her room, I remember feeling shocked by her appearance. She was bone-thin, with tiny wisps of hair remaining on her head, and so weak from the chemotherapy and the cancer that it took all her energy to talk to me. Despite her labored breathing, she spoke to me for over an hour about her fears and the pain of her many losses. Eventually, she collapsed back into her bed from exhaustion. This woman was an art teacher who felt devastated because she was no longer able to do even the simplest everyday things, never mind the activities that fulfilled her. She showed me photographs of herself and her family, pointing out that she felt like a shell of her former self. A strong, healthy woman peered at me from the photographs. She was an avid reader who was now too weak to turn the pages of a book, a former dancer now unable to stand without assistance. She felt comfort in knowing that, should she no longer be capable of tolerating her situation, she could end her life. That sense of control, paradoxically, sustained her. This woman was the first of many people with cancer I would come to know.

I felt completely drained after that session and overwhelmingly sad. I turned to my supervisor for support. I still feel angry about what transpired. As I expressed my sadness, my supervisor asked me, "Did you give this patient a Beck Depression Inventory?" I realized at that moment how easy it is to distance oneself from the pain of another person's experience. It is much easier to have clients complete a paper-and-pencil inventory than it is to share in the intensity of their emotions. I felt abandoned by my supervisor and grew afraid that I too might eventually find ways to distance myself from patients. Fortunately, there was a professor in my graduate program whose main research and clinical focus was death and dying. He gave me the opportunity to speak freely and fully about my experience. After shedding many tears, I finally felt some relief. I am still grateful to him for allowing me my pain and sadness at another human being's suffering.

For 2 years, I worked as a clinical and research associate in the Psychology Department at Roswell Park Memorial Institute in Buffalo, New York. In my first 2 months, I familiarized myself with medical terms, various medications, and cancer protocols. It was intellectually challenging to learn about the many different diseases that fall under the umbrella word *cancer*. Not only was I completely naive about the disease, but I was also unprepared for the toll it would take to be fully present to people who were in such emotional or physical pain. As difficult as these experiences were, I was inspired by the strength I saw in so many who struggled through and survived the illness or who transcended the experience but ultimately succumbed to the disease.

Within 1 year of returning to New York City, my experience with cancer hit closer to home. Shirley, my mother and best friend, was diagnosed with cancer. My mother had large, warm hands; an easy and quick sense of humor; and the deepest capacity for offering empathy that I have ever known. If I or any other person that she loved was troubled, we knew we would always find a nurturing hug and an understanding presence. Even now I can hear her saying, "Remember, I'm in your corner." A visit to "Shirley's kitchen" (as a plaque on the refrigerator proclaimed) meant plenty of food, lots of laughter, and generous portions of empathy. My friends often congregated in my house when we were young. Shirley would buzz around cleaning (she was a real "balabusta," an excellent homemaker), yet she would always find time to entertain us with a funny story, feed us delicious snacks, and ask us how we were doing—not to be polite, but because she genuinely wanted to know. With all of her talents for taking care of others, she often neglected her own needs.

For months my mother sought help from various doctors for her debilitating fatigue. None of them diagnosed her cancer. As a psychologist, I thought her fatigue was related to feelings of depression she was experiencing, especially because the doctors she consulted gave her a clean bill of health. Finally, after she began to report extreme back pain in addition to the fatigue, she was diagnosed with multiple myeloma. I vividly recall sitting in the oncologist's office as he told us the diagnosis. At first, I felt as though my world was crumbling around me. Then, almost immediately, I felt like I was outside the room looking down at a scene where a doctor was telling a perfect stranger she had cancer.

Despite my urging to get a second opinion, my mother refused, because she did not want to hurt the doctor's feelings. As is true for many women, she felt compelled to protect this man that she did not even know, rather than do what was necessary to protect herself. Months later we learned that she had been misdiagnosed again. She was being treated for the wrong cancer. I was angry—angry at the medical establishment, angry at my mother for not being more assertive in her medical care, angry at myself for misattributing her fatigue to psychological causes, and angry at God. At the same time, I was relieved because her new diagnosis offered her a better prognosis. My family was flooded with renewed hope. Unfortunately, the correct diagnosis came too late; I still wonder whether she would be alive today if she had been correctly diagnosed from the beginning.

It is almost a cliché to say that living with cancer—whether you are the patient, family member, or significant other—is like being on an emotional roller coaster, but it is true. These ups and downs came frequently and more and more intensely through my mother's 2-year illness. I rejoiced with her when, after her chemotherapy, her hair grew back enough that she no longer believed she needed to wear a turban, scarf, or wig. I accompanied her to her first haircut, and we were both giddy, because on some level, having her hair back represented health. Months later, the oncologist called me into the office alone and said that there was nothing else he could do for my mother. He thought that trying additional experimental treatments would only cause her more pain and prolong the inevitable. The tears come even now when I think of this moment. To watch my beautiful mother, so full of love and warmth, life and laughter, suffer the indignities of the disease and the medical intervention was intolerable. She died in December 1989, 22 months after her initial diagnosis.

My experience moved from the professional to the personal, but the story that follows, written by my coauthor, colleague, and friend, begins with a mother's illness.

"You look just like your mother." Everybody has said so—ever since I was a little girl—so it must be true. I never thought so. But now, at the age of 46, I see that they were always right. In fact, my mother and I have more in common than our appearance. We are both great cooks but lousy at cleaning house. Oh, we can do it; we just prefer not to—it's not a priority. We can sew clothes and curtains, upholster and refinish furniture, grow beautiful flowers and vegetables. We have a lot of energy and the stamina to teach ourselves to do things from books. We are alike in numerous ways, except for one very important way. My mother has cancer. I do not, at least as far as I know.

I'll never forget the day I learned my mother was ill. My doctoral internship would begin in less than 3 weeks, and I had to clean, move, unpack, and be ready to begin. My apartment had been emptied. All that remained were some houseplants, suitcases full of clothes, and the dregs that always seem to be left after the moving van has driven away. There were still carpets to be cleaned, floors to be mopped, and holes to be spackled in order to get that all-important security deposit back. It couldn't have been a worse time for my mother to announce that she had found blood in her urine. I can't explain why, but I just felt it was serious. The stress of moving caught up with me in that moment, and I burst into tears and cried out, "Mama, I don't want you to be sick." I felt like I was 6 instead of 36, and my mother and I clung to each other in the middle of that empty apartment and cried. We didn't talk to each other about our feelings, but I know we were both afraid. I promised my mother I would return from Delaware in less than 24 hr to accompany her to see a specialist. Everything was already moving so quickly.

The news was not good. Seeing my mother being examined by a stranger was difficult for me. Suddenly I was the person in charge, the adult, the caregiver, and my mother was the vulnerable one, the one who was unable to make rational decisions for herself. I was not ready for this. The next days were spent getting ready for the surgery that was hastily scheduled. There were forms to complete, insurance matters to research, and still an empty apartment to clean.

I drove my mother to the hospital early the day of the surgery. After saying good-bye to me, she was placed on a gurney and wheeled out of her room. Once again I felt uncomfortable seeing my mother so vulnerable. I spent most of that day alone in the hospital with my fears, while my mother was alone with strangers. In the late afternoon, the surgeon came to me and told me that her prognosis was good. Early detection and immediate surgery followed by chemotherapy suggested that she would be healthy again. I was relieved, yet uneasy. That was nearly 10 years ago, and my mother is still in remission, and I am still uneasy at times. Each year as the time for her checkup approaches, she becomes anxious. So do I. We still don't talk about this experience very much. Yet there is always a little uneasiness in both of us.

No one was there to help us deal with this unexpected and frightening turn in our lives. My husband and friends listened to me and supported me, but my mother had only her minister and me, and I am not sure that either of us was very helpful to her. Certainly, no one helped us process and make sense of this event.

Every time I work with a client with breast cancer, I remember my experience with my mother and her illness. Without that experience, I'm not certain that I would have the patience to listen to the stories, the fears, the frustrations. Each client comes to me at a different stage in the cancer experience. Some clients begin therapy before the diagnosis, and suddenly our work changes to include the crisis of the unexpected illness. Others come during the period of breast reconstruction, and others enter therapy while in remission. No matter when they come, they always talk about their struggle with the disease and their frustration that family members don't really understand how they feel, both physically and emotionally. I listen to their stories, and occasionally cry with them as I empathize with their pain. Other times I encourage them to go on; sometimes I just listen. Always I remember my mother.

> *This book was born from our experiences with our mothers, our clients, and with each other. We forged a deep connection when, soon after we met, we shared our stories of our mothers' illnesses. However, it was not our personal experiences alone that instigated the writing of this book; the proliferation of managed health care in the United States escalated our already substantial concerns about women's health issues.*

Policies and actions of health maintenance organizations (HMOs) and preferred provider organizations (PPOs) have negatively affected the professions of medicine and psychology and, in some cases, have led to such questionable practices that legislators have stepped in to regulate the industry. For example, when some managed care companies reduced hospital stays to 24 hr for women having mastectomies, prompting the term *drive-through mastectomies,* the outcry was so great that states passed legislation mandating longer hospital stays. State and federal efforts have been initiated to curtail abusive practices by managed care corporations such as "gag clauses," which preclude physicians from assisting with patients' appeals or informing patients of out-of-plan options; refusing women direct access to their obstetricians and gynecologists; and providing financial incentives to doctors who deny care, particularly expensive diagnostic and treatment procedures.

The story of one woman who died from metastatic breast cancer will sound familiar to many of you who have directly experienced frustrations with managed care or have heard such stories from friends or family members. This particular account was excerpted from the Wellness Web, and even an abbreviated version does not dilute its impact (Joyce, 1998).

Janet did her homework before choosing a particular HMO; her oncologist was a preferred provider, as was another reputable oncologist in the area. Furthermore, a hospital from which she had previously received excellent care and a university-based hospital offering specialized cancer care were represented. Janet never could have anticipated the nightmare that eventually unfolded; namely, a seemingly endless series of denials and delays in requests for medical services from her HMO.

At the outset, her request for a second opinion was denied for no justifiable cause. To make matters worse, she was blocked from seeing her oncologist until the denial of the second opinion was fully processed by the HMO. In the meantime, Janet's breathing grew worse, and her primary care physician directed her to the Urgent Care department at her hospital. The Urgent Care doctor ordered blood tests and a chest X ray but didn't think a transfusion was necessary. The next day, still having trouble breathing, she was finally permitted to see her own oncologist, who recommended a transfusion. Unfortunately, the HMO would not authorize her admission to the hospital. To complicate matters further, Janet's primary care physician did not contact her until late the next day, at which point she directed Janet to the emergency room of a local hospital. The emergency room doctor, who saw her after many hours elapsed, refused to do a transfusion unless she repeated her blood work and chest X ray, the results of which wouldn't be ready until the next day. When she finally received the transfusion, the doctor did not administer the Lasix her oncologist had recommended, resulting in a serious respiratory problem. Janet's condition worsened and she needed home health care, but it was not authorized; her only other option was to enter a hospice. Hospice care was not covered by Janet's HMO, but her secondary Medicare policy did cover it. Even though they were not paying for it, the HMO would not provide a referral to Janet's hospice, and, despite her repeated phone calls to resolve the situation, the HMO did not call back for several weeks. In the meantime, Janet was experiencing severe pain from her bone metastases, and the HMO refused to authorize referral to a pain specialist—although it did authorize a visit to an anesthesiologist. Radiation to her bones also became necessary, and here, too, there were significant delays in authorization. The story goes on and on, ultimately culminating in Janet's death from metastatic breast cancer (Joyce, 1998).

Not all stories are as dramatic as Janet's, but negotiating the managed care system frequently frustrates providers and patients alike. In medical situations in which time is of the essence, managed care companies have often fallen short. Busy phone lines prevent providers from reaching HMO representatives, and slow responses prohibit patients from obtaining care in a timely fashion. The routine practice by HMOs and PPOs of restricting patients' choices of physicians to specific providers at times results in patients' receiving substandard care. Networks may not include cancer experts or may include providers who have little experience with cancer diagnosis and treatment. A National Cancer Institute panel agrees that women with breast cancer are better off being treated by specialists at cancer centers who have substantial experience treating other women with the same diagnosis and who are also more likely to be proficient at state-of-the-art diagnostic techniques and treatments. Yet directors of managed care companies acknowledge that they typically will not cover "out of network" providers because there are no definitive data to suggest that local oncologists cannot provide appropriate care. In fact, comprehensive cancer centers, often those associated with major medical schools, may offer some women the best chance of survival.

In defense of HMOs, some studies have found that they are superior to fee-for-service providers with respect to early detection. Breast, cervical, and colon cancer and melanomas were diagnosed significantly earlier in HMO patients than others, as were cancers in elderly individuals whose HMOs covered routine screenings like mammograms, Pap smears, and fecal blood tests. Furthermore, in those instances in which plan physicians acknowledge that they cannot handle a particular case, the patient may be given permission to go out of the network.

Our concern about managed care is focused squarely on its impact on the quality of care patients receive; however, we also worry about its impact on health professionals such as doctors, nurses, psychologists, counselors, and social workers. Cost-cutting efforts of managed care companies have resulted in reduced payments to health care professionals, consequently increasing patient caseloads. Again, consumers suffer when managed care companies hire unqualified, lower-paid workers to draw blood, remove intravenous tubing, or take blood pressure and when they force health care providers to reduce the amount of time spent with each patient. Such practices lead to serious health consequences for patients and growing frustrations for health care providers. Fees for service continue to be reduced, paperwork requirements justifying additional sessions and longer hospital stays continue to increase, and control by professionals to determine appropriate diagnostic and treatment procedures continues to erode. Many managed care companies are delinquent in their payments to health providers. Consequently, some health care providers have banded together, withdrawing from the managed care system and taking back control of patient care, and others have quit practicing altogether.

Nevertheless, it is clear that managed care companies are here to stay, at least for the foreseeable future. It makes sense for mental health professionals to publicize the roles they can play in health care and to pursue more visible lobbying efforts at local, state, and national levels to ensure that behavioral health issues are included in policy formation, research grants, and service allocations. Fifty to 70% of all visits to primary care physicians are by patients who have no identifiable physical illness but whose complaints stem from psychological factors (Gaus &

DeLeon, 1995) that can be addressed by mental health professionals. Behavioral and psychoeducational approaches, in particular, have been effectively used with a wide variety of psychosomatic and health-related problems (Siegel, 1993). Effectiveness has been demonstrated for relatively brief interventions focused on skill building and modification of lifestyle behaviors as well as cognitive-behavioral interventions to reduce pain, hasten discharge from the hospital, and reduce emotional distress that precipitates requests for medical services. Mental health professionals can directly intervene with women with breast cancer to ensure quality patient care and actually reduce health care costs—contributions consistent with the goals of managed care; however, they must continue documenting and publicizing the cost-effectiveness of their techniques.

We also encourage all health professionals—including physicians and mental health professionals—to become advocates for women with breast cancer in the larger political sphere. Such advocacy can take the form of lobbying congresspersons to support continued funding of breast cancer research as well as health care reform proposals such as The Patients' Bill of Rights. In March 1998, the Democrats introduced this proposal to Congress with the backing of the American Medical Association and the major labor and consumers' unions, but Congress has recently defeated this bill. A less active form of advocacy, but a worthwhile one, is voting for politicians who have a documented record of support for women's health care issues.

In the past, primarily women have advocated for women. When breast cancer was "unmentionable," women who were survivors of mastectomy volunteered to help newly diagnosed and treated women cope with the inevitable emotional turmoil. Women in the 1970s brought breast cancer out of the closet, making it permissible to utter the words aloud, and began to demand input in treatment decision making. In the 1980s, a few notable women began forming foundations and projects devoted to raising money and promoting research and breast cancer as a political cause. In the 1990s, largely as the result of women's efforts, research money to the tune of $430 million was appropriated for breast cancer research. Clearly, as women became alarmed about the growing prevalence of breast cancer, they formed grassroots organizations to advocate for increased research funding and better patient care. Their efforts made a significant difference, but there is still more to do. Without women who are willing to participate in clinical trials, little information will be gathered, and the knowledge base will not be enhanced.

Increased funding has yielded medical breakthroughs over the past several years that are enormously exciting. In fact, the many new developments in genetics, diagnostic testing, and prevention significantly delayed the completion of this book. Just as we thought we had put the finishing touches on the medical chapter, another major research study was published. However, there is still much to be learned; little is known about the causes of breast cancer, including, for example, the possible link between environmental toxins and the etiology of breast cancer. Furthermore, all women do not yet have access to high-quality diagnostic and treatment procedures.

Fortunately, because of the Mammography Quality Standards Act of 1992, women who do have mammograms are assured that national standards regulate how mammograms are taken and who administers them.

We focused this volume on breast cancer because it affects so many women—a staggering one out of eight women in the United States is diagnosed with the disease. Women with all types of cancer have concerns about surviving the disease and coping with treatment side effects, but there are unique concerns associated with breast cancer. Changes in physical appearance often affect women's body image, their identities as women, and their sexuality. Mental health professionals are unlikely to have specialized knowledge about medical and psychological aspects of the disease. We provide this information here. Not everything we discuss is applicable to all women; however, an understanding of the medical and psychological aspects of breast cancer is critical to good mental health treatment.

There is much we want to offer to other mental health professionals who work with women with cancer. We hope readers will gain specific knowledge about cancer and skills for assessing and intervening with clients in culturally sensitive ways. Equally important, it is our hope that mental health professionals will learn to acknowledge their own fears and to develop the courage to be fully present when working with their clients. Only when they develop skills that empower women and forgo their own tendencies to protect themselves can they positively influence the lives of women with cancer. This book reflects our deep commitment to helping women (those who have breast cancer and those who fear it) by providing information and helping them to draw on their psychological and emotional resources.

2

Breast Cancer

What You Need To Know

Some facts about breast cancer:

- Breast cancer is the most prevalent cancer among women.

- It is estimated that, by the year 2000, there will be 1.5 million new cases of breast cancer in the United States. Women in the United States have among the highest rates of breast cancer in the world. Particularly at risk are urban women of higher socioeconomic status, married women, and women living in the northern United States.

- In the general population, approximately 75% of new cases of breast cancer occur in women age 50 and older, and 13% of initial breast cancer diagnoses occur in women between 40 and 49 years of age.

- Breast cancer is less prevalent in women under 40, but younger women tend to experience higher mortality from the disease.

- The overall incidence of breast cancer increased from the early 1970s to the early 1990s and then decreased approximately 0.6% from 1991 to 1995. Because of advances in medical research and earlier detection, overall survival rates have increased.

- Breast cancer is the second leading cause of cancer death in women in the United States overall, but it is the leading cause of cancer death in Filipino and Hispanic women in the United States.

- Although the disease is more common in White women across all age groups, it occurs more frequently in Black women under the age of 45. Black women are also more likely to die from the disease.

- One in eight women in the United States will be diagnosed with breast cancer (based on a life span of 90 years).

Mental health professionals have skills that can improve the well-being of women worried about getting breast cancer as well as those who have already been diagnosed with the disease. Without specialized knowledge about the disease and its treatments, however, mental health professionals are likely to be less effective. This chapter aims to familiarize mental health professionals with breast cancer, relevant diagnostic tests, and both traditional medical and alternative treatments. Professionals who are familiar with cancer terminology and with practices that promote early detection can be stronger advocates for their clients and much more helpful to them.

WHAT IS CANCER?

There is not a universal definition of cancer. [1] In the traditional medical systems of South Asia, Latin America, and Africa, cancer's meaning is related to the intervention of evil spirits. Cancer is looked upon as a punishment or an act of aggression toward the patient and is treated by priests and shamans who are considered to have supernatural abilities and great magical powers. These healers identify deities, ghosts, or other agents and then determine how to overcome or placate them. In Chinese medicine, cancer is attributed to naturalistic causes and is explained in impersonal systemic terms. Cancer patients are seen as having unbalanced equilibriums. In order for the patient to recover, the balance of humors must be restored; this is usually accomplished by curers who acquire their knowledge of herbs and treatment skills from more experienced healers. In Western societies, cancer is perceived as a disease (actually as more than 100 different diseases) to be treated by scientifically trained doctors. The doctor establishes the physical basis of complaints, takes a history, and embarks upon an examination of the patient and a treatment plan that usually consists of some type of therapy. Although this chapter takes a primarily Western medical perspective on cancer and its treatments, we have included a critical section on alternative or complementary treatments. A majority of physicians in the United States are not knowledgeable about these treatments and do not recommend them to their patients, but there is anecdotal evidence supporting the efficacy of some of these healing methods, and numerous patients seek them out.

ABOUT BREAST CANCER

Although many individuals would view breast cancer as one type of cancer, there are actually several different types and combinations of types of breast cancer. Breast cancer is labeled according to where it arises, whether it is invasive, and the appearance of the cells. Breast cancers can begin in glands called ducts (86%) or lobules (12%). These cancers are often referred to as adenocarcinomas. In rare cases, breast cancer can arise in the surrounding tissue. Cancer is also described as invasive (infiltrating) when it has spread into the surrounding tissue. Noninvasive carcinomas may be called *ductal* (or *lobular*) *carcinoma in situ* or *intraductal carcinoma*. Various names may be present in the pathology report, based on the appearance of the cells. For example, papillary carcinoma cells have small projections or papules, whereas tubular cancer has tube-shaped cells.

Once the pathologist identifies the type of cancer, the next step is to determine how aggressive the cancer is. It is difficult to say with any degree of certainty how aggressive an individual's cancer is, but there are certain signs that suggest aggressiveness. For example, poorly differentiated cells tend to be more aggressive than well-differentiated or normal-looking cells. The more quickly cells divide and the greater the number of cells that are dividing, the more aggressive the cancer. These two factors are used to grade the aggressiveness on a scale from I to IV, with IV being the most aggressive. Other signs of aggressiveness include the presence of cancer cells in the blood or lymphatic systems, the presence of numerous blood vessels associated with a tumor, and the presence of necrosis or dead cancer cells.

There are other measurable characteristics of tumors that can indicate how a tumor might behave. Whether a tumor is sensitive to hormones, for example, may indicate how aggressive it is and also whether it is likely to respond to hormone therapy. Tumors that are sensitive to estrogen (estrogen receptor positive) tend to be slower growing and can be treated using hormones; they thus have better prognoses. Tumors in postmenopausal women tend to be estrogen receptor positive and, on average, have better prognoses, whereas tumors in premenopausal women tend to be estrogen receptor negative. For information on other tests that provide information about the aggressiveness of tumors, see Love (1995).

There is a relatively new theory that the term *breast cancer* is actually used for three different diseases. One is a very aggressive type that develops and spreads so quickly that it can become lethal in the time between a woman's annual mammograms. It has been estimated that from 13% to 17% of breast cancers are of this type, and women in their 30s and 40s are more likely to have it. A second type develops and then spreads within 5 to 10 years. A third type is so slow growing that it may never spread, or it may take so many years to spread that no treatment is needed other than to remove the tumor. This type is hypothesized to account for 10% to 15% of breast cancers. As scientists become better able to differentiate these types of cancers, treatments may be more appropriately tailored so that women with very slow-growing tumors may be spared the experience of adjuvant chemotherapy.

Staging

Carcinoma in situ (either interductal or lobular) is noninvasive cancer that is found in only a few layers of cells. It is considered by some physicians (e.g., Love, 1995) to be precancer because it has not spread into surrounding tissue. Ductal carcinoma in situ (DCIS) used to represent less than 1% of all breast cancers, but because of increased mammography rates, by 1997, 13% of all new cases (with some treatment centers reporting 20% to 40%) are DCIS.

Stage I cancer, considered early-stage breast cancer, is diagnosed when the cancer cells have not spread beyond the breast and the tumor is no more than 1 in.

across. Stage II breast cancer means that the tumor is 1 to 2 in. across and the cancer has spread to underarm lymph nodes. In Stage III breast cancer (locally advanced disease), the tumor is more than 2 in. across, and the cancer is spread more widely in the underarm lymph nodes or to other tissues in the breast. Stage IV breast cancer is metastatic breast cancer, meaning that the cancer has spread from the breast to other parts of the body. The liver, bones, and lungs are the areas to which breast cancer most commonly spreads. When cancer returns despite what seemed to be successful treatment, the term *recurrent cancer* is used. If the cancer returns in the breast or chest wall, it is considered a local recurrence. If it returns in another part of the body, it is considered metastatic disease or distant disease.

"Most cancers have been around eight years before they can be seen on a mammogram and 10 years before they can be felt as a lump" (Love, 1995, p. 265). Once a malignancy has been diagnosed, many women believe that they need surgery immediately and pressure themselves to make treatment decisions. Contrary to popular belief, breast cancer generally spreads rather slowly, taking approximately 100 days, on average, for one cancer cell to split. "It takes 100 billion cells to have a centimeter's worth of cancer" (Love, 1995, p. 265). It should be noted, however, that different types of cancers grow at different rates and that all cancers have the ability to spread microscopically before they can be detected. Furthermore, cancers tend not to grow in an orderly fashion. The average time a tumor takes to double in size is 260 days, but the range is from 10 to 7,051 days.

> What we see on a mammogram or feel on physical exam isn't the cancer cells themselves, but the reaction the body forms to the cancer cells. Until the cluster of cancer cells grows to a critical size, the reaction won't form. That critical size varies from person to person and from cancer to cancer. Some cancers will incite a large reaction when the malignancy itself is very small, and you'll feel it comparatively early in its growth. Others provoke no reaction until they're quite large. . . . So the idea that cancer is always detectable when it is small and early simply isn't true. (Love, 1995, p. 268)[2]

SCREENING TECHNIQUES

Screening can lead to early detection. Women are advised to perform monthly manual examinations of their breasts and the area under their armpits, to obtain annual clinical examinations by physicians, and to undergo regular mammograms. The importance of these screening behaviors cannot be overemphasized. We recently learned about a friend's sister, a 33-year-old Long Island, New York, resident, who was diagnosed with bilateral breast cancer. She had felt a small lump in her breast about a year ago but had dismissed it because she had no family history of breast cancer and believed that breast cancer tended to strike older women. She gave birth 4 months ago to a baby boy and during a postpartum exam mentioned the lump to her physician. The doctor dismissed it as being a clogged milk duct. Three more months elapsed before the lump grew noticeably bigger, and she was referred for a mammogram that revealed lumps in both breasts. A subsequent biopsy indicated that the tumors were malignant. A follow-up MRI revealed a mass at the base of her spinal cord. Tragically, the cancer had metastasized to her bones. We can't help but wonder how her prognosis would have differed had she obtained a mammogram when she first discovered the lump.

For those readers unfamiliar with mammograms, they are X-rays of the soft breast tissue. Radiology technicians ask women to place one breast at a time on a film plate. The breast is then compressed so that as much surface of the breast as possible can be X-rayed. This compression may cause some discomfort and even minor pain. To reduce discomfort, women should schedule mammograms right after they have menstruated, when their breasts are less tender. Large-breasted women get more accurate pictures than do small-breasted women, because they can more easily position their breasts on the film plates.

The "picture" that results from mammography shows areas of density that appear as shadows. Some shadows indicate abnormalities that may need further examination. Younger women get less-accurate pictures, because their breasts are more dense, thus potentially obscuring abnormalities. As women age, their breasts contain more fat, and so abnormalities are more easily seen. Although mammography reveals lesions that are too small to be discovered by manual examination, the technology could be improved. In any case, mammography alone is an insufficient screening tool and should be conducted in combination with manual examinations.

According to the Harvard Women's Health Watch (1998), there are promising new developments in high-technology imaging processes, such as digital mammography, an X-ray technique that allows the image of the breast to be stored on a computer disk and then displayed on a high-resolution monitor where specific sections may be magnified and contrasts can be adjusted. The Image Checker displays the breast image from a mammogram on a video screen and marks features that have characteristics of cancer; thus, the same radiologist who initially read the mammogram can reconsider the results, eliminating the need for review by a second radiologist. Positron emission tomography (PET) scans may reveal the metabolic process of cancer cells through the use of radioactive substances, allowing detection of tumors in dense breast tissue and those that have metastasized. As of 1999, clinical trials of PET scans are being conducted. Another method, high-definition ultrasound, was recently approved by the Food and Drug Administration (FDA) to be used in conjunction with mammograms for a more detailed picture of some lesions. Still another method, magnetic resonance imaging (MRI), may detect all cancers accurately without using radiation, but MRI also detects many benign lesions and may require up to an hour in an enclosed space. A more efficient open MRI that is breast-specific is being designed "as are dyes that are preferentially absorbed by breast tumors" (Harvard Women's Health Watch, p. 5). Another procedure, Miraluma imaging (scintimammography), has received FDA approval, and radiologists are testing it in clinical trials at several cancer centers. In this procedure, a vein in a woman's arm is injected with a dye that flows into the blood vessels in the breast. The dye accumulates in malignant cells more than in benign cells because they have more blood vessels. A special camera is used to photograph the breast tissue, and the dye in malignant cells projects a brighter image. This procedure may make it possible to determine whether the cancer has metastasized to the lymph nodes and may help determine characteristics of malignant tumors, but it cannot be used for tumors smaller than 1 cm, and it dispenses a higher level of radiation than mammography. Another new alternative for identifying breast lumps is the T-Scan 2000. Using electrical shocks, the T-Scan measures the electrical conductivity of cells. Healthy cells conduct substantially more electricity than do cancer cells, and thus possible tumors appear to be bright white spots on a computer screen. The T-Scan can be used when a mammogram is unclear. With the use of the T-Scan, some biopsies could be avoided.

In addition to palpating their breasts for any lumps, women should carefully observe their breasts as a part of breast self-examination. They should look for retraction of the nipple or any other obvious changes in the size or shape of their breasts, or redness, scaliness, dimpling, or puckering. Women should report to their physicians any sign of discharge from the nipple, as well as any other change that is not related to a menstrual period. After menopause, any change at all should be reported to one's physician.

DIAGNOSIS OF BREAST CANCER

Mammograms will show abnormalities such as scar tissue or fat necrosis (these may appear as pseudolumps), solid masses (benign tumors such as fibroadenomas or malignant tumors), calcifications (which may be benign, cancerous, or precancerous), lymph nodes, and cysts (fluid-filled lumps). Expert radiologists may be able to diagnose some benign conditions based on the shape, size, or clustering pattern of the abnormalities. If a small, round lump is revealed by mammography, the patient might be referred for an ultrasound to determine whether it is a solid mass or a cyst. If it is a solid mass, the patient might be referred to a breast surgeon for consultation, and a biopsy may be recommended.

Biopsy

Biopsies are generally performed to determine whether a lump is cancerous, precancerous, or benign. Biopsy results also furnish information about the cells and breast tissue; for example, if the tumor is malignant, the biopsy results could indicate the type of cancer and how aggressive it is. When a woman or a physician finds a lump through manual breast examination, a mammogram may not be ordered, but instead, a biopsy may be performed. If the lump is not palpable, surgeons utilize the mammogram results to locate the tumor and guide the biopsy.

At the writing of this book, four types of biopsies are routinely performed. Two are done with needles, and two are done by surgical cutting. We describe all four, from least to most invasive. The fine-needle biopsy takes a few cells out; a large-needle (tru-cut or core) biopsy takes a small piece of tissue; the incisional biopsy takes a larger piece of the lump; and an excisional biopsy takes the entire lump. When an excisional biopsy is performed, the pathologist can examine the margins of the removed tissue. If cancer cells appear only in the center of the tissue and the margins are "clean," it is a positive sign suggesting that all of the cancerous tissue was removed. If there are cancer cells all the way up to the border of the removed tissue, there is a greater chance that there is still malignant tissue in the breast.

A new type of biopsy, mammotomy or mammotome biopsy, is a faster, more accurate, and less painful procedure than core biopsy. As in the fine-needle biopsy, a hollow, very thin needle is inserted into a nick in the breast, rotated, and, as in the core biopsy, used to remove tissue rather than just a few cells. In fact, this less-invasive method removes more tissue than the core biopsy.

Another new technique available at major medical centers is the sentinel node biopsy. Doctors inject a blue dye and a radioactive tracer that illuminates the sentinel node (which is the first node that malignant cells would encounter as they leave the breast). If this node is cancer-free, it is likely that all other nodes are also cancer-free. A recent study of 107 women indicated that in the 100 women for whom the sentinel node was identified, diagnosis as positive or negative for cancer was 100% accurate. A sentinel node biopsy is preferable to surgical removal of several lymph nodes because it reduces nerve damage and lymphedema. The type of biopsy to be performed should be decided by a woman in consultation with her physician.

Generally, when a biopsy is performed, the woman is given the results, and if further treatment is warranted, it is done at a later time. This is in contrast with the one-stage process, where a woman gives her consent prior to the biopsy to have a mastectomy performed if cancer is detected. Current medical knowledge of how cancer is spread suggests no reason for a one-stage process: However, some physicians or women may prefer this method because only one surgery is needed.

TREATMENTS FOR BREAST CANCER

Many women would be surprised by the variability in breast cancer treatment; for example, physicians from different geographical locations may show preference for different techniques or procedures. Recommendations may differ according to whether physicians are or are not affiliated with cancer research institutions.

Treatments for breast cancer are either local, that is, the breast itself is treated, or systemic, in which case the entire body is treated. Surgery and radiation are local treatments, and chemotherapy, hormone therapy, and bone marrow replacement therapy are systemic treatments. Depending on a variety of factors (e.g., the type of cancer, the size of the tumor, the age of the patient), breast cancer may be treated with local, systemic, or a combination of treatments. Breast cancer can recur regardless of the type or types of treatment women have.

Surgical Treatments

There are several different surgical procedures: (a) the radical mastectomy (only used when the tumor has spread to the chest muscles), (b) the modified radical mastectomy (currently the most commonly used surgical procedure), (c) the total (or simple) mastectomy, and (d) breast-conserving surgeries. These procedures are described from most to least invasive. In radical mastectomy, the surgeon removes the entire breast, the chest muscle, all of the lymph nodes under the arm, and some additional fat and skin. This operation was standard for over 100 years, the first one having been performed in 1857 (Love, 1995). Today this surgery is only used when the tumor has spread to the chest muscles.

In modified radical mastectomy, the surgeon removes the breast, some of the lymph nodes under the arm, and the lining over the chest muscle. In total (or simple) mastectomy, the entire breast is removed. Postoperatively, a woman who has had a total mastectomy may experience phantom breast pain and/or itchiness and numbness around the scar. Her chest will be flat and possibly concave. In addition, she may experience an unpleasant tingling sensation when her chest is touched. Surgeons place drains in the skin below the scar to remove the fluid that accumulates around the incision. Unfortunately, after the drains are removed, fluid sometimes continues to accumulate.

In breast-conserving surgeries, the tumor and a margin of healthy tissue around it are removed. The amount of tissue removed varies from patient to patient. Although these procedures may be referred to as lumpectomies, more accurately they should be labeled as partial or segmental mastectomy, quadrantectomy, or wide excision. (There has been a dramatic increase in the use of lumpectomies during the 1990s.) Although lumpectomy suggests that the surgeon will remove only the tumor and a small area of surrounding tissue, in fact, some surgeons remove a wider area of tissue. Side effects from lumpectomy include decreased sensation in the breast, a spot that may be permanently numb, and a change in the size and shape of the breast. Once a total or partial mastectomy is completed, lymph nodes are removed and then analyzed by a pathologist.

Risks from the removal of lymph nodes are the same whether one has a lumpectomy or total mastectomy. These include lymphedema, phlebitis (an inflammation of the vein), and the accumulation of fluid leading to swelling of the armpit. When scarring prevents the lymph fluid from draining effectively, lymphedema or swelling of the arm occurs. Infection appears to increase the chances of developing lymphedema. Approximately one tenth of lymph node surgery patients develop this complication, which can develop either soon or not for years after the surgery. Once it develops, treatment options are limited, so prevention is emphasized. Lymphedema can be painful and disfiguring, and in rare cases it can develop into lymphangiosarcoma.

If nerves are cut during lymph node surgery, a woman may experience loss of sensation in the back of the armpit, a sensation of tiredness in the arm, and winged scapula (an extended shoulder blade when one's arm is extended). A new technique, sentinel node biopsy, detects whether cancer has spread to the lymph nodes without requiring women to have the more invasive traditional underarm surgery, thus reducing discomfort and functional limitations.

Systemic Treatments

Systemic treatments may be used prior to surgery in rare breast cancers such as breast inflammatory disease, or to shrink a locally advanced tumor so that breast conservation is possible or so that the tumor can be better managed with radiation. A 1997 study by Bernard Fisher of the University of Pittsburgh found that women who had chemotherapy followed by lumpectomy had the same low rates of recurrence as women who had mastectomy followed by chemotherapy (Fisher et al., 1997). Systemic treatments may also be used following cancer surgery, at which point they are considered adjuvant treatments, or they may be used when the cancer has metastasized. The detection of cancer cells in the lymph nodes suggests that the breast cancer has spread beyond the local region of the breast. Generally, in this case, a systemic treatment—either chemotherapy or hormonal treatment—will be recommended; however, even in node-negative women, chemotherapy may be prescribed. Recent studies suggest that systemic treatment alone may be as effective as surgery in combination with systemic treatment in women over the age of 70 (Love, 1995, p. 351). When systemic therapy is indicated, women with breast cancer are referred to medical oncologists (specialists in hormones and chemotherapy).

In chemotherapy, drugs enter the bloodstream and travel through the body to kill cancer cells. Because these drugs cannot discriminate between rapidly dividing healthy cells and cancer cells, healthy cells are destroyed along with the cancer cells. The death of cells in the digestive tract, bone marrow, and hair follicles can cause nausea, vomiting, fatigue, and hair loss. Unfortunately, there are many potential side effects from chemotherapy, which vary depending on the particular drugs prescribed.

Chemotherapy drugs may be administered orally, intravenously, or by intramuscular injection, and treatment may commence prior to surgery or 4 to 12 weeks after surgery. The course of drug therapy usually spans 3 to 6 months but is sometimes longer. Generally, a combination of drugs is used. Typically used drug combinations are CMF (cyclophosphamide, methotrexate, and fluorouracil); CAF (cyclophosphamide, Adriamycin, and fluorouracil); and CA (cyclophosphamide and Adriamycin). Although most chemotherapy protocols can be administered on an outpatient basis, the woman may require a hospital stay depending on the drugs given and her health. Chemotherapy treatments are typically spaced so that the body can recover before the next treatment.

Chemotherapy seems to work better in younger women. The reasons for this are not entirely clear. One hypothesis is that for premenopausal women, chemotherapy kills cancer cells and also has a hormonal effect (a chemical meno-pause); that is, estrogen is blocked and tumor growth is retarded. Women in their 20s and early 30s will likely resume their menstrual periods and retain their fertil-ity; however, there is a risk of permanent menopause. A woman who is close in age to her natural menopause is less likely to resume menstruation (Love, 1995).

Hormonal therapy is used to block cancer cells from receiving the hormones they need to grow. This can be accomplished through the surgical removal of the ovaries or the oral administration of the drug tamoxifen, an estrogen blocker. Tamoxifen is typically taken two times each day for 3 to 5 years, and it has fewer side effects than most chemotherapy protocols. Nevertheless, there are potential side effects, including hot flashes, nausea, and vaginal dryness, discharge, or bleeding. (Women who bleed should consult their physicians.) Much less common are headaches, bone pain, depression, and endometrial cancer.

Tamoxifen is most effective in women with estrogen-positive tumors, but it also works in about 5% to 10% of estrogen-negative tumors. Current research indi-cates that this hormone treatment may not only arrest the development of cancer cells but may also kill some cancer cells, improving overall survival by 2 years. Tamoxifen has reduced the rate of recurrence by 40% in women with early-stage breast cancer. The effects of this drug appear to be lowest in women under 40, with maximal benefit in women over 50 (Love, 1995), although recent research sug-gests that tamoxifen may be more effective with premenopausal women than pre-viously thought. As of 1999, research suggests that tamoxifen be discontinued after 5 years because long-term use may result in risks that outweigh potential benefits.

Radiation Therapy

Radiation therapy (also known as radiotherapy) uses high-energy rays to dam-age cancer cells and stop their growth. Once a tumor is surgically removed through lumpectomy (or after mastectomy in patients who have a high risk for a local recurrence), radiation therapy is used to kill any remaining cancer cells that reside in the breast area (Love, 1995). After the surgical incision has healed and comfort-able movement of the arm is restored, radiation treatments can begin. Typically, small dots are tattooed onto the chest to guide the administration of the radiation treatments. The radiation is administered to the breast and the lymph nodes—so a large area is treated—while the surrounding area is protected with a shield. Exter-nal radiation treatments are given 5 days a week for about 5 to 6 weeks. Once this phase of the radiation treatment is completed, a "boost" may be given; that is, an extra dose of radiation is directed only at the site of the tumor. This boost can be given by a machine that directs an electron beam at the site, or small radioactive pellets may be implanted in the breast for about 36 hours.

Side effects from radiation include asymptomatic rib fractures, a "sunburn" or severe skin rash, fatigue, swelling and sensitivity of the breast, feelings of depression, thickening or darkening of the skin, crusty nipples, and an increased risk of lymphedema. Sometimes radiation produces numbness in the fingertips, and rarely it causes an increased risk for other types of cancer.

Bone Marrow Transplant

Bone marrow transplants are considered experimental procedures and have been used with advanced cancer patients who have not responded to adjuvant chemotherapy. They enable women with breast cancer to receive much higher chemotherapy doses than can normally be tolerated. Because chemotherapy depletes blood cells, extremely high doses result in death. In the transplant procedure, bone marrow stem cells are removed prior to a course of high-dose chemotherapy that may last from 3 to 8 days; the stem cells are then reintroduced into the body 24 to 48 hours after chemotherapy is completed. The transplanted bone marrow restimulates production of blood cells over a period of time. Posttransplant, the woman is isolated to prevent infection. When a woman's blood counts are at their lowest, she is likely to feel completely fatigued, very depressed, and bored. Nausea and diarrhea, bleeding from the bladder or rectum, mouth sores, and loss of appetite are only a sample of the potential side effects. Various drugs have specific side effects, and women also vary in the degree to which they experience symptoms. Although most women are able to leave the hospital a few weeks after the transplant (when their blood cell counts return to normal levels), it may take a few weeks for them to feel better and several months for them to regain their normal energy levels. High-dose chemotherapy with stem cell rescue is difficult to endure. Empirical evidence regarding this treatment's effectiveness has been mixed, and the results are inconclusive (Zujewski, Nelson, & Abrams, 1998). Some physicians caution against the use of high-dose chemotherapy other than in clinical trials (Gradishar, 1999). However, a review of drug therapy in the treatment of breast cancer published in the *New England Journal of Medicine* (Hortobagyi, 1998) reported that high-dose chemotherapy regimens may be effective as a first treatment for metastatic breast cancer.

Herceptin 2

Approximately 30% of women with breast cancer have a surplus of a protein called Her-2/neu, which is a docking port for growth factors that instigate the spread of the cancer. A new antibody, Herceptin 2, is being used on an experimental basis for women who do not respond to traditional cancer treatments. This drug blocks the effects of Her-2/neu and represents an exciting breakthrough in the treatment of malignancies because, unlike chemotherapy, which kills cancer cells as well as normal cells, Herceptin 2 fixes the genetic defect directly. Thus, it does not cause the aversive side effects associated with chemotherapy. Breast cancer activists are largely responsible for the fact that this drug is now being tested in clinical trials. Pharmaceutical companies had discontinued research on Herceptin 2 because they did not believe it would be financially feasible, but pressure from breast cancer advocates ultimately persuaded them to reinitiate the research.

Taxanes

New drugs, known as the taxanes, are quite promising as treatments for metastatic breast cancer. Studies that have compared docetaxel (Taxotere) and paclitaxel (Taxol) suggest that docetaxel is the most effective single agent for fighting advanced breast cancer (Crown, 1998). The success of paclitaxel added to standard adjuvant therapy suggests that the taxanes reduce tumor size, but their overall impact on survival rates is still unclear (Miller & Sledge, 1999). Rigorous clinical trials continue to evaluate the effectiveness of the taxanes in combination with or substituted for conventional chemotherapy treatments for early-stage and metastatic breast cancer (Ravdin, 1999).

CLINICAL TRIALS

Clinical trials are research studies that examine new treatments to determine if the new treatment is superior to the standard treatment. Typically, a clinical trial is the last step in testing the efficacy of a new treatment. Usually, there are three phases to a clinical trial. Phase I of a trial usually has a small number of participants and focuses on determining effective dosages and methods of administration. Phase II includes more participants than Phase I—approximately 20 to 50 participants—and attempts to determine if the treatment works. Phase III compares the standard treatment with those Phase II treatments that appear to be effective. All the new options are at least as good as the standard of care, but the new treatments may be superior to the standard of care. Phase III trials generally have thousands of participants, and individuals are randomly assigned to the various treatment options.

Women with breast cancer can learn about clinical trials by asking their physicians about treatment options including clinical trials. Pharmaceutical companies, teaching hospitals, and the Internet may provide information about clinical trials. The National Cancer Institute's clinical trials information resource (http://207.121.187.155/NCI_CANCER_TRIALS/zones/TrialInfo/Resources/) can help one find a clinical trial, or women can call 1-800-4-CANCER.

Women can also contact a Comprehensive Cancer Center to learn about participation in clinical trials. Comprehensive Cancer Centers were created under the National Cancer Act of 1971 and are located throughout the United States. To become a Comprehensive Cancer Center, an institution must be awarded a grant from the National Cancer Institute that funds research and information services related to cancer. Every 3 to 5 years the institution must be reviewed in order to have the grant renewed. Only those institutions that continue to meet the National Cancer Institute's criteria are renewed.

Experimental treatments are not typically covered by insurance companies. However, not all clinical trials are considered experimental treatments, so participation in clinical treatments may or may not be covered by insurance. Treatments that are similar to standard treatments are more likely to be covered by insurance. It is important to contact the insurance company before beginning participation in a clinical trial to determine how much, if any, of the treatment will be covered. Often sponsors of the research, such as pharmaceutical companies, cover some of the expenses. However, they may not cover all expenses, leaving patients financially responsible. We urge women who meet the inclusion criteria and who are financially able to volunteer for participation in clinical trials. Counselors may explain the benefit of clinical trials, particularly if physicians haven't, but should in no way coerce their clients to participate.

RECONSTRUCTION

Breast reconstruction procedures have improved rapidly over the last 20 years, and more women are requesting reconstruction after mastectomy. Women must decide whether to have breast reconstruction and, if so, when. Reconstruction can be performed at the time of mastectomy or after the physical healing from the initial surgery has occurred. Currently, immediate reconstruction is the favored option, in part because it is associated with psychological benefits. Women who choose reconstruction must also decide whether they will have prosthetic reconstruction (saline or silicone implants) or autogenous reconstruction (the use of their own tissue to fill in under the skin flap). Physical complications from immediate autogenous or prosthetic reconstruction do not significantly differ from those of delayed reconstruction.

Autogenous reconstruction allows for a more natural feel and contour and more symmetry with the opposite breast. However, the surgery is longer, more complex, and typically requires more time in the hospital prior to discharge than prosthetic reconstruction. Plastic surgeons sometimes perform a "tummy tuck" in conjunction with the reconstruction. Tissue and fat removed from the abdomen are used in reconstructing the breast. Improvements in autogenous breast reconstruction have resulted in outcomes that usually exceed the expectations of patients. With a skin-sparing mastectomy, excellent cosmetic results are often achieved.

The use of silicone implants has been very controversial. Many women have complained of health problems (including various autoimmune disorders) from leaking silicone implants. As of 1999, however, scientific evidence does not support a link between autoimmune disease and silicone implants.

Women may be less concerned about the safety of saline implants, but saline implants generally do not achieve as good a cosmetic result as silicone implants do. For women with bilateral reconstruction, the outcome is somewhat better, because surgeons can generally achieve a greater degree of symmetry between the two breasts. Medical personnel should inform women of the possible risks, the cosmetic outcome of the procedures, and the resulting lack of sensation in the reconstructed breast.

ALTERNATIVE OR COMPLEMENTARY TREATMENTS

Western medicine sees breast cancer as an enemy to be fought with drugs, surgery, and radiation. The language used to describe the process is replete with military analogies—"the war against cancer" or "she lost her battle with cancer." Alternative medicine views disease differently. For example, practitioners of Chinese medicine believe that cancer is always present and that a weakened immune system allows the cancer to grow and spread. Instead of waging a war, the alternative caregiver works to strengthen the body's immune system and to improve the overall health of the patient. Alternative therapies generally focus on the psychological aspects as well as the physical aspects of the disease.

Some individuals turn to alternative therapies out of desperation when conventional medicine has not produced a cure and they see no hope. Others seek alternative care as a complement to conventional medicine. These treatments are generally labeled complementary as opposed to alternative treatments. Still others seek help from an alternative caregiver because they feel dehumanized by their conventional cancer treatment and are dissatisfied with the information physicians provided them with respect to diagnosis and treatment. Cultural and personal beliefs may also influence the type of treatment sought. Finally, some women seek alternative therapies as the treatment of choice and reject conventional medical treatment altogether.

Women who become disillusioned with physicians who do not encourage lifestyle changes or active participation in treatment decisions may prefer alternative caregivers who treat them with interest and respect, who listen with empathy and concern, and who thoroughly explain procedures. On average, alternative caregivers spend over four times as much time with patients as do physicians (Spiegel, 1998). Caregiver and patient work in tandem to make treatment decisions that are most appropriate for that individual. Women who participate in alternative treatment perceive themselves to be "partners" in their health care rather than "recipients" of information that they do not understand. Seminars and groups designed to promote hope are common elements of alternative treatment programs.

Many physicians cite a lack of empirical evidence as the reason they are skeptical about claims attributed to various alternative therapies. We fully support this hesitation to recommend alternative therapies when no evidence exists to support their efficacy and when other medical treatments are available that have demonstrated even modest effects. However, if a woman has exhausted all conventional treatments, we believe that alternative treatments can offer some hope. Although many substances are approved for use in other countries, the enormous research costs necessary to provide evidence to the FDA for drugs to be approved in this country has impeded the use of alternative substances in the United States. Proponents of alternative therapy suggest that the lack of funding for research studies is the result of business and politics. They claim that because drug companies develop new drugs solely for profit, these companies are unwilling to study alternative drugs, which may be less expensive to the consumer, consequently yielding smaller profits for the manufacturer. Furthermore, national funding for testing alternative approaches has been a relatively low priority, despite the initiation in 1991 of an Office of Alternative Medicine (recently renamed the National Center for Complementary and Alternative Medicine) at the National Institutes of Health in Bethesda, Maryland.

What Are Alternative Therapies?

Alternative therapies may include the use of substances that have not been approved by the FDA, such as laetrile. Alternative treatments can also include dietary changes or regimens; techniques such as hypnosis and acupuncture; or the use of herbs, vitamins, and other natural products. Some of these alternative therapies have their roots in ancient healing practices such as Chinese medicine, Indian traditions, and folk practices, whereas others have been developed in recent times by individuals who have been dissatisfied with Western medicine. Some of these approaches may make conventional treatments more tolerable, and others are thought to reduce the cancer activity.

Acupuncture, a procedure in which thin needles with the circumference of a human hair are placed into acupuncture points in the body, has been found to reduce the number of medications needed in some cancer treatments and to be helpful in treating nausea associated with chemotherapy and with anesthesia following surgery (Rosenfeld, 1996).

A low-fat, high-fiber diet is thought to be effective both in preventing cancer and in retarding the growth of early cancers (Rosenfeld, 1996). Nutritional scientists reason that the same high-fat diets associated with the onset of cancer may also promote the growth of cancer tumors. Consequently, they recommend diets that may slow the growth of tumors. As of 1999, scientific studies do not support a relationship between dietary fat and breast cancer.

The use of herbs and plants to promote healing has been a practice for thousands of years, up until the present. For example, the anticancer drug Taxol is made from the bark of the yew tree. Herbalists suggest that teas brewed from herbs, poultices, or tablets made from plants or herbs may be useful in cancer treatment. Although little evidence exists to support the use of many herbs for medicinal purposes, some alternative therapists believe that various herbs stimulate the immune system and that some may retard the growth of cancer cells. Other herbs are thought to alleviate the side effects associated with conventional medical treatment, such as nausea, loss of appetite, fatigue, or hair loss.

Oxygen therapy, that is, the inhalation of extra oxygen through a mask, may be helpful for individuals undergoing radiation therapy, because the oxygen promotes the growth of tissue and blood vessels. Some individuals claim that it may also reduce the side effects of chemotherapy.

A number of products marketed by health food stores have been promoted as cancer treatments. For example, melatonin, a hormone, and Coenzyme Q10

(CoQ10), an antioxidant, may be useful in treatment of women with advanced breast cancer. Shark cartilage, also available in health food stores, is thought to interfere with the growth of the capillaries that feed cancerous tumors, thereby restricting the growth of the tumor. Empirical testing has failed to support shark cartilage as an anticancer agent. Clearly, we must step up the evaluation of alternative substances in this country so that women with breast cancer can avail themselves of a wider array of legitimate treatment options.

Decisions regarding the use of alternative treatments should be made thoughtfully. An excellent source of information is *Dr. Rosenfeld's Guide to Alternative Medicine* (Rosenfeld, 1996). Dr. Rosenfeld describes various treatments and regimens and presents evidence for their efficacy, where it exists. He also discusses possible harmful effects.

SUMMARY

The goal of this chapter is to introduce mental health professionals to cancer in general and, more specifically, to breast cancer, diagnostic tests, and traditional medical and alternative treatments. Mental health professionals are in an excellent position to help their clients with breast cancer become educated consumers, but they must first become educated themselves. Informed counselors can communicate more effectively with their clients about the disease and its treatments. Furthermore, teaching clients how to access information about breast cancer and its treatments so that they can more fully understand their options and make an informed choice about doctors and hospitals is a tremendous service. We still tend to view physicians as godlike, but they are human and make mistakes just like the rest of us; a second opinion, and even a third, is not a waste of time. Some women also do not realize that there are differences among physicians with respect to training and experience and that they are better off choosing a physician in whom they can legitimately have confidence. We are not saying that women must be active participants in treatment decisions, because not all women want to take that degree of responsibility, but we do believe that taking time to research physicians and hospitals is critical. Most women will get at least three or four references before hiring a contractor or a baby-sitter, but they tend not to put effort into what may be one of the most important decisions in their life, namely, choosing cancer specialists.

Notes

1. Because of its clarity, comprehensiveness, and up-to-date content, we relied heavily on *Dr. Susan Love's Breast Book* for basic information about diagnosis and treatment of breast cancer, in addition to recent articles from medical journals. Given that the focus of this book is the psychological rather than the medical aspects of the disease, we refer the reader to Dr. Love's book for more detail about breast cancer and its treatments. Because medical information is rapidly changing, we caution that the information in Dr.

Love's book may be outdated. The National Cancer Institute website (at www.nci.nih.gov) is regularly updated and is replete with comprehensive, up-to-date information. It is important that counselors remain well-informed. It is exciting that there is new genetic information about breast cancer, and our hope is that breast cancer research continues to be funded so that ultimately we will have a cure and a way to prevent the disease.

2. Mental health professionals can use this information in their work with clients who were first diagnosed with more advanced breast cancer. These clients may unnecessarily blame themselves for not detecting it sooner when, in fact, their cancer may not have been detectable.

3

Risk Factors and Prevention

A colleague recently recounted with dismay her experience at a cancer seminar several years ago. Apparently, the seminar leader, after presenting information on cancer risk factors, distributed a risk survey to participants. After it was scored, the presenter interpreted the meaning of several score ranges (e.g., 0-10 or 10-20). This colleague, whose score was considerably higher than the ranges offered to the audience, confronted the presenter at the end of the seminar and inquired about her individual risk. She was told by this "expert" that she had a 150% chance of getting cancer in her lifetime. She knew that this was statistically impossible, but she was still alarmed. Despite her attempts to dismiss the seminar leader's gloomy prophecy, as she told her story, we could hear an undercurrent of anxiety.

Our colleague is not alone in her fear of developing breast cancer. Popular talk shows, newspapers, and magazines are quick to inform us that one in eight women will develop breast cancer, a scary prospect. And if a mother or sister has had breast cancer, we're informed that our breast cancer risk increases even more. These statistics are alarming when they are not offered in the proper context, and they lead many women to overestimate their risk. For some women, worrying can escalate to preoccupation, intrusive thoughts about developing breast cancer, compulsive checking for lumps, and overuse of medical services. Other women are so frightened that they cope through denial and avoidance: They do not get mammograms, do breast self-exams, or go for annual physical checkups (Lerman et al., 1993). Recent research indicates, however, that moderate anxiety about developing breast cancer is correlated with *better* screening practices (Diefenbach, Miller, & Daly, 1999). Women who are well-informed are more likely to reject myths about breast cancer that potentially inhibit them from adhering to recommended screening guidelines.

WHAT ARE THE RISKS FOR BREAST CANCER?

Risk factors for breast cancer include age; genetics; hormonal factors; lifestyle factors such as diet, alcohol use, and exercise; personal or family history of breast cancer; and environmental factors. Although no specific carcinogens for breast cancer have been definitively identified, there are data to suggest that further exploration is necessary. Risk factors do not include bruises or bumps to the breast, fibrocystic breast conditions, history of fibroadenomas, overactive or aggressive fondling of the breasts, not wearing a brassiere, or wearing an ill-fitting brassiere, although some women continue to believe that one or more of these conditions or events can cause breast cancer.

Beliefs in the connections among personality, stress, and the development of cancer are widely held, despite the contradictory results of many studies in this area. Women with breast cancer tend to believe that "stress" or "depression" was a factor in their development of breast cancer (Roberts, Newcomb, Trentham-Dietz, & Storer, 1996), and in fact, the growing research in psychoneuroimmunology does suggest that stress reduces immune function. Reviews of the literature either report no relationship between breast cancer and psychosocial factors or a weak association. Those reporting no association tend to criticize the studies they reviewed on methodological or conceptual grounds, stating in essence that if the empirical studies were stronger, an association would have been revealed. A meta-analysis of studies investigating the role of psychosocial factors (i.e., anxiety/depression, childhood family environment, conflict-avoidant personality, denial/repression coping, anger expression, extroversion/introversion, stressful life events, and separation/loss) in the development of breast cancer was recently conducted (McKenna, Zevon, Corn, & Rounds, 1999). Effects were found for denial/repression coping, separation/loss experiences, and stressful life events. Conflict-avoidant personality was significant as well, but the finding was less robust. "Results overall support[ed] only a modest association between specific psychosocial factors and breast cancer and are contrary to the conventional wisdom that personality and stress influence the development of breast cancer" (McKenna et al., p. 520).

Age

One in eight women will get breast cancer, but this statistic is not as ominous as it sounds. Too many women identify eight of their best friends and conclude that one of them is destined to get breast cancer. This isn't exactly the way it happens. The one-in-eight statistic represents a "lifetime" risk. As Table 3.1 reports, breast cancer risk increases as women age. By age 70, a woman has a one-in-fourteen chance of developing breast cancer; by age 85, she has a one-in-nine chance, and her risk continues to worsen as she ages. Understanding these statistics may help to decrease some of the apprehension women feel about the possibility of developing breast cancer.

TABLE 3.1 Average Risk of Developing Breast Cancer

By the Age of	Average Risk
25	1 in 19,608
30	1 in 2525
35	1 in 622
40	1 in 217
45	1 in 93
50	1 in 50
55	1 in 33
60	1 in 24
65	1 in 17
70	1 in 14
75	1 in 11
80	1 in 10
85	1 in 9
Ever	1 in 8

Genetic Factors

Although genetic mutations have recently been identified as causing breast cancer, the overwhelming majority of breast cancer patients (approximately 90% to 95%) do not have hereditary breast cancer. Some individuals, however, do carry mutated genes (*BRCA1* and *BRCA2*) that are associated with breast cancer. *BRCA1* produces an abnormal protein that does not do its job of inhibiting cell division. Consequently, cell division is uncontrolled, and cancer develops. This defective protein has been implicated in cases of familial breast cancer. A flaw in another gene, *BRCA2,* was discovered in 1996, and this flaw appears to account for over 30% of the genetically transmitted early-onset breast cancers not connected to *BRCA1.* In nonhereditary breast cancer, the protein itself is not defective, but it is located in the cytoplasm rather than the nucleus of the cell. The outcome is the same: cell division is uncontrolled, and cancer develops. Scientists estimate that women with a genetic mutation have between a 56% and an 85% chance of developing breast cancer by age 70, regardless of their family history. Mutations in the *BRCA2* gene are believed to cause breast cancer in young women. These genetic mutations are commonly found in women of Eastern European descent, particularly Ashkenazi Jews (Egan et al., 1996; Offit et al., 1996) and in those who have a first-degree relative (i.e., a mother or a sister) with breast cancer (Egan et al., 1996).

Hormonal Factors

Evidence mounts that the hormone estrogen is related to the development of breast cancer. Laboratory experiments have confirmed that estrogen is a growth factor for most breast cancer cells. Women's estrogen levels surge during menstruation, and the more menstrual periods a woman has, the greater her risk for breast cancer. Women with the lowest rates of breast cancer have had their first child by the age of 20, a greater number of completed pregnancies, late onset of menstruation, and early onset of menopause. Breastfeeding also has been shown to reduce the risk of breast cancer, perhaps because it tends to delay the resumption of menstruation after pregnancy. Women who were breastfed as infants also may have a reduced risk of developing breast cancer.

Birth control pills (which all contain estrogen) are associated with breast cancer during the period in which they are taken and for up to 10 years afterward (Collaborative Group on Hormonal Factors in Breast Cancer, 1996). More specifically, current pill users are 24% more likely to get breast cancer than non-pill users. Once oral contraceptives are discontinued, however, breast cancer risk is lowered so that after 5 years the added risk reduces to 16%, and after 10 years it essentially disappears. The age at which birth control pills are first used also may be related to breast cancer risk. Teenagers who are given estrogen at 14 or 15 years of age to regulate their periods or for birth control may be at higher risk. Adolescent girls may be less vulnerable to breast cancer if they have irregular periods, and therefore fewer periods, but more research is needed before any definitive conclusions can be reached.

Hormone replacement therapy (HRT), a treatment for postmenopausal women that is typically a combination of estrogen and progesterone, has also been associated with increased incidence of breast cancer, uterine cancer, and gallstones. However, a recent study of 37,000 women participating in HRT revealed only a small increased risk of developing slow-growing, highly curable breast tumors. Over 11 years, women undergoing HRT were no more likely to develop fast-growing, life-threatening breast cancers than women who were not undergoing HRT.

However, HRT has clear health benefits: reduced morbidity from osteoporosis, possible reduction in cardiovascular mortality, and decreased risk of colorectal cancer and Alzheimer's disease. For many women, the health benefits of HRT outweigh the increased health risks. Most women do not realize that mammograms may be less accurate for women taking estrogen (Laya, Larsen, Taplin, & White, 1996); however, accuracy can be maintained by discontinuing HRT for a short period of time before screening (Black & Fletcher, 1996). Decisions to briefly interrupt HRT should be made with input from physicians, because menopause symptoms could return. In general, we recommend that women, together with their physicians, consider their personal and family health histories when making any decision about HRT.

Lifestyle Factors

High-fat diets, lack of exercise, deficiency of certain vitamins or fiber, and alcohol intake may increase the risk of breast cancer. Diets high in fat have in the past been linked to increased risk of breast cancer, but this relationship may be a spurious one. Nearly 89,000 women participating in the Nurses' Health Study recorded their eating habits from 1980 to 1994. The results of this study contradicted earlier studies. The researchers found no evidence of increased risk of breast cancer with increased consumption of animal fat, polyunsaturated fat, saturated fat, or transunsaturated fat, nor did it appear in this study that a low-fat diet reduced breast cancer risk (Holmes et al., 1999).

Adult weight gain has also been associated with increased breast cancer risk. Huang et al. (1997) found that postmenopausal women who had gained between 22 and 41 pounds after age 18 and had never used HRT had a 61% higher risk of developing breast cancer than women who gained less than 5 pounds. It is important to keep in mind that 73% of breast cancers have no relation to dietary fat, and it is still unclear when during a woman's lifetime is the critical period for reducing fat intake. Love (1995) suggested that the period between menarche (the onset of menstruation) and menopause may be the most crucial period in which to have a low-fat diet; however, more research is needed on the relationship between high-fat diets and breast cancer.

Moderate physical activity (2 to 3 hours per week) appears to significantly lower breast cancer risk, as does the consumption of vegetables containing antioxidants such as vitamins A, C, and E. Researchers have reported that women who eat the most fruits and vegetables reduce their risk of breast cancer by approximately 50%. It has been hypothesized that the fiber and antioxidants in fruits and vegetables may protect against cancer. However, antioxidant supplements are not as effective as eating fruits and vegetables.

Vegetables such as broccoli, carrots, kale, and lettuce; folic acid; and soy proteins are also being studied as potential factors in cancer prevention. The consumption of soy has been suggested as one reason why women living in Asia have low rates of breast cancer. Reputable studies have indicated that drinking four to six cups of green tea daily provides protection against many cancers (Rosenfeld, 1996). These teas are also more common in China and Japan than in the United States. A breast cancer prevention diet (Arnot, 1998) recommends daily intake of soy protein (35 to 60 g), flaxseed (25 g), fish oil (10 mg), and a low-fat diet that particularly avoids omega-6 fatty acids.

Alcohol use is associated with increases in breast cancer, but further study is needed to establish cause (Colditz, 1990). Women in their 30s who drink two or more alcoholic beverages per day may have a 70% to 80% increased risk of developing breast cancer. A 1998 research review suggested that alcohol consumption raises estrogren levels in postmenopausal women who are on estrogen replacement therapy (Purohit, 1998). It is premature to recommend, on the basis of this finding, that women on HRT refrain from drinking, but it might suggest why alcohol use has been associated with increased breast cancer risk. Breast tumors in women with advanced breast cancer seem to grow particularly quickly when alcohol is ingested.

Smoking may be a risk factor for developing breast cancer, and it has been established that smokers have a 25% greater risk of dying from breast cancer than nonsmokers do. This risk is much higher for heavy smokers. Women who smoke over two packs a day have a 75% greater mortality risk from breast cancer than do nonsmokers (Katzenstein, 1994).

Personal History of Breast Cancer

Women who once had breast cancer are at increased risk for a new primary breast tumor. If a woman had a mass that was diagnosed as atypical hyperplasia or as lobular carcinoma in situ, she is also at increased risk for breast cancer. Women with familial breast cancer (defined as one or more first- or second-degree relatives with breast cancer), but with no confirmation of a genetic defect, are also at increased risk. However, a history of fibrocystic breast disease does not increase a woman's chances of developing cancer.

Environmental Factors

Although specific environmental carcinogens related to breast cancer have not been identified, there is mounting suspicion that a relationship exists. Given that approximately 70% of women diagnosed with breast cancer have few or none of the known risk factors, activists have increasingly questioned whether environmental factors cause breast cancer. Concerns have been raised about exposure to DDT, PBBs, PCBs, vehicle exhaust, low-frequency electromagnetic fields, foods cooked by high-temperature methods, radiation, and contaminated drinking water. Although a link between environmental factors and breast cancer has yet to be uncovered, researchers have noted unusually high rates of breast cancer in certain geographic locations and in women who are concentrated in certain occupations. For example, high breast cancer rates have been found in Long Island, New York; in 7 out of 10 towns in Massachusetts (particularly those around Cape Cod); and in areas of Maine. Some individuals suggest that toxins (pesticides and other chemicals) in the water or fallout from bomb tests may be responsible.

A link between radiation and breast cancer has been confirmed (Love, 1995). Breast cancer rates rose in women exposed to radiation at Hiroshima and Nagasaki, particularly for women in their early 20s and younger. Women in their 50s and 60s exposed to the radiation suffered no effects. Furthermore, women who had radiation treatments to their chest in late adolescence and early adulthood had strikingly high rates of breast cancer later in life. Flight attendants appear to have increased rates of breast cancer. Exposure to radiation on planes is being considered as a potential risk factor. Radiation does not pose a danger to most passengers; however, traveling on long flights on a regular schedule may be problematic.

Individuals who work on the night shift (e.g., nurses, automobile workers) have also been identified as having elevated rates of breast cancer. These workers, who are exposed to light at night, produce less melatonin. Lowered production of melatonin by the pineal gland may be associated with increased risk of breast cancer, but the relationship between pineal gland functioning and breast cancer is not clearly established.

Further, studies of electromagnetic fields (EMF), to which people are exposed via sun, X rays, power lines, appliances, and computer terminals, suggest that exposure to EMF may also be a possible causal agent in breast cancer. Although physicists have concluded that electromagnetic fields do not affect genetics, such fields may affect the functioning of the pineal gland, thus lowering melatonin production. In the laboratory, human breast cancer cells exposed to melatonin stop growing or dramatically decrease their rate of growth. When EMFs are applied, the cells begin growing again. Nevertheless, most scientists remain skeptical about EMF as a causal factor in breast cancer because laboratory conditions do not approximate normal exposure in humans.

The DNA in breast cells is most susceptible to damage during adolescence and pregnancy, when breast tissue cells are multiplying the fastest. Tumors resulting from this damage may not appear for many years. More investigation of these environmental factors is clearly warranted, and we hope the results will benefit today's young girls as well as future generations.

LOWERING PERSONAL RISK

All women are entitled to complete information about the risks and benefits of specific lifestyle habits and available treatments. In order to evaluate individual risk, women must discuss with their doctors their personal and family history and the risks and benefits of possible treatments. For women at risk for heart disease and osteoporosis, for example, HRT may be indicated. By the same token, HRT may be contraindicated for women who have a higher risk for breast cancer.

It seems that most women could benefit from eating a low-fat diet, eating two to four servings of fruit and three to five servings of vegetables per day, and engaging in 2 to 3 hours of exercise per week. An overwhelming majority (86%) of women who responded to a national survey of women aged 18 to 65 (conducted by *Glamour* magazine and funded by Hanes Hosiery) revealed that they would restrict their intake of highly desired but unhealthy foods and would exercise more if they knew it would reduce their breast cancer risk. Unfortunately, most women ranked obesity, lack of exercise, and alcohol consumption as the lowest on a list of breast cancer risks. They believed that the three most important risks were heredity (91%), smoking (53%), and environmental factors (37%). In a separate section of this survey, injury to the breast was cited most often as a risk factor. Also, many women (particularly women in the 18- to 39-year-old age group) were confused about when and how often they should get mammograms. These survey results dramatically illustrate women's misconceptions about breast cancer. Educating women about breast cancer risks could potentially have an impact on women's health if information were delivered in a way that would motivate women to comply with recommended guidelines.

POPULATIONS AT INCREASED RISK

In addition to women who carry the mutated genes *BRCA1* and *BRCA2,* some other groups of women may be at greater risk for developing or dying from breast cancer. Chronic psychiatric patients, African American women, and lesbians warrant more focused attention. According to one study, chronic psychiatric patients had a more than threefold greater risk of breast cancer than did general hospital patients, and a ninefold greater risk compared to the general population (Halbreich, Shen, & Panaro, 1996). This finding is potentially explained by the fact that chronic psychiatric patients are often homeless, have poor diets, tend to be heavy smokers and alcohol abusers, and have poor access to health care. In any case, this study should be replicated before definitive conclusions can be reached.

African American Women and Breast Cancer

Racial and ethnic groups differ in the extent to which risk factors for breast cancer exist. For example, on average, African American women consume more nitrates and meat and not enough fiber relative to their protein, fat, and carbohydrate intake. As a group, they have insufficient intake of thiamine, riboflavin, vitamins A and C, and iron, and they have a tendency toward obesity. Premenopausal obesity in particular has been associated with breast cancer risk, and according to Gillum (1987), approximately 50% of African American women are overweight by as early as the third decade of life.

About one fourth of all women who find symptoms that suggest breast cancer wait 2 to 3 months before they seek medical care (Mor et al., 1990, cited in Lauver, 1994) . Although some studies suggest that women of color wait longer than white women to seek care, other studies suggest that the difference in the amount of time is neither statistically nor clinically significant (Coates et al., 1992). African American women who delay diagnostic testing and treatment may do so for a variety of reasons. First is that medical services are less available to and underused by African American women, primarily because of low socioeconomic status (Guidry, Aday, Zhang, & Winn, 1998). Economic demands necessitate that some African American women continue to work in order to provide for themselves and their families. Also, African Americans tend to demonstrate a great tolerance of symptoms and tend not to seek medical help (Long, 1993). Furthermore, some African American women do not have confidence in physicians who practice Western medicine, believing that they do not understand and therefore can not effectively treat illness as well as healers who practice folk and popular medicine can (Snow, 1983). Clearly, outright avoidance or delays in seeking medical care can result in more deaths from breast cancer.

Although a greater percentage of white than African American women are diagnosed with breast cancer when all age groups are considered, incidence and mortality rates are significantly higher in African American women under the age of 50 (Long, 1993). Younger African American women also have increased mortality rates, regardless of the stage of the disease. In fact, from 1980 to 1991 the breast cancer death rate rose by 21% for Black women, during which time the death rate for White women rose less than 1%. More recent data (through 1993) show that death rates among Black women dropped for all groups under age 70, but above age 70 the death rates increased.

African American women tend to be diagnosed with advanced disease for other reasons as well. African Americans are less likely to have routine mammograms or to use other screening methods (Forte, 1995). Older African American women tend to leave decisions to physicians, who tend not to recommend breast screening for poor, older women. Black women as a group are also less likely to receive information from their physicians about breast cancer risk and have insufficient awareness of ongoing national chemoprevention trials (research studies to evaluate specific drugs for use in breast cancer prevention). In comparison to White women, Black women have less positive attitudes toward clinical trials, greater mistrust of cancer researchers, greater doubts about the ethics of clinical trials, and a strong preference for being treated by a Black scientist (Mouton, Harris, Rovi, Solorzano, & Johnson, 1997). According to Royak-Shaler (quoted in DeAngelis, 1995, p. 37), Black women incorrectly cited risk factors not known to cause breast cancer, such as bumping or bruising a breast and smoking, and they often neglected to name actual risks, such as family history.

Quality of care also tends to differ for African American and White cancer patients. African American women are less likely to undergo liver scans, radiation therapy, progesterone receptor assays, postmastectomy rehabilitation, and adjuvant chemotherapy. The underutilization of these diagnostic tests and treatments likely contributes to the higher mortality rates for African Americans and is probably tied to differences in socioeconomic status, health insurance coverage, and cultural attitudes toward Western medicine.

Finally, Black and White women differed on other factors, such as immune functioning. Lake-Lewin, Kunzweiler, and Kunick (1990) found that immune functioning was compromised to a greater extent in African American women than in White women, and African American women tended to develop more aggressive forms of breast cancer at earlier ages (Freeman & Wasfie, 1989; Krieger, 1990). Satariano, Belle, and Swanson (1986) suggested that African American women and White women who are 65 years of age or older when they develop cancer may be more similar in behavior or susceptibility than are women who are diagnosed in early adulthood and middle age.

Lesbian Women

Suzanne Haynes, an epidemiologist at the National Cancer Institute, suggested that the lifetime breast cancer risk for lesbians may be as high as one in three (Brownworth, 1993). She based this risk estimate on results of the National

Lesbian Health Care Survey (Bradford & Ryan, 1988) and on existing studies of breast cancer risk factors. Lesbians may be at greater risk for developing breast cancer, in part, because they are less likely to conceive children and are less apt to obtain mammograms. It is clear that some lesbians avoid seeking medical care and are therefore vulnerable to delays in diagnosis and treatment (Simkin, 1991; Stevens & Hall, 1988; Trippet & Bain, 1992). "The reasons for the difference in frequency of contact with the health care system are multiple; they include institutionalized homophobia and heterosexism in the health care system, erroneous beliefs held by lesbians that they are immune to certain health problems, and financial barriers to care" (Peterson & Bricker-Jenkins, 1996, p. 34). Stevens and Hall (1988) found that almost three quarters of their sample of lesbian women believed that physicians reacted to their sexual orientation with shock, embarrassment, condescension, fear, pity, or unfriendliness. Not surprisingly, several studies have shown that lesbians prefer female physicians, and ideally, lesbian physicians (Lucas, 1992). Health care professionals tend not to ask about sexual orientation, and most gay women do not volunteer that information. Consequently, doctors ask medical history questions that are based on heterosexist assumptions, for example, questions about birth control and intercourse.

Fortunately, more attention is being paid to lesbian health issues. Two large studies, the Harvard Nurses' Study and the Women's Health Initiative of the National Institutes of Health, are collecting data on lesbian patients to see if they are more at risk for certain diseases and to identify potential preventive measures. In addition, the American Medical Association issued a policy statement directed at eliminating insensitivity toward lesbians.

SCREENING GUIDELINES AND PRACTICES

The American Cancer Society recommends that women do monthly breast self-examinations beginning at age 20 and that they receive manual breast examinations from their gynecologists or family physicians every 3 years until age 40—at which point yearly clinical breast examinations are recommended. The National Cancer Institute and the American Cancer Society have not always agreed about mammography screening guidelines, but both organizations agree on annual mammograms after 50 years of age. The American Cancer Society recommends that women be screened first at age 40 and then every year thereafter. The National Cancer Institute recommends that women in their 40s have mammograms every 1 to 2 years. These are only guidelines, and women should consult with their physicians to determine how often they should undergo a clinical breast examination and when a baseline mammogram should be performed. Physicians may tailor the frequency of exams and mammograms to a woman's personal and family medical history.

Mammograms

Regular mammography, in conjunction with clinical breast examinations, decrease mortality rates from breast cancer (30% to 35% reduction in women over age 50, 17% reduction in women aged 40 to 49). However, mammography is not perfect; mammograms fail to detect approximately 13% of breast cancers, and approximately 60% to 80% of the lesions they do detect are benign. Unfortunately, women have not participated in mammography screening as frequently or as regularly as has been recommended, although mammography rates appear to be increasing. Detection rates from mammography are predicted to rise because of improvements in technology.

Inner-city Hispanic women are less likely to be screened for breast cancer than are non-Hispanic women, perhaps because of several misconceptions: Some Hispanic women do not see themselves as susceptible to breast cancer, others do not believe that breast cancer is curable, and some believe that a breast exam given by a physician makes a mammogram unnecessary or that they would not benefit from having a mammogram (Fulton, Rakowski, & Jones, 1995).

Inner-city Hispanic women are not alone in their misconceptions about mammography screening. Women of many racial and ethnic backgrounds do not obtain mammograms because they are asymptomatic (Rimer, Keintz, Kessler, Engstrom, & Rosan, 1989), or they underestimate their risk of developing breast cancer because they have no family history of the disease or because they take vitamins and exercise. Other women do not get screened for the opposite reason: They fear being diagnosed (Fox & Stein, 1991). As a group, high-risk women are not screened any more regularly than low-risk women are (Kaplan, Weinberg, Small, & Herndon, 1991), but more-educated women are screened more regularly than less-educated women. Higher incomes and insurance coverage are also positively related to mammography utilization.

The women least likely to have regular mammograms are women over 60. This is not surprising, because women typically heed the recommendations of their physicians with respect to screening, and physicians are less likely to refer older women for mammograms. A recent analogue study (Marwill, Freund, & Barry, 1996) found that physicians made decisions about whether to refer women for mammograms based on their implicit judgments about the woman's quality of life. For example, women who were depicted as quite elderly, as nursing home residents, or as demented were less likely to be referred.

If their physicians recommend a mammogram, and if they trust their physicians, older women are very likely to get screened. Those women who perceive themselves to be vulnerable because of a personal or family experience of breast cancer, who perceive the expected benefits to outweigh the perceived risk of adverse effects, and whose social networks support mammography are also more likely to engage in the screening. Studies have indicated that a moderate amount of anxiety motivates women to engage in breast cancer screening. According to some researchers (e.g., Lerman et al., 1993), when anxiety is low there is little motivation to get screened, and when anxiety is high, avoidance is common. A recent meta-analysis (McCaul, Branstetter, Schroeder, & Glasgow, 1996) and another empirical investigation (McCaul, Schroeder, & Reid, 1996) both dispute the claim that there is a curvilinear relationship between anxiety and screening. McCaul, Schroeder, and Reid reported that the greater the worry and the greater the perception of personal vulnerability, the more likely women are to perform breast self-examinations and to obtain mammograms and clinical breast exams.

The conflicting findings regarding whether anxiety prompts avoidance or motivates screening may be clarified to some extent by examining the role of personality. A study by Schwartz et al. (1999) revealed that distress (defined as intrusive thoughts and worries about having a relative diagnosed with breast cancer) was not related to mammogram utilization for highly conscientious women with a family history of breast cancer, but it was associated with less mammogram use in women who are not conscientious. Perhaps personality factors like conscientiousness are moderators of health-promoting behaviors.

In any case, to increase participation in mammography screening, both women and physicians should be targeted. For educated White women (those with at least a high school diploma), messages that inform women that they are responsible for detecting breast cancer have been found to be more effective for increasing mammography screening than neutral information about breast cancer or messages that emphasize that doctors are responsible for detecting breast cancer (Rothman, Salovey, Turvy, & Fishkin, 1993).

Other methods for increasing screening have been implemented successfully. A 12-page booklet describing the importance of screening and offering clear advice about how to reduce fears about mammograms was mailed to women who were not following recommended screening guidelines; the increase in mammography adherence was 13%. More intensive intervention efforts may be necessary for those women with abnormal mammogram results who do not follow up. Telephone calls designed to reduce fears and other barriers to participating in mammography screening yielded a 24% increase.

A relatively new program offered by the American Cancer Society provides women who are frightened about obtaining a mammography with a "buddy" who will accompany them to the appointment. This seems like an excellent idea to increase mammography screening, but the program has yet to be evaluated. Another service designed to increase screening in economically disadvantaged areas is the provision of mobile mammography units.

More research needs to be conducted that will help health educators understand the optimal ways to promote screening in women with different coping styles. Materials designed to promote awareness of breast cancer screening must be at reading levels appropriate to the target population. Screening information must be made available in different languages and through written, pictorial, and oral methods so that diverse groups of women can be reached.

Breast Self-Examination

Beginning at age 20, a woman should examine her breasts monthly (5 to 7 days after her period begins) to become familiar with how her breasts typically feel so she is more likely to detect changes. Postmenopausal women should pick a date each month to examine their breasts, perhaps their birth date, because it is easy to remember.

Most breast lumps are discovered accidentally by women themselves (e.g., washing in the shower or bath), and most of the lumps prove to be benign. Although an overwhelming majority of women (96%) know about breast self-examination (BSE), only 20% to 25% of women regularly perform them. When asked why they do not do BSEs, many women say that they aren't confident in their ability to detect a problem, especially if their breasts tend to be lumpy, or they say that BSE makes them anxious. Many women have never been shown the proper way to perform a BSE. One study that used a very small sample (Millar & Millar, 1992) found that women in their 40s were less likely to do BSE than women in their 30s, even though women in their 30s had greater doubt about the efficacy of BSE than did women in their 40s. Women in their 30s also believed themselves to be at greater risk for developing breast cancer in the next 10 years than did women in their 40s (even though the opposite is true). A number of factors made low-income women over 40 years of age more likely to engage in BSE: if their physicians encouraged it, if they were proficient at it, if they knew when they should examine their breasts each month, if they felt confident, and if they were more educated (Morrison, 1996).

Genetic Testing

One option for women with family histories of breast cancer is genetic testing. Tests for the *BRCA1* gene are currently available, although their psychological and social impacts have not been adequately determined. If a woman tests negative, it does not indicate that she is free from breast cancer risk. Over 90% of all women who develop breast cancer do not have this gene mutation. A potential adverse consequence of receiving a negative test result is that women will be falsely reassured, their sense of personal vulnerability will decrease, and they may be less vigilant about screening.

In 1998 Congress approved a proposal introduced by President Clinton prohibiting insurance companies from denying coverage to people who are in high-risk groups based on their genetic testing results. This is a huge step forward; however, because this is recent legislation, it is unclear whether women with family histories of breast cancer will avoid genetic testing. There are other concerns women have about knowing their genetic status. If they test positive they may be plagued by questions, such as: Will this be the day I find a lump? Should I tell my boyfriend that I have a *BRCA1* mutation, and if so, when? When should I tell my daughter that she may have inherited this mutation? Should I share this information with other family members? Other considerations are the cost of genetic testing (between $300 and $3,000, depending on the complexity of the DNA analysis) and worries about the confidentiality of the results; for example, could employers or potential employers find out?

In a study by Lerman et al. (1995), only 43% of the women who participated in genetic testing wanted to know their genetic status, largely because they worried about the impact on insurance coverage. As would be expected, women who received negative test results (no genetic mutation) were significantly less depressed and more likely to function well at 1-month follow-up. Women who received positive test results (a mutation in *BRCA1*), surprisingly, did not experience increased distress. This suggests that there may be psychological benefits to knowing one's genetic status, particularly for women who are worried. Knowing one's status appears to reduce distress for those women not actually carrying the mutation but does not appear to increase distress for those women who do have *BRCA1* mutations (at least in a sample of well-educated and knowledgeable women). More research is necessary for a comprehensive understanding of the psychosocial consequences of genetic testing for breast cancer. Suggested areas for study would be the incidence of depression, anxiety, remorse for transmitting the defective gene to offspring, or survival guilt for testing negative when other family members tested positive for the genetic mutation; possible impairment in vocational, social, and sexual functioning; and appetite or sleep disturbances (Lerman & Croyle, 1996).

Genetic testing for breast cancer raises many ethical and legal issues. Will physicians be legally bound to inform patients' relatives of their shared susceptibility, or will they be banned from doing so? Does submitting a child to invasive genetic tests constitute parental abuse, or does lack of testing represent negligence on the part of parents? Can a physician refuse to test a child if he or she believes that it is premature or not in the child's best interest? And what about the proliferation of for-profit genetic testing centers? How can we assure that proper pre- and posttest counseling is occurring? These questions remain largely unanswered.

Women are entitled to a comprehensive explanation of the risks and benefits of accepting, rejecting, or postponing genetic testing. Risks inherent in the testing process as well as in facing the test result should be fully discussed. Women have the "right to know their genetic prognosis and a right not to know it" (Dickens, Pei, & Taylor, 1996, p. 814).

MEDICAL AND SURGICAL APPROACHES TO BREAST CANCER PREVENTION

Healthy women who have a strong family history of breast cancer or are at genetic risk are eager for preventive interventions. Prior to 1998, these options were limited to regular mammograms, clinical and self breast examination, and lifestyle changes to lower risk. Unfortunately, women who choose these measures often continue to feel vulnerable. Until 1998 only one other option was available, and it is a rather drastic measure: prophylactic mastectomy. Some healthy women who have the *BRCA1* or *BRCA2* mutation have opted for bilateral mastectomies. Fortunately, they now have another choice. In 1998, the Breast Cancer Prevention Trial was completed. Findings suggested that when healthy women who were at increased risk for breast cancer were administered tamoxifen, their breast cancer incidence was significantly reduced (United States Department of Health and

Human Services, 1998). Prophylactic mastectomy and tamoxifen are both options for prevention of recurrence as well.

Prophylactic Mastectomies

Because it is impossible to remove all breast tissue, even total mastectomies do not guarantee freedom from breast cancer. Why then would women choose such a drastic option? Stefanek, Helzlsouer, Wilcox, and Houn (1995) reported that women who had the surgery expressed more worry about developing breast cancer and were more likely to have had previous breast biopsies than women who did not undergo prophylactic surgery.

Removing 95% or more of the breast tissue should significantly decrease the risk of developing breast cancer (Lopez & Porter, 1996). Data from several studies make a strong case for prophylactic mastectomies, indicating a substantially reduced incidence of breast cancer in women who had the surgery compared with the incidence in age-matched controls (see Lopez & Porter). Women with a genetic mutation who have had prophylactic mastectomy reduce their breast cancer risk by as much as 85%. Much more research is needed, however, before any definitive conclusions can be drawn.

If prophylactic mastectomy is elected, "skin-sparing total mastectomy (not subcutaneous) with autogenous tissue reconstruction is the preferred approach" (Lopez & Porter, 1996, p. 231). After the surgery the breasts appear small, but after 3 months they grow to their full capacity. Women can choose their cup size prior to surgery. Nipples are typically grafted or tattooed onto the breasts 6 months after the initial surgery to give the implants time to settle.

Women who elect to have prophylactic mastectomies with reconstruction report many psychological benefits. For instance, they are no longer plagued by fears of developing breast cancer because they know they have done everything possible to reduce their chances. Another advantage is that their new breasts may be firmer than their original breasts. On the other hand, women with implants cannot have mammograms and they lose almost all or all sensitivity in their breasts. Furthermore, some women may be confronted by people who disapprove of their decision to have a bilateral mastectomy before they were even diagnosed with cancer.

Tamoxifen Trials

The Breast Cancer Prevention Trial was a randomized study of tamoxifen, a drug that when taken for 5 years had been found to markedly reduce cancer recurrence in women who had breast cancer. In the prevention trial, tamoxifen was administered to healthy women who were at increased risk of breast cancer because they were 60 or older or had other combinations of risk factors. In addition to assessing whether the tamoxifen could help prevent breast cancer, the study also examined other benefits, such as protection against heart attacks and osteoporosis.

In women over 50, tamoxifen reduced the risk of invasive breast cancer by 51% and of noninvasive cancer by 30%; the drug appeared to reduce osteoporosis, but it elevated the risk of blood clots in the veins and lungs, endometrial cancer, and premalignant overgrowth of the endometrial lining. In women aged 35 to 50, tamoxifen reduced the risk of invasive breast cancer by 46% and of noninvasive cancer by 73% with no added risk of endometrial cancer or blood clots (Harvard Women's Health Watch, 1998).

Surgical Removal of Ovaries

In one small study, 43 women who tested positive for a mutated *BRCA1* gene but who had no history of breast or ovarian cancer had their ovaries surgically removed. A control group consisted of women who also had *BRCA1* mutations and no history of breast or ovarian cancer. After 10 years, the women who had undergone the surgical procedure had a 67% reduction in the incidence of breast cancer, and between 5 and 10 years, there was a 72% reduction (Rebbeck et al., 1999).

Other Prevention Research

Clinical trials are under way to test the efficacy of raloxifene, a drug believed to have fewer adverse effects than tamoxifen, in preventing breast cancer in high-risk women. In a recent randomized double-blind clinical trial conducted in 25 countries, the Multiple Outcomes of Raloxifene Evaluation (MORE; Cummings et al., 1999), postmenopausal women who were diagnosed as having osteoporosis were treated with raloxifene over 3 years to determine whether it would reduce their risk for fractures. Secondarily, the participants were monitored for occurrences of breast cancer. Raloxifene increases bone density, and in this trial it was found to decrease the risk of vertebral fractures, but not of other types of fractures. Further, invasive breast cancer risk was substantially reduced. There was no evidence of increased risk for endometrial cancer; however, an increased rate of thrombosis and pulmonary embolus was observed. Finally, hot flashes were reported by study participants. Although the news about raloxifene is good, this does not mean that postmenopausal women should routinely take the drug as a preventive measure. Rather, such decisions should be made by a woman and her doctor and should be based on the woman's health risk history.

Additional breast cancer prevention studies are examining dietary interventions and the impact of environmental toxins. The Women's Health Initiative has enrolled 70,000 women over age 50 in a series of clinical trials to measure the effectiveness of a low-fat diet (% of calories from fat), calcium and vitamin D supplements, and HRT for breast cancer prevention. Research is also being conducted on a synthetic form of vitamin A, other vitamins including C and E, vegetables, and phytochemicals, which are naturally occurring chemicals found in fruits and vegetables. Investigations of environmental toxins are also under way. Fat tissue is being removed from the breasts of women with and without cancer so that levels of 80 toxins (e.g., dioxins and PCBs) can be compared.

SUMMARY

The purpose of this chapter is to introduce mental health professionals to research on breast cancer risk factors and on screening and prevention methods. Mental health professionals who are informed about breast cancer can be helpful to all their female clients, whether or not they have breast cancer. For healthy women who are worried about getting breast cancer, they can serve as advocates for early detection and can educate women about ways to lower their personal risk. They can help women to take a proactive approach to their health by adopting healthier diets and exercise routines, regularly visiting their gynecologists, and adhering to recommended screening guidelines.

4

The Breast Cancer Experience

The breast cancer experience can be divided into several phases. In this chapter, the experiences of women with breast cancer are discussed as they encounter prediagnosis, diagnosis, treatment, and recovery. The last part of the chapter discusses the experiences of women whose illness is terminal.

COMMON RESPONSES DURING THE EARLY PHASES

Prediagnosis

A woman discovers a lump or her doctor tells her that her mammogram shows something unusual but not to worry about it, that "in six months we'll do another mammogram to see if anything has changed." Such discoveries lead many women to seek consultations with other doctors or advice from friends and family. Feelings of fear and even panic are intermingled with confidence that nothing is wrong. Visits with doctors, examinations, and diagnostic tests are sandwiched between business meetings or family activities.

This prebiopsy period is, for many women, one that is highly anxiety provoking. Many women find it hard to concentrate because thoughts of cancer and death keep intruding. Nevertheless, decisions must be made about whether to proceed with evaluations or diagnostic tests and the types of tests to be performed. Some women trust their doctors implicitly when told that an abnormality on their mammogram is nothing to worry about. Such women may not see their situation as severe enough to warrant a second opinion or to have any diagnostic tests performed. However, friends or significant others may respond with fear and concern that a woman's medical care is inadequate. They may tell of friends or relatives who had similar experiences only to have cancer diagnosed at a later date, or they may question her doctor's competence. These anecdotes often evoke or heighten her anxiety.

"Just yesterday everything was fine. I'm the same person today as I was yesterday, only today I discovered a lump while taking my morning shower. I didn't have time to think about it then—I was late for work, and I had an important meeting first thing. But now everything is quiet and the moment that I found the lump has intruded into my day. My partner is out of town, so I can't even ask for a 'second opinion.' But I know that the lump wasn't there before, and now I must do something. I'll call my doctor. She will see me tomorrow; she has always been responsive if I have a problem. I'm glad that I don't have to wait a long time to see her. I can't do anything else right now. I tell myself, 'There is no point getting upset until I know what this is all about.' And so I'll put this out of my mind, at least until tomorrow."

On the other hand, the woman who receives information from a physician who appears worried may feel immediately anxious and believe her situation to be very serious (Shapiro et al., 1992) even before she knows her diagnosis. She may convince herself that she has cancer and feel paralyzed by fear.

Seeking medical attention. Early detection of breast cancer is associated with a better prognosis, and early detection is partly dependent on how quickly women seek medical care once they identify symptoms. About 20% to 25% of women wait 2 to 3 months after they discover symptoms before they seek medical care (Lauver, 1994).

A number of factors are associated with care-seeking behavior. Women who are concerned about their symptoms, believe that it is useful to seek medical advice, generally seek routine medical care, and have a medical care provider who is affordable and accessible are likely to seek care promptly (Coates et al., 1992; Lauver & Ho, 1993). Even when women are not anxious, their physicians seem to be able to influence them to follow up on suspicious symptoms (Lauver & Ho, 1993). On the other hand, for women who do not have a general practitioner or other regular physician, anxiety seems to be the key: It motivates them to seek medical attention. If a woman does not have a physician and she is not anxious, then she is likely to seek care later rather than sooner (Lauver, 1994). In addition, age, financial resources, and optimism are factors that may influence when women seek help. Young women who are less optimistic, have few economic resources, and have little experience with medical procedures may delay their medical care. However, when women have a friend who has had breast cancer, they are likely to seek help promptly.

Misconceptions about cancer may also prevent women from seeking care. Mathews, Lannin, and Mitchell (1994) uncovered some of these in a study of rural African American women (e.g., a belief that "once cancer has been activated," it is best to avoid diagnostic procedures such as X rays or mammograms and treatments such as radiation and surgery so that the disease isn't "stirred up" any further).

Another explanation for not seeking prompt care was "the lump wasn't hurting me or bothering me in any way so I thought I should leave it alone." Other women revealed that they believed that cancer is an incurable, degrading, and humiliating disease, so why seek help if there is nothing doctors can do? They believed it was better to put their cure in God's hands.

Distress and coping. Distress may be exacerbated as women begin to understand that they are dealing with uncertainty about the future. Although various risks have been identified, there is no known cause of breast cancer and no guaranteed cure; consequently, distress associated with uncertainty is woven through the entire cancer experience. This very unsettling ambiguity persists even after treatment has ended and women have survived the experience; they continue to worry about recurrence. How well women deal with ambiguity in general may be associated with how well they cope with the cancer experience.

How women cope during the prebiopsy phase varies. Optimists are less likely to use avoidance coping, choosing instead to focus on the positive as they approach the biopsy. As would be expected, they are likely to feel more positive as they await their biopsy results. Younger women who are less optimistic, feel threatened, and engage in more cognitive avoidance are likely to be more distressed than are older women and those who tend to be more optimistic or use other coping styles.

Information needs at prebiopsy. A woman referred to a breast surgeon for consultation about her symptoms may need information about biopsy options, potential outcomes of diagnostic surgery, and whether pain is associated with the biopsy. She may want to know how soon she will learn the results of the biopsy, and what the next step might be if, in fact, the tumor is malignant. Some studies suggest that physicians fail to provide adequate information because they may underestimate their patients' need for details and their ability to understand sophisticated technical terminology (Cawley, Kostic, & Cappello, 1990; Faden, Becker, Lewis, Freeman, & Faden, 1981). Consequently, women who have a "need to know" may want to do some homework prior to consulting with a surgeon. In this way, they are prepared to ask questions and can avoid feeling like they are being railroaded into procedures with which they are uncomfortable. Other women may be comfortable allowing their physicians to determine the type of procedure needed at this time.

Prior to biopsy, women should understand the difference between a one-step and a two-step procedure. Although the one-step procedure is used less frequently today, some women may prefer it. In any case, women should have the opportunity to choose between the two procedures. The National Cancer Institute (National Institutes of Health, 1996) suggests that a one-step procedure alleviates the psychological stress that can occur during the time—sometimes up to 2 weeks—between diagnosis and surgery and that can arise from the extra cost of two surgeries. This may be particularly important to women who are elderly or in ill health. On the other hand, time between diagnosis and surgery may give some women the time they need to adjust to their situation, gather information, and make decisions about their preferred treatment.

Diagnosis and Its Aftermath

Although almost 80% of biopsied breast lumps turn out to be benign (Internet, Breast Cancer Network [on-line], 1997), anxiety is high during the process of diagnosis (Andersen & Doyle-Mirzadeh, 1993). As would be expected, those individuals who receive news that their tumors are benign experience lower levels of distress than do those individuals who receive a cancer diagnosis (Devlen, Maguire, Phillips, & Crowther, 1987; Stanton & Snider, 1993). Weisman and Worden (1976) suggested that the cancer diagnosis precipitates an existential crisis and that it takes approximately 100 days for a woman to change her view of herself as a healthy person to a view of herself with a serious illness. Upon learning of the diagnosis, many women become more depressed (Andersen & Doyle-Mirzadeh (1993), tense, angry, fatigued, and confused (Stanton & Snider, 1993). Many individuals report that receiving the cancer diagnosis was the most stressful part of the entire process (Roberts, Elkins, Baile, & Cox, 1989). Anxiety may escalate as women imagine the possible treatments they will undergo and the impact the illness will have on their daily lives (Andersen & Doyle-Mirzadeh, 1993). In one study of 44 breast cancer patients, approximately 25% of women had severe anxiety reactions at the time of diagnosis (Hughes, 1981). Some women believe that their diagnosis is a death sentence or that if they live, they will be horribly disfigured. They may imagine themselves to be a burden to their family or believe that they can no longer fulfill the sexual activities of a relationship. They may think their marriage is doomed. Physiological symptoms of anxiety may include muscle tension, shakiness, restlessness, abdominal distress, frequent urination, difficulty concentrating, and sleep disturbances (Andersen & Doyle-Mirzadeh, 1993). It may be helpful for women to bear in mind that symptoms of depression and anxiety at diagnosis have no predictive effect on their psychological status 3 months later (Schwartz et al., 1999).

Some women enter a state of denial ("This can't be happening to me") or have feelings of depersonalization (i.e., they watch themselves as if from a distance when attending meetings with doctors and having medical examinations and treatments). What once seemed like a stable and somewhat predictable world now seems unsafe and out of control. Many women no longer trust their bodies, and wonder, "How could my body betray me like this?"

Upon learning that her tumor is malignant, the woman with breast cancer may have to wait several weeks before other tests are conducted that will yield information about the stage of the cancer and whether it has metastasized. Fears that the cancer has spread and that she may die become paramount. This time period is particularly stressful because information is incomplete and a woman does not really know what her situation is. She may experience physical pain as a result of diagnostic surgery, and this pain may escalate as she anxiously awaits the test results. At the same time, she is faced with overwhelming technical information, numerous treatment decisions, grueling treatment, and possibly issues of reconstruction. But despite her personal health crisis, the rest of her life does not stop, and she must make arrangements regarding her family, her job, and other aspects of her life.

Clearly, the process of diagnosis is extremely distressing, yet some women seem to fare better than others during this phase. Younger women (under age 55) report greater overall distress than older women (Cimprich, 1999). In addition, according to Stanton and Snider (1993), women who are generally optimistic, seek social support, and cope through focusing on the positive tend to have more energy. On the other hand, women who use avoidance coping experience higher levels of distress at diagnosis. Finally, women who blame themselves for their cancer at the time of diagnosis are likely to experience greater distress at that time and throughout the year after the diagnosis (Glinder & Compas, 1999).

Initially, it is difficult to differentiate symptoms of major depression from depression that is a reaction to a potentially life-threatening illness. As time elapses, however, individuals who are simply reacting to their health situation are likely to feel less depressed once treatment begins, and the depression may completely disappear once treatment is concluded. In individuals who are experiencing physical pain, depression is more likely to be a response to their medical situation (Andersen & Doyle-Mirzadeh, 1993). It is important for counselors and psychologists to understand that periods of depression and anxiety can return at times of follow-up medical appointments, suspected or actual recurrences, anniversary dates, and so on.

Decision making and decision-making styles. In Western societies, communication with the patient and families has shifted from a paternalistic approach to one in which the patient is viewed as a health care consumer with rights to information and access to health care professionals. Informing people about their cancer diagnoses, obtaining their informed consent, and incorporating their expressed preferences in treatment management decisions are increasingly standard practices. Although some individuals prefer not to know their cancer diagnosis, a 1977 information-rights law makes it likely that patients will be told (Dura & Ibanez, 1991). In other countries and cultures, even in some European countries, physicians do not necessarily inform the patient but instead tell the closest relative. Regardless of who knows the diagnosis, treatment decisions must be made fairly soon after diagnosis—some doctors believe within 1 month (Lange, 1997).

Numerous issues must be considered, and questions can be mind-boggling: What types of treatment are best for my situation? What is the best treatment facility? How will I find the best surgeon? Who will pay for my treatment? Will the insurance company limit my treatment options? If I need a mastectomy, do I want reconstructive surgery? What kind of reconstructive surgeries are there? If I do want reconstruction, when should I have it done? What does reconstruction entail, and is it safe? Are any of these treatments safe? And if I go through all this, will I really get better? In addition to the practical concerns and questions, many women have unspoken fears about cancer treatments and reconstruction. For example, women may be suspicious of radiation because they associate it with the bombing of Hiroshima. Chemotherapy drugs are toxins, and women may perceive them to be similar to toxins that may have made them sick in the first place. They may be fearful of reconstruction, having heard of women who have had problems following silicone implant surgery.

Women are expected to consult with a variety of specialists, such as plastic surgeons, breast surgeons, and oncologists, at a time when they are seriously stressed. Doctors may throw around words such as *mastectomy, lumpectomy, reconstructive surgery, chemo, radiation,* and others that may be completely foreign. Yet women must choose among these options. At a time when women need the help and support of others, their friends may be hesitant about offering help for fear they are intruding at a very emotionally charged and personal time.

Pierce (1993) identified three types of decision-making styles that affect how women make decisions about their care and treatment.

1. Deferrers. Pierce referred to women who want to make their decisions quickly and with as little conflict as possible as deferrers. Often these individuals defer to their physicians. These women experience no conflict or distress, have no need for additional information, and do not mull over alternatives. They quickly identify unacceptable options and rule them out. They are satisfied with their treatment decisions and don't anticipate that they will reject their decisions at a later time.

2. Delayers. These women consider two or more options as viable but can not identify one option as being superior—all the options seem equally good or bad. Although these individuals feel a great deal of conflict going back and forth between or among options, once an identifiable difference is detected, a decision is made, and they feel satisfied with their decision. Delayers are not likely to seek additional information, but if they do, it is likely to be information gleaned from women's magazines or popular books.

3. Deliberators. These women feel they are responsible for their treatment decisions and use a decision-making strategy in which they gather technical information, evaluate that information, and consult with experts. These women do not make decisions until they feel confident that they have all the information—and that it is complete and accurate. Risks and possible negative outcomes are considered, and a decision is finally made when one option meets their personal criteria. For this group, the decision-making process is stressful and fraught with conflict. Nevertheless, these women experience a greater sense of control and more confidence about their decisions. This confidence ultimately reduces their conflict and decreases their uncertainty; however, some uncertainty does linger, and they express concern that they might regret their decision later. Of the three groups, these women experience the most distress, and their decision-making process requires a great deal of time and effort.

Information needs. Obviously, women with different decision-making styles require different amounts and types of information. Some women prefer to read magazines, books, and pamphlets that give a cursory explanation, whereas others prefer technical journals that give detailed, sophisticated information. Physicians may or may not provide the amount or type of information women need. Women who wish to participate actively in their treatment decisions are likely to be dissatisfied if they do not receive information about all treatment options and the risks and benefits associated with each (Hack, Degner, & Dyck, 1994). In one study regarding treatments for epilepsy (Faden et al., 1981), physicians routinely presented the benefits of a treatment, and they frequently withheld information about the risks. Physicians also withheld information about treatments other than the one they recommended. In addition, about one fifth of the doctors in the study admitted that they would withhold information that they thought would make the patient more anxious. On the other hand, patients indicated that they wanted to know about risks associated with treatment so they could make informed decisions and so their expectations of treatment would be accurate. Patients also believed that the final decision about type of treatment should rest with them. Doctors disagreed. They believed they should make the final decision about which treatment a patient should have. Nurses may be in a unique position to bridge the gap between patients and their doctors by providing information and support to women as they make primary treatment decisions (Monson & Harwood, 1998). Similarly, patients thought that if they had detailed information about the treatment, they would be more likely to comply. Doctors, on the other hand, believed that patients would be distressed by the information, less confident in the treatment, and less likely to take the treatment as prescribed. At least one study of breast cancer patients (Cawley et al., 1990) reported that 25% of the patients did receive all the information they wanted prior to lumpectomy. Of that group, only 61% of women between 60 and 70 years old felt that they had been well-informed, compared to 85% of the 50-year-old women.

In fact, some doctors, based on their experience, believe that women are more interested in being told which breast option is best.

Dr. I. Craig Henderson, a breast cancer specialist and adjunct professor at the University of California in San Francisco, said he used to present the panoply of treatment alternatives to patients and ask them to choose. But now he realizes that patients often want him to provide hope, not options.

> If you lay out a buffet, what you're saying is, "Oh, you can do almost anything and it will work equally well," but the message is, it will work equally badly. . . . Most patients . . . want a sense that there is something their doctor believes in. (Kolata, 1997)

Some doctors also believe that patients prefer them to make the treatment decision so that if the treatment is unsuccessful, they can blame the doctor rather than themselves.

> There is a fair body of literature, and even more common experience, to suggest that bad outcomes feel worse if you made the choice yourself. . . . many patients try to get enough information to be sure that whatever choice their doctor suggests is in the right ball park. Then . . . they are very happy to lay off the responsibility.
>
> Others . . . will learn enough to decide for themselves what they think the right choice is. If their doctor advises them differently, they will find another doctor

who says what they want to hear. That way, the doctor can still be responsible for the patient's decision. (Kolata, 1997)

Research studies also suggest that not all individuals have the same information needs (Hack et al., 1994; Perez, Allan, Humm, & Wynne, 1995; Steginga, Occhipinti, Wilson, & Dunn, 1998). Some patients want to be educated but prefer that their physicians make the final treatment decision because they believe only physicians have the expertise necessary to make these decisions. Although there is not much information about the psychological benefits and disadvantages of receiving technical information, some studies suggest that if women are given the choice to participate in their treatment, anxiety and depression may diminish (Fallowfield, Hall, Maguire, & Barum, 1990; Morris & Ingham, 1988). Educated women tend to want more information, as do those whose coping style is to actively monitor their situations. Such women will be dissatisfied when doctors do not offer sufficient information. On the other hand, individuals who prefer to avoid their situations are likely to feel overwhelmed and anxious when presented with too much detail. Similarly, they may feel anxious if they sense a pressure to participate in treatment decision making.

In states where physicians are legally bound to inform patients about treatment options, "higher rates of breast conserving surgery have been found, suggesting that patient participation in medical decision-making does have an effect on the type of treatment selected" (Hack et al., 1994, p. 279).

More support for patients' becoming active in treatment decision making is found in a study by Baumann, Deber, and Thompson (1991). Doctors were presented with vignettes depicting women who were diagnosed with various forms and various stages of breast cancer. Doctors who reviewed these vignettes were very confident that their treatment choices were the best. There was, however, an astounding lack of agreement across physicians regarding treatment recommendations. This research suggests that women with the exact same type of breast cancer in the exact same stage of breast cancer would get very different treatment plans from different physicians (Baumann et al., 1991). The importance of women's seeking an independent second opinion cannot be overemphasized. No matter how confident a physician appears when communicating treatment recommendations, a different physician may have a different perspective.

There are no advantages to physician overconfidence. For example, overly confident physicians may not comprehensively outline breast cancer treatment options and may thereby lessen patients' roles in their own health outcomes. This may be particularly alienating for women who prefer to take an active role. Furthermore, physicians who are overly confident may refuse to refer patients for an independent second opinion. An independent opinion is one in which the referring physician releases only test results and medical history to another physician, not his or her assessment of the patient's situation. In addition, the physician the woman consults for a second opinion should not be in the same medical group, have common financial interests, or be related in any way to the referring physician. A second opinion should be truly independent.

Clearly, treatment decision making is a complicated process for physicians and their patients. Physicians are trained to evaluate vast amounts of information and then make a reasonable treatment decision, and most physicians are confident about their recommendations. This confidence is likely to have a calming influence on patients, but at the same time, physician overconfidence may limit a woman's options and potentially impede her attainment of health.

Reconstruction. Another critical decision that must be made prior to surgery concerns reconstruction. Women who are considering reconstruction express worries about postsurgery discomfort and surgical complications (Anderson, Rodin, & Ariyan, 1994). As breast-conserving surgeries have become the norm, more reconstructive techniques are available to women who have undergone breast surgery. At the time they first consult with a plastic surgeon, many women have already determined when they will undergo reconstruction and the type of reconstruction they prefer (Corrall & Mustoe, 1996). Women who choose reconstruction tend to have greater concerns about appearance (Anderson et al., 1994). Research suggests that women who have immediate reconstruction are less psychologically distressed than women who choose reconstruction sometime after the initial medical treatment has been completed (Franchelli et al., 1995; Jozwick, Rouanet, Sobierajski, & Pujol, 1995). In fact, more immediate breast reconstructions are being performed for this reason (Wickman, Jurell, & Sandelin, 1995).

Hospitalization: Surgery and the Postsurgical Period

Once a treatment protocol is decided on, women move into the next phase of the cancer experience. Individuals who are hospitalized for a surgical procedure have much to fear: They may experience physical pain as a result of the procedure, their bodies may be damaged by the surgery, and they risk death. This phase may include surgical procedures to determine how far the cancer has spread locally, for example, a lymph node dissection, followed by chemotherapy to shrink the tumor, followed by surgical removal of the lump. Now women have a new set of challenges, and once more their emotions may ebb and flow as they confront each new experience. Fear of surgery and anesthesia may be replaced by anxiety as women wait for the pathology report. Women who choose a lumpectomy may fear that they made the wrong choice and that a mastectomy would have been more effective. Women who choose mastectomy may be fearful that they will regret not having preserved their breast. Fear of chemotherapy—the procedure and its side effects—becomes salient for women at different times. For those who have chemotherapy to shrink the tumor prior to surgery, the fear emerges soon after diagnosis. In individuals who delay chemotherapy until after surgery, this fear is postponed.

Very few studies have examined psychological reactions to breast cancer surgery, but studies of women undergoing surgery for benign reasons show that women are anxious prior to surgery and less anxious once surgery is completed.

Further, individuals who sustain high anxiety levels postsurgery are likely to have a slower recovery (Andersen & Doyle-Mirzadeh, 1993).

Again, how women manage their distress depends on a number of factors. Women with early-stage breast cancer with a good prognosis were found to be most angry, anxious, and depressed the day before surgery, but by 7 to 10 days after the surgery, their levels of distress had dropped significantly. Pessimistic breast cancer patients experienced more distress prior to surgery, immediately after surgery, and during the year following surgery than did more optimistic women. As was true in earlier phases of the breast cancer experience, women who accepted their situation tended to experience less distress than those individuals who coped by using denial (Carver et al., 1993).

> The overall picture that emerges . . . is one of optimists as engaged copers, planful and active during the period when there are plans to be made and actions to engage in, trying to make the best of a situation that they are also trying to accept as real. People at the other end of the optimism dimension in contrast, show evidence of trying to escape from the reality of the situation and of tending to experience a disengagement from their other life goals. (Carver et al., 1993, p. 380)

When women are highly distressed prior to surgery, they are more likely to use denial or disengagement. The use of these ineffective coping mechanisms leads to a snowball effect, in which high levels of distress have been observed even 6 months later (Carver et al., 1993).

Pain after surgery. How women tolerate pain after their breast surgery may be related to their cognitive coping strategies. Butler, Damarin, Beaulieu, Schwebel, and Thorn (1989) found that patients who catastrophized or did not use adaptive cognitive coping strategies experienced more intense pain after general surgery. One study (Jacobsen & Butler, 1996) found that following breast cancer, younger women tended to catastrophize more than older women, and women who catastrophized also experienced more intense pain. The use of adaptive cognitive coping strategies, surprisingly, was not associated with less pain.

THE MIDDLE PHASES OF THE CANCER EXPERIENCE: THE POSTHOSPITAL PERIOD AND ADJUVANT TREATMENT

Following initial treatment for breast cancer and discharge from the hospital, a woman enters the next phase of treatment. She may be emotionally and physically exhausted from her ordeal, but she has little time to recuperate before she must face new issues and challenges. If a woman has a good prognosis, has not undergone disfiguring surgery, or both, it may surprise her that treatment may continue for 6 months or longer after her surgery, or that her physicians may wish to continue to meet with her for up to 2 years after her initial treatment. An individual with a poor prognosis expects treatment to continue postsurgery.

Regardless of prognosis or type of initial treatment, it isn't unusual for women after they return home from the hospital to reevaluate earlier treatment recommendations and decisions. Those women who have undergone extensive surgery will need to adjust to their new body image. Simultaneously, many women resume the activities of daily living in between treatments and examinations. Several other issues become salient during this phase, including fears of recurrence, decisions regarding additional treatments, and worries about treatment side effects. Each of these issues poses new challenges, and women respond to these stressors in various ways.

How women cope, the general quality of their mood, and their level of interpersonal effectiveness prior to diagnosis are associated with physical and psychological outcome 1 year after breast surgery. Schag et al. (1993) found that women who were classified at time of diagnosis as high risk for psychosocial morbidity (e.g., they had a history of depression, had undergone numerous stressors prior to diagnosis, exhibited poor or limited coping skills, or had long-standing marital problems) had more physical and psychosocial distress 1 month after surgery than individuals who were classified as low risk (e.g., they had no history of depression, had few stressors prior to diagnosis, exhibited good coping skills, or had sound marital relationships).

Physical Issues

Following hospital discharge and for up to several months afterward, women typically have difficulty going about their daily routines and report problems with physical activity; pain; discomfort at the site of the surgery; and tenderness of the breast, chest wall, and arm. These problems tend to dissipate for most women, except those initially classified as high risk for psychosocial morbidity. A full year later, these women reported greater weight gains and more psychological distress than individuals who were classified as low risk (Schag et al., 1993).

During the year following surgery, women are concerned about their bodies, their scars, their clothing, and wearing prostheses. By the end of the year, most women generally resolve issues related to their appearance, but those women classified as high risk continue to be concerned. Similarly, anxiety related to medical situations, concern about the future, and feelings of anger, though common during the month following surgery, are more likely to persist in high-risk women (Schag et al., 1993).

Physicians and mental health professionals may minimize the physical and psychological issues experienced by women postsurgery, particularly if the women appear to be in remission. The fact that women appear to have "beaten the cancer" (a primary concern prior to the surgery) does not mean that they are not facing other very legitimate problems. There is a litany of physical symptoms that women can experience even after the physical healing of their surgical scar. For example, most women enter a premature menopause or are at an age where they are naturally approaching their menopause. The hormone replacement therapies typically prescribed to ease the considerable symptoms of menopause are not rec-ommended for women who have been treated for breast cancer. It is critical that professionals acknowledge how uncomfortable menopausal symptoms can be (McPhail, 1999). After all, women can be thankful that they are in remission and still be unhappy about the unpleasant symptoms they experience.

Some women worry about developing lymphedema. Lymphedema can occur years after the completion of treatment for breast cancer, and so these women may be concerned about cuts, burns, insect bites, and other things that may increase the risk of lymphedema. Women who develop lymphedema are often frustrated by their appearance and struggle to find clothes that are comfortable or that conceal the condition.

Reconstruction

Some women opt not to have immediate reconstruction but wait until surgery and adjuvant treatments are completed before deciding. The decision about whether to have reconstruction is a personal one. Women tend to weigh many factors, including feelings about their current appearance and the reality of undergoing many procedures over many months. If a woman decides to proceed with recon-struction, she may consider various types of reconstruction in collaboration with her physician.

Those who have chosen to forgo reconstruction must begin the process of adjusting to their new bodies. They may feel frustrated at the difficulty they have finding prostheses and clothes that fit properly. They are likely to fear that their sexual partners will no longer find them attractive. They may also be fearful about having their scars touched, either because they fear their partner's reactions or because of the pain to their breast, arm, and chest.

Recurrence

Breast cancer can recur at any time—just a few weeks or months after initial treatment for breast cancer has been completed or years later—although typically it recurs during the 2 years following diagnosis (Payne, Sullivan, & Massie, 1996).

> Because it is a slow growing cancer, it can spread to another part of your body and go undetected for 10 or even 20 years. The longer you go without a recurrence, however, the less likely a recurrence is, and the more treatable it will be if it does happen. . . . Therefore, you're wise to think of breast cancer as similar in some ways to a chronic disease, like high blood pressure . . . that you'll always have in your life. You're also wise to remember that, like other chronic disease it's very likely something you can live with. (Love, 1995, p. 271)

Site of the recurrence and type of cancer. When breast cancer recurs, it may be at the same site as the original cancer. This type is referred to as a local recurrence. In this case the cancer is seen not as a cancer that has spread, but instead is referred to as *residual*; that is, it was not treated completely the first time. Another type of localized recurrence is one that is invasive. This type of cancer seems to be particularly aggressive. A third type is an entirely new cancer in a different area of the breast. Finally, a woman may develop a regional recurrence; that is, the cancer recurs in the lymph nodes (Love, 1995). When a local or regional recurrence is detected, physicians run tests to determine if the cancer has metastasized to other sites in the body. It is not uncommon for physicians "to downplay local and regional recurrences because they are not as life-threatening as metastatic disease can be" (Love, 1995, p. 473).

Recurrence jitters. For women whose disease has been in remission and who have physically recovered from their ordeal, the emotional scars of the cancer experience linger. Nearly all women are fearful that their cancer will recur (Peters-Golden, 1982), and anecdotal evidence suggests that women continue to worry about the possibility of recurrence. Pains and illnesses like the flu often raise concerns that the cancer has recurred, and checkups and anniversary dates typically precipitate or increase levels of anxiety. It is hard to adequately capture in words the free-floating anxiety some women feel after they complete breast cancer treatment. Fears that one small undetected cancer cell remains and is spreading to the lymph nodes, the other breast, and even other regions of the body can escalate. These fears can become all-consuming for some women, whereas for others, such fears emerge only with specific reminders like pain or anniversary dates. Once a woman perceives that her body has betrayed her, she may always feel vulnerable.

How women respond to recurrence. Women who have a recurrence of cancer may be even more distressed than when they were initially diagnosed, and some individuals report that the recurrent phase was the most stressful phase of the entire course of illness (Northouse, Dorris, & Charron-Moore, 1995). Cella, Mahon, and Donovan (1990) found that for some patients, recurrence diminishes hopes for a cure or a remission of the illness. Recurrent breast cancer, in fact, may cause more psychological distress than breast cancer that is initially diagnosed as terminal (Silberfarb, Maurer, & Crouthamel, 1980).

At recurrence, symptoms are likely to be more severe, and patients perceive their illness as more serious than they did when they were initially diagnosed (Munkes, Oberst, & Hughes, 1992). For some women, death becomes a more real possibility than before. They worry about the pain they will endure, and there is fear that death will be painful. Anger and depression may be more intense than at initial diagnosis, and anxiety will return (Northouse, Dorris, & Charron-Moore, 1995). Women who respond to recurrence with hopelessness and uncertainty about the future tend to have more severe physical symptoms and greater difficulty fulfilling their social, family, and occupational roles (Northouse et al., 1995). These women may also experience greater disruption in their sex life and in their life roles (Silberfarb et al., 1980). It appears that women are most distressed and have the most difficulty with their psychosocial roles when they are "very surprised" or "not at all surprised" by the recurrence. It is easy to understand why those who are very surprised are quite distressed; they have further to fall. In other words, they were confident that their treatment was successful, and now they feel even more betrayed by their bodies and perhaps their doctors and God. Women who are not at all surprised may be pessimists by nature who typically use less effective coping mechanisms.

Another factor that can exacerbate stress at this period is the strain that recurrence might cause between women and their doctors (Cella, Mahon, & Donavan, 1990). Medical personnel tend to withdraw more from patients with recurrence than from those initially diagnosed or from those who are terminally ill (Silberfarb et al., 1980). The combination of women's more pessimistic feelings about their recovery (Worden, 1989) and the potential guilt (conscious or not) that some physicians experience may seriously strain a relationship that was once strong.

Time of recurrence. The time of recurrence may affect how women react. When recurrence occurs soon after the initial treatment, women are robbed of time to adjust to the disease and the aftermath of surgery. They now face an all-too-familiar process once again. Women feel frightened and discouraged and may question whether they received the appropriate treatment in the first place. They may give up hope and see death as the only outcome to their illness (Payne et al., 1996).

On the other hand, women who have had several years when they were free of the disease have had time to recuperate from the physical effects of treatment. These women have also had an opportunity to adjust psychologically; to adapt to any body changes; and to resume their social, work, and family roles. They have moved on with their lives, even though they may have had to make accommodations to their illness—for example, the use of prostheses. Because they thought they had beaten the disease, they tend to feel even more betrayed by their bodies. With recurrence comes a tendency to reevaluate previous decisions. Women may question whether a mastectomy would have been better than the lumpectomy that they had. They may wonder if prior treatments such as hormone therapy caused their recurrence. And they may wonder about the efficacy of cancer treatment—after all, it didn't work before, why should it work now?

Adjuvant Treatments

About 75% of women who are diagnosed with breast cancer are likely to survive for up to 5 years provided they receive adjuvant chemotherapy. Adjuvant treatments are systemic treatments (e.g., chemotherapy or hormonal therapy) provided in addition to radiation of the breast, breast surgery, or both (Love, 1995). These treatments are intended to prevent cancer from occurring in other sites in the body. Although adjuvant therapy is recommended, not every woman decides to participate in these treatments. Some women choose alternative treatments, such as special diets, to treat their cancer after surgery.

Even when women agree to adjuvant treatment, they may not always follow through. How well people comply with their treatment depends partly on their

"Now that I am back to work, everyone expects things to be fine. But you know what? I'm not fine. I'm still tired, I can't find clothes that look right, I'm gaining weight, and I'm worried that my arm is going to swell up. Each time I have to take a pill or see my doctor, I'm reminded that I have this awful disease. People tell me I should be thankful that I'm OK again. But I can't be OK again until I can put this whole thing behind me. When will that be? When I finish my adjuvant treatment? When I'm no longer surprised to see a scar each time I undress? When? Will I ever be able to put this behind me, or will I always worry that the cancer will recur?"

mood and attitude about cancer. One study (Ayres et al., 1994) found that women who exhibited more physical energy, a fighting spirit, and higher levels of anxiety and depression were more likely to be compliant. Individuals who were hostile or guilty were less likely to be compliant. It is possible that hostile individuals have poor relationships with health care providers and consequently refuse treatment or deny that chemotherapy was recommended. Individuals who usually feel guilty may believe that they are responsible for their disease or that they are a burden to others and therefore deserve to be sick. As a result, they may be reluctant to undergo treatment (Ayres et al., 1994).

The severe side effects of chemotherapy (e.g., nausea and vomiting) are another obstacle to compliance. Some individuals develop anticipatory nausea (they become nauseated as their next treatment approaches). Sometimes just waiting in the clinic is enough to elicit nausea (Andrykowski & Jacobsen, 1993; Morrow & Dobkin, 1988), and the more chemotherapy treatments that are administered, the more likely one is to develop anticipatory nausea (Morrow & Dobkin, 1988). To make matters worse, women who develop anticipatory nausea tend to experience more severe nausea after receiving their chemotherapy treatment than do individuals who do not experience anticipatory nausea (Tomoyasu, Bovbjerg, & Jacobsen, 1996).

There may be psychological barriers to compliance with adjuvant treatment as well. Women who agree to adjuvant treatment are reminded each time they receive another treatment that the cancer experience is not yet over. These women have been found to experience more psychological distress (i.e., anxiety including fears of recurrence and depression) than do women who did not receive additional treatment (Ganz, Polinsky, Schag, & Heinrich, 1989).

THE LIVING-DYING INTERVAL AND THE TERMINAL PHASE OF BREAST CANCER

Although breast cancer is 95% curable if caught at the early stages, not all women will survive. Some women are forced to confront the fact that their cancer has metastasized and is very likely terminal. This recognition may occur during the initial diagnostic phase or may occur at a time of recurrence of the disease. We all live with the knowledge that we will die eventually and may even accept that this is the natural order of things. Yet when we actually learn that our illness is killing us, we experience this knowledge of our death as a crisis. On top of her fears of pain and medical treatment, the woman who learns that her illness is terminal must also confront her own mortality. She must "reorient [her] life, values, goals, and beliefs to accommodate this sudden realization" (Rando, 1984, p. 199).

The Living-Dying Interval

Having one's disease classified as terminal does not necessarily mean that death is immediately forthcoming. Some women must learn to live with the knowledge that they will die sooner rather than later, but not in the very near future. Although all of us know that we will die at some time, we usually do not fret about it. In fact, in Western culture, we tend to put thoughts of our death firmly out of our minds and make plans for our future. When women learn that their cancer is terminal, this knowledge of their death forces them to recognize that they do not have as much time left as they had thought. This time between learning one's illness is terminal and the actual time of death is sometimes referred to as the living-dying interval (Pattison, 1977, 1978). For the woman with breast cancer, this interval can be many years: Between 5% and 10% of women diagnosed with metastatic breast cancer survive for 5 years (Ashby, Kissane, Beadle, & Rodger, 1996), and there are reports of women living as long as 10 years after being diagnosed as terminal (Love, 1995).

The living-dying interval can be a difficult time, because women must prepare for their own death while they are still very much alive and coping with their illness. Rando (1984) identified several issues that arise when a woman learns that she is dying: (a) she may need to give attention to unfinished legal and financial business; (b) she may feel depressed and grieve for the loss of her self and her loved ones; (c) she may have to make decisions about her further medical treatment; and (d) she may anticipate the loss of her physical abilities and increased pain associated with her illness and death. How each of these issues is addressed can make a difference in the quality of her life before death. For the woman with breast cancer to die a death with minimal psychological conflict, it is critical that she be allowed to participate fully in planning for her death and the remaining months of her life should she so desire:

1. She may want to complete legal and financial business, such as writing a will or reviewing one written previously. She may want to be sure all debts are taken care of and that she has provided for any survivors, particularly her children. She may want to be certain that she knows who will care for her minor children after her death.

2. She may grieve for the loss of her self and her loved ones. As she grieves for the loss of her self, she will grieve for her physical self and also for her ideal

self. She will recognize at some point that she will no longer be able to physically carry on as she had in the past. She will slow down and be unable to participate in life as fully as she has. It may be difficult for her to accept that she will no longer have energy to work and play as she has in the past. At the same time, she may be angry or feel cheated that she will miss out on future events, such as the marriage of her daughter and the birth of her grandchildren, or opportunities, such as her long-awaited promotion. She may be angry at herself as she recalls past behaviors of which she is not proud. She may also grieve the loss of her entire world and all those individuals that make up her world. She will be concerned about her survivors and the grief they will feel, and she may encourage her partner to seek a new relationship or encourage her children to move on after her death.

3. Decisions about further medical treatment must be made. She may want to decide about the extent of her palliative care and where she wishes to spend her last months and days, and she may consider a hospice. Discussions with her partner or family may focus on how to ensure that her wishes are fulfilled.

4. Plans for the future may be made. For example, she may wonder how to continue living a quality life as long as she is physically able. Perhaps she will want to realize dreams that have gone unfulfilled in the past. There may be people she wishes to see or places she has always wanted to visit, or perhaps she wants to make plans to continue working at her job.

5. She will anticipate the loss of her physical abilities and the pain associated with her illness and death. She may need to get information about how to minimize her pain, or she may find that some of her fears are unrealistic. Nevertheless, great anxiety may be associated with the unknown. She may fear that she will become a burden to her family and partner, and she may need to work out some resolution to this problem.

6. The woman who is dying because her breast cancer has metastasized may consider various medical interventions that may slow or hasten the dying process. She may decide that certain physical losses are unacceptable to her and may ask for help in terminating her life, or instead she may decide that her physicians must do everything possible to keep her alive as long as possible. She may need to consult other physicians who are more expert at helping her to die comfortably.

How Women Respond to the News That Their Cancer Is Terminal

Death anxiety and the meaning of death. Some authors (e.g., Solomon, Greenberg, & Pyszczynski, 1991) write that self-esteem results from the notion "that one is a valuable part of a meaningful universe" (p. 73, cited in Larson, 1993). Perhaps that is why so much anxiety results when one's existence is threatened—because one will no longer have a meaningful place in the universe. It is difficult for us to accept that we will no longer exist, and some find this reality incomprehensible. Research in thanatology suggests that this concept of nonexistence is quite stressful and that all people experience some degree of death anxiety. Further, it is this very anxiety that leads to a denial of death, which can allow us to live our daily lives without being overwhelmed by the knowledge of our eventual mortality.

For most women, awareness that their breast cancer is terminal leads to an acute crisis characterized by intense death anxiety. This anxiety is different from fears expressed by women at diagnosis or during treatment (e.g., a fear that cancer will be diagnosed or a fear of the medical treatment); this anxiety is a response to a recognition that death is a reality—that one will soon cease to exist and that there is nothing that can be done to change the situation. Our usual methods of problem solving are inadequate. Because none of us has had the experience of dying, we cannot know how to face death.

Strong religious beliefs help many women to find meaning in life and death. All religions attempt to give individuals a framework for understanding death; that is, these religions teach that the individual continues after death in some way. Western religions speak of an afterlife where individuals are reunited in death. Eastern religions speak of reincarnation. These beliefs may provide solace for some women who are terminally ill and may help them to derive meaning as they move through the death process. Similarly, some individuals who do not have strong religious beliefs may find that the process of dying provides an opportunity for human growth and that one can achieve a greater understanding of herself and her life by engaging in the process. It is important that the counselor of a client with terminal breast cancer understand how that client has derived meaning in her life and how she finds meaning in death.

Physical status and age. How a woman responds to the knowledge that her cancer is terminal is partly dependent on the symptoms she experiences. The woman who has few symptoms and little pain is likely to cope more effectively with her cancer than the woman who experiences pain or other physical symptoms. Pain may serve as a reminder of one's illness and signal that the disease is progressing and that death is approaching. Women's anxiety may skyrocket and consequently reduce the body's natural ability to manage the pain. As the pain increases, so does the anxiety; as the anxiety increases, so does the pain. This snowballing effect may leave the woman feeling physically unable to participate in many of the activities that gave meaning to her life. Consequently, she may begin to feel hopeless and depressed, and as she participates even less frequently in the activities she enjoys, her levels of depression further increase.

How a woman responds to the terminal diagnosis may also be influenced by her age. An older woman who has lived fully may have concerns about dying with dignity or about being a burden to her family. A younger woman may feel great terror at the thought of dying before she has had a chance to participate fully in living.

How women learn of their prognosis. How women learn that their disease is terminal may influence the feelings they have. Some women may be told directly by their physicians, others may overhear a conversation, and others may know intuitively that their cancer has spread (Kagan et al., 1984; Rando, 1984). Sometimes family members may know that the illness is terminal before the patient knows. Nevertheless, patients may have detected that something is wrong by the behavior

"Who does that doctor think she is? She wants me to consider hospice care. I just know I can beat this thing. I've read books and numerous articles, and I've seen people on talk shows who were told their cancer was terminal, and guess what? They beat it; well, I'm going to beat it, too! My doctor is just not listening to me. She is treating me differently now that she sees me as hopeless. Can you believe she told me I failed the chemotherapy? What a joke—if anything, the chemotherapy failed me. By the way, other people are treating me differently, too. The changes are subtle, but they hit me over the head like a ton of bricks. Even my family members are standing further away, not touching me as much, and friends are definitely calling less often."

exhibited by medical personnel or family and friends. Some reports suggest that nurses avoid individuals who are dying, that doctors may make fewer visits, and that family members may have difficulty talking about future plans if they don't expect them to be realized. Such clues tend to be picked up by patients who are ignorant of their medical status, and as a result, they recognize that they are dying without anyone having told them directly.

Although patients often react with anger when told that their illness is terminal, Kagan et al. (1984) believe that patients who are not told directly end up feeling particularly angry with their physicians. Giving a patient full information about her prognosis allows her to make informed decisions about further treatment (Kagan et al., 1984). Knowing their prognosis gives individuals an opportunity to complete personal business before death (Doka, 1997; Lair, 1996).

The site of the metastasis affects how women respond. Breast cancer can metastasize to various sites in the body. Generally, the cancer is likely to spread to the bones, brain, lungs, and liver, and less often to the brain and spinal column (Love, 1995). When women learn that their breast cancer has metastasized to the liver or the brain, they may experience additional fears. Misconceptions—for example, "liver metastases mean death is imminent" or "brain metastases always impair cognitive functioning"—are likely to instigate tremendous anxiety (Payne et al., 1996). Personal meanings associated with the particular site also may affect reactions. For example, one woman whose sister had been institutionalized at a young age because, as her father had explained, "She had a bad brain," believed that her brain metastases indicated she too had a bad brain and was being punished. These thoughts resulted in uncontrollable crying fits that diminished when her history was fully explored.

Palliative Medical Care

Women whose breast cancer is terminal may continue to receive medical treatment, but their treatment is no longer curative; rather, it is palliative treatment.

Such medical treatment is aimed at reducing cancer-related pain as well as other symptoms associated with the spread of the disease, for example, nausea, drowsiness, vomiting, and shortness of breath (Ashby et al., 1996). There is no reason for women to endure pain related to their illness because analgesics are available that greatly reduce or completely eliminate pain (Love, 1995). Treatments are offered to patients provided that their efficacy at controlling symptoms outweighs their toxicity. There is no question that palliative care can make women more comfortable and improve their quality of life during the last months of their lives, and women may feel more comfortable knowing that they do not have to face a painful death. Women who are suffering from chronic pain as a result of metastatic cancer can be referred to a pain specialist for further assistance (Love, 1995).

Palliative medical treatment can be administered in a hospital, a hospice, or even at one's home. If a woman chooses to enter a hospice, she can expect to find a more homey atmosphere with professionals who tend to prioritize the woman's comfort. When sufficient pain medication is available, women can more easily focus on preparing themselves psychologically or spiritually for death. If a woman prefers to die at home or in the home of a relative, it is critical that there be a physician available to prescribe pain medication as needed. It is not unusual for the oncologist who was involved in the woman's active cancer treatment to withdraw when his or her patient is dying. Family members often need to advocate strongly for their loved one to ensure that adequate pain medication is administered. If the original doctor is not providing adequate palliative care, he or she may need to be replaced.

The woman who is dying of breast cancer has the right to decide how involved she wants to be in choosing her palliative medical care and where she will receive this care: Some have the interest and energy to participate actively, whereas others relinquish decision making to doctors and family members.

The Terminal Phase of the Living-Dying Interval

Pattison (1978) suggests that the terminal phase of the living-dying interval "is not precise and is roughly thought to begin when the dying person starts to withdraw into herself and respond to those internal bodily signals that tell her she must now conserve her energy" (Pattison, cited in Rando, 1984, p. 222).

The Lazarus effect. Some women come very close to death and then experience a sudden remission in their illness. Sometimes women live for years with their illness in remission only to experience a relapse that puts them close to death again. This alternation between death and remission makes patients and their families wary and uneasy. They may be afraid to be too hopeful for fear that their hopes will be dashed again. Yet when the woman is on the brink of death, her family fears losing her. The situation becomes further complicated when family members accept that death is imminent only to have their loved one bounce back once more. Family members sometimes find it too painful to reengage after they finally come to terms with their impending loss; the fear of suffering the pain associated with the loss of their loved one once again can feel like too much to bear. Women with breast cancer who experience this alternation between life and death feel confused if others disengage and withhold their love, support, and companionship, and they may feel abandoned by their family.

SUMMARY

From prediagnosis through treatment and possible recurrence and death, the woman who negotiates the breast cancer experience will feel as if she is on a roller coaster. How women cope with the experience depends on their general level of psychological and physical functioning prior to the illness. How women respond, and their physical and psychological needs, will vary with the course and phase of the illness. Diagnosis is acutely stressful, particularly for younger women, who tend to have more intrusive thoughts about the disease. Using problem-focused engaged coping during this time period seems to reduce distress, perhaps in part because women are confronted with technical information and asked to make decisions about their diagnosis and treatment. They experience medical procedures that can be painful and debilitating—all with no guarantee that their illness will remit. Clearly, the experience is an emotional and taxing one for the woman with breast cancer and for her significant others.

5

How To Do a
Psychosocial Assessment

Strangers peering and poking at their naked breasts, purple lines drawn on their bodies that indicate areas for radiation therapy, paper gowns, and cold steel tables are the things that women with breast cancer come to know all too well. Diagnostic and treatment procedures for breast cancer can be dehumanizing. Technological advances in cancer treatment, coupled with increasing pressures on physicians to provide cost-effective service, lead to more rushed and less personal treatment, with the result that many women with breast cancer feel like they are being treated as objects. Psychological assessment may be equally invasive and dehumanizing if the counselor is not sensitive to the client and her situation. A clinical interview allows the mental health professional to gather information and at the same time to demonstrate respect for and interest in the client as a whole person, not just a body part.

Although we strongly recommend a clinical interview in the assessment of women with breast cancer, we also recognize the benefits of psychometrically sound instruments. Such measures may also be useful in certain circumstances, such as when the client is too weak to participate in a fairly lengthy interview or when the counselor has worked hard to understand the client and is still confused (Table 5.1). Paper-and-pencil tests are not shortcuts to understanding clients, but they may serve to clarify issues or symptoms. Familiar measures such as the Profile of Mood States, Symptom Checklist 90R, Beck Depression Inventory, or the State-Trait Anxiety Inventory may be helpful in determining the level and quality of psychological distress.

It is particularly important that assessment instruments incorporate a range of symptoms and signs that will encompass possible idiosyncratic or cultural differences in the expression of distress. In European cultures, for example, it is more common for people to report depressed mood, feelings of guilt, and suicidal ideation. However, in Chinese culture, dysphoria is regarded as a source of shame to the individual and to the family. Consequently, dysphoric feelings are less likely

Table 5.1 Useful Assessment Instruments for Women with Breast Cancer

---

Cancer Inventory of Problem Situations (Schag, Heinrich, Aadland, & Ganz, 1990): A psychometrically sound 131-item measure of problems cancer patients may experience (i.e., activity, anxiety in medical situations, changes in physical appearance, cognitive difficulties, communication with medical staff, control in medical situations, dating relationships, domestic chores, eating, employment, finances, pain, physical abilities, prostheses, relationships with family and friends, self-care, side effects from treatment, significant relationships, sleeping, transportation, worry). Total severity rating, total number of problems, and average intensity scores can be calculated.

Measure of Adjustment to Illness Scale (Watson et al., 1988): This scale assesses adjustment to cancer diagnosis through five categories (i.e., Fighting Spirit, Avoidance, Fatalistic, Helpless, and Anxious Preoccupation).

Melzack-McGill Pain Questionnaire (Melzack, 1987): This measure is useful for monitoring pain experienced by cancer patients. It assesses perceived pain intensity and sensory, affective, and cognitive components of pain.

Multidimensional Health Locus of Control (Wallston, Wallston, & DeVellis, 1978): This instrument assesses whether people view their health status as the result of internal factors or chance or as under the control of powerful others. These beliefs have implications for health-related behaviors.

Psychosocial Adjustment of Illness Scale-Self-Report (Derogatis & Lopez, 1983): This instrument assesses how people are coping with major health problems; the instrument was developed for use with cancer survivors.

Quality of Life Index (Parker, Levinson, Mullooly, & Frymark, 1989): This instrument has also been used with cancer survivors to assess functioning with respect to activities of daily living, self-care, health status, support, and attitude.

Sickness Impact Profile (Bergner, Bobbit, Carter, & Gibson, 1981). This self-report measure assesses functional status and impact of sickness applicable to any disease or disability group.

---

to emerge through instruments or interview content, and distress is more likely to be expressed through somatic symptoms.

As in general counseling practice, good clinical interviewing skills are necessary to assess a client with breast cancer. Mental health practitioners should also have specialized knowledge about the disease and its treatments and should be familiar with the literature in health psychology. For example, if counselors do not know that adequate preparation for surgery hastens discharge from the hospital, reduces postsurgical pain, and actually speeds recovery, they may fail to inquire about their clients' understanding of the impending procedure. Cultural factors, such as race-ethnicity and gender role socialization, and biological factors, such as physical status and stage of the disease, are often neglected or minimized by counselors. These two factors, in addition to clients' affective, cognitive, and behavioral functioning, must be assessed when working with women who have breast cancer. It is important that the client's current status, changes since the illness, and prior history be obtained for all of these factors (Belar & Deardoff, 1995).

The emphasis mental health professionals place on each assessment factor differs based on the purpose of the assessment. Assessments may be conducted to plan appropriate treatment, to distinguish psychological from somatic reactions, or to answer physicians' questions about the client's psychological status. For example, mental health professionals may be consulted to explain a client's disturbing behavior on the hospital ward or to assess the potential for suicide. Physicians also may ask psychologists to assess the patient's ability to cope "with the illness, [her] compliance, preparation for surgery, presurgical screening, [and] diagnostic and treatment issues associated with chronic pain, and of course, neuropsychological evaluations" (Belar & Deardoff, 1995, p. 40).

Counselors can assess client functioning by directly interviewing the client; by speaking to friends, family members, nurses, and doctors with the client's written consent; and, when possible (e.g., in a hospital setting), by directly observing clients in interactions with others. However, therapists should not rely only on patients' reports of their moods and psychological symptoms. Research has shown that some women who are experiencing difficulties in functioning in their sexual, vocational, and social roles may not disclose psychological symptoms or problems with mood (Nelson, Friedman, Baer, Lane, & Smith, 1994).

In summary, a comprehensive psychological assessment includes gathering information from various sources, being knowledgeable about the disease and its treatments, and being sensitive to the woman as a person. The remainder of the chapter will discuss target areas that mental health professionals should address as they assess women with breast cancer.

ASSESSMENT TARGETS

Affect and Mood

Mood is affected both by a breast cancer diagnosis and by its treatment. Although anxiety, anger, depression, and guilt are common in women who are diagnosed with breast cancer, these feelings are intermittent or short-lived for women who cope successfully. A woman's anxiety is raised from the moment a lump is discovered, and the anxiety may recur years after treatment has been completed, for example, prior to yearly checkups or on anniversary dates. Feelings of sadness are related to the loss of a woman's identity as a healthy person and, for the woman who has had a mastectomy, the loss of her breast. A woman may wonder "Why me?" and be angry at herself, the medical establishment, healthy people, and God. Many women report an overwhelming sense of alienation from others and decreased pleasure in social activities.

Mood tends to reflect the phase of the illness and is affected by the various challenges presented by the illness and its treatment. For example, anxiety may predominate prior to surgery, whereas depression may follow the loss of a breast. The individual whose mood seems unaffected may be denying the emotional impact of breast cancer, or she may be uncomfortable expressing her feelings. Inappropriate affect also should be noted by the counselor.

Counselors must rely on observation of the client's nonverbal behaviors, such as foot tapping, eye contact, facial expressions, and tone of voice, as well as self-report in order to assess the client's mood. It is important, however, to interpret within the context of the client's culture. Standardized measures of mood may also be used, for example, the Profile of Mood States. It is critical to know if a client has been diagnosed with an affective disorder, such as depression or bipolar disorder, prior to the diagnosis for breast cancer, so that the client's current psychological status is not misunderstood as a situational response to the crisis of diagnosis or treatment.

Body Image and Sexual Functioning

Breast cancer is stressful not only because it is potentially fatal but also because women who are diagnosed with the disease face the very real possibility of losing a body part that has been sexualized and glorified by many cultures. A woman's feelings about her body and her level of sexual desire, sexual activity, and sexual satisfaction will be affected by the diagnosis and the course of treatment. How the woman with breast cancer views her body can affect her intimate relationships and her psychological well-being and may influence treatment decisions.

Family attitudes toward sex and intimacy, cultural values, and the individual's ability to be open about sensitive issues will influence whether or how the counselor broaches these issues. The counselor must recognize that some women may perceive discussions about body image and sexual functioning as embarrassing and invasive. Because some women feel more comfortable speaking to other women about their feelings of femininity and physical attractiveness, the gender of the therapist may be an issue.

Because of the sensitive nature of this topic for some women, the counselor may choose to begin discussions of these issues with a comment rather than by asking direct questions. For example, the counselor might say, "Some women find it uncomfortable to talk about how they feel about their breasts or how satisfied they are with their sex life, and yet these are areas that may be troubling you." The counselor might acknowledge how difficult it is to articulate fears about these issues: "Even though you may be concerned about changes in your sex life or how others will respond to your not having a breast, you may feel hesitant about expressing these worries" or "Because you have always considered sex a private matter, you may feel uncomfortable discussing it with me." Counselors must assess how important a woman's breasts were to her self-image prior to diagnosis, as well as her current feelings about her body and sexuality; decisions regarding mastectomy and reconstruction may hinge on these feelings, values, and attitudes. If the woman has a partner, it is imperative to assess his or her reactions to the breast cancer experience and the woman's changed body. Although it is relatively rare for women who have had mastectomies to be rejected by their sexual partners, many partners do have fears and concerns that could hamper the couple's sexual functioning or reduce their sexual enjoyment. The woman who feels good about her appearance and femininity despite her surgery will project an air of confidence that can reduce her partner's potential discomfort.

Sexual satisfaction may decrease in women who feel less attractive sexually and who are concerned with their partners' reactions to them. Some women report decreases in sexual desire in the months following mastectomy; anxiety, fear, depression, and fatigue all contribute to this lack of desire. Many women want closeness, touching, and cuddling, but they may not feel ready for sexual intercourse. One study found that 8 years or more after their original surgery for breast cancer, half of a sample of sexually active women reported feeling less sexually attractive, having difficulties becoming aroused and lubricated and achieving orgasm, and feeling dissatisfied with their level of sexual activity. They attributed these problems to the cancer experience (Polinsky, 1990). Although many women are reluctant to have their partners see their scars following mastectomies, those who have shown their partners their scars shortly after the operation are more likely to resume their normal sexual functioning soon after surgery, because both people in the relationship have become comfortable with the woman's appearance. The sooner normal sexual functioning is resumed, the better the woman's overall psychological adjustment.

Not all women suffer losses in self-esteem, body image, or sexual functioning as a result of mastectomy. Women who mourned the loss of their breast, took steps to improve their bodies because they realized they could look attractive, and believed that their sexuality was not a function of their physical appearance tended to cope more successfully with respect to their body image and sexual functioning (Kahane, 1990). A woman's self-image and sexuality do not appear to be much affected by whether she had breast reconstruction or decided to wear an external prosthesis (Reaby & Hort, 1995).

It should be noted that chemotherapy contributes to the difficulty women with breast cancer may experience in sexual functioning. Aside from the fatigue, hair loss, and weight gain that make many women feel unattractive, the drugs themselves are likely to cause vaginal dryness and make sexual intercourse quite painful.

Culture

Culture has been defined as the values and behaviors shared by a group. Broadly defined, it includes ethnic and racial heritage, as well as age, gender, religion, lifestyle, physical and mental ability, and socioeconomic status (Corey, 1996). Although therapists are trained to focus on psychological dynamics rather than social influences, it is a mistake to ignore the impact of popular culture on how women view themselves. Culture influences how people communicate, develop and maintain intimate relationships, perceive health and illness and their interactions with medical and mental health professionals, and seek and cooperate with treatment. Culture also defines roles for men and women. For instance, women are socialized to be physically appealing to men. In the United States, girls and women are bombarded by images of women with tiny waists and large breasts. Many women strive to meet this male-defined standard of beauty, sometimes at the risk of their own health. Understanding cultural beliefs and gender role socialization is crucial to working effectively with women with breast cancer.

If counselors fail to understand their clients' cultural backgrounds, miscommunication is inevitable. For example, in an attempt to put an African American grandmother with breast cancer at ease, a counselor greets her by her first name. The client interprets this as a sign of disrespect and terminates counseling prematurely. Another counselor discusses treatment options with a Latina client who reluctantly participates and does not follow through on homework assignments. The counselor erred in not including family members in an early consultation. For many Hispanics, the entire family and not just the individual who is ill make decisions about medical treatment. Both of these situations illustrate how a lack of understanding of cultural practices interferes with the counseling process.

Although counselors should be sensitive to the impact of culture, they must also understand that there are greater differences among people within a particular cultural group than there are between cultural groups. When counselors overemphasize cultural differences, their perceptions may be equally inaccurate and result in improper treatment. For example, if the counselor assumes that all Asians are highly intelligent, she may provide information about breast cancer that is too sophisticated and technical for the client to comprehend.

One way to understand the impact of culture is to assess the level of acculturation, that is, the language spoken, the customs the person observes, and generational status (e.g., immigrant, first generation, etc.). It is also important to consider religious beliefs and health locus of control. As an individual becomes more acculturated to the dominant culture, he or she may respond in ways that are similar to the traditional or to the assimilated culture. For example, an Asian client who adheres strongly to her traditional cultural values avoids eye contact with her counselor as a sign of respect for authority. On the other hand, if the client is highly acculturated, that same lack of eye contact may indicate anxiety, anger, or depression. When acculturation is not considered, counselors may draw erroneous conclusions that adversely affect treatment decisions.

Age and Developmental Stage

Age can affect how women adjust to a breast cancer diagnosis and treatment. Older women generally have an easier time coping than do younger women. For example, women over 40 years of age who have mastectomies tend to have significantly higher self-esteem and fewer concerns about their femininity than women in their 30s (Penman et al., 1987). Younger women are more likely to express concerns related to physical affection, sexual relations, family interactions, and intimacy than are older women. They are more likely to voice fears about getting too close to their husbands—cuddling may be scary, and sex may seem out of the question. Some women may reject themselves and be fearful that their partners will reject them.

Age may also affect a woman's choice of treatment options. A younger woman, for example, may opt for a mastectomy with no follow-up radiation or chemotherapy rather than a lumpectomy with follow-up treatment, either because she fears developing cancer 20 or 30 years down the road as a direct result of the radiation or because she fears that the follow-up treatment will impair her fertility. On the other hand, a mastectomy results in greater disfigurement, which may also be a more relevant issue for the younger woman. Clearly, treatment decisions may be fraught with greater anxiety for younger women. A younger woman who develops cancer may also be frightened by the statistics that report that breast cancer in younger women is tied to higher mortality.

The counselor must also take into account each woman's individual developmental stage when assessing age as a factor in a woman's adjustment to breast cancer. A 25-year-old is likely to feel cheated by a diagnosis of Stage IV breast cancer, whereas an 80-year-old woman who has accepted her own mortality may be better able to accept the diagnosis. On the other hand, age is not the only factor. An 80-year-old woman who has not accepted that death is a part of life or who has just recently found happiness may feel as cheated as the younger woman with the same diagnosis. In general, however, studies suggest that age is a fairly good predictor of emotional adjustment; older women who are diagnosed with cancer seem to have better adjustment than do younger women (Meyerowitz, 1980; Penman et al., 1987; Vinokur, Threatt, Caplan, & Zimmerman, 1989), although older women may be less likely to express a wide range of emotions (Kaye et al., 1988).

The literature on women's identity development is particularly relevant to understanding their adjustment to breast cancer. Developmental theorists (e.g., Gilligan, 1982) suggest that women in early adolescence "lose their voice" and submerge their own needs in order to please and serve others. One way they learn they can please boys and men is through physical appearance. This focus on meeting the needs or standards of others results in an alienation from self. When women undergo mastectomy, they may not cope effectively with their perceived loss of physical beauty because this loss could represent a total loss of identity. Older women, particularly postmenopausal women, place less importance on physical beauty, tend to feel more comfortable with themselves, and are less preoccupied with what they believe others want them to be. In general, women who focus on developing their inner selves and interests remain responsive to others yet are able to maintain appropriate boundaries. Such women have an easier time coping with mastectomy.

Life circumstances (e.g., presence and age of children, career stage, relationship status) that are linked to age and developmental issues also affect women with breast cancer. Women with young children will have different worries than women with adult children or no children at all. They worry about their ability to care for their children while undergoing treatment and also agonize about who will care for their children if they should die from the disease. Women with female children may worry that their daughters are genetically predisposed to breast cancer. Well-established career women may be concerned about how their illness will affect further success and achievement. Women who have lost partners to separation or death may fear becoming physically intimate with someone else. Women who have recently retired or whose children have recently left home may be anticipating starting a new life when they are diagnosed with breast cancer. Thus, developmental issues and life circumstances affect clients' adjustment and should be explored.

Socioeconomic Status

Socioeconomic status influences women's psychological adjustment and physical well-being. Mental health professionals should assess their clients' financial resources in order to determine whether additional social services are needed. If women have adequate health insurance coverage and the resources to pay for treatments outright or to cover the copayment or deductible, stress is reduced. If they have the resources to pay for increased child care costs, transportation to the hospital, and home health aides, stress is reduced. If they have the financial resources to tolerate a loss in income, stress is reduced.

Financial instability raises stress directly, in the ways we have mentioned, and indirectly through its association with minority group status and education. Lower-income women who are also minority group members encounter obstacles related to their racial-ethnic minority status as well as to their financial standing. (These obstacles are discussed in various ways throughout the book.) In the United States, respect and stature in the community are intimately tied to economic resources; in other countries, family ties to royalty, education, or religious affiliation may afford people high status. Furthermore, lower-socioeconomic-status women may be less educated in general and less educated about cancer diagnosis and treatment in particular. They are likely to lack health insurance completely or to have inadequate coverage; even those who are insured may be less proficient at negotiating the insurance maze. Finally, the medical care in poorer communities may be substandard, and in rural low-income communities there may be no access to comprehensive cancer centers with state-of-the-art diagnostic and treatment procedures. It is difficult to untangle the effects of low socioeconomic status, racial minority status, and education; however, it is clear that financial resources can facilitate the journey toward health and well-being for women with breast cancer.

Religious Beliefs

The research on the relationship between religiosity and psychological adjustment to breast cancer is not entirely consistent, but most research supports the benefits of religion and spirituality. Terminal cancer patients with strong religious orientations tend to be less fearful of death and more willing to make use of social supports. Women with breast cancer who feel close to God, pray, and attend religious services tend to be more satisfied with their lives, feel better emotionally, and experience less pain (Johnson & Spilka, 1991). Similarly, spirituality, religion, and prayer lower distress in patients diagnosed with various forms of cancer (Hagopian, 1993) as well as in those diagnosed specifically with breast cancer (Mickley, Soeken, & Belcher, 1992). Empirical research investigations indicate time and again that no one religion is superior to any other with respect to promoting well-being in women with breast cancer. However, cancer patients who use the church for emotional support may more easily deny impending death (Gibbs & Achterberg-Lawlis, 1978).

In contrast, Spiegel, Bloom, and Gottheil (1983) found that women in families that deemphasize religious orientation reported better moods. Some religious beliefs make it more difficult for women to cope, such as when illness is perceived as punishment for having not done enough good deeds. Women who hold these beliefs are likely to feel responsible and more depressed and guilty for being ill. Counselors must assess the role of religion in the client's life regardless of whether religion functions as a stressor or a support in a person's life.

Recent research by Pargament (1997) reveals three coping styles used by individuals who are fairly religious. People who use the self-directing style rely on themselves rather than God for support. Users of the deferring style tend to passively defer responsibility to God for their illness outcomes. Finally, those individuals who use a collaborative style view God as an active partner in their coping with the illness as well as in illness outcomes. Pargament's research suggests that people of the same faith can use their religion to cope in very different ways, perhaps explaining in part why there are no significant differences among religions. In other words, there are more within-group than between-group differences in religious coping. All three styles have been associated with lower psychological distress, but the question of whether these particular styles affect illness outcomes has not yet been answered.

Clergy are in a position to provide comfort and spiritual support to women with breast cancer, by helping them to view God as a partner in, rather than the sole source of, their recovery. The philosophy that God helps those who help themselves can empower women to seek prompt medical attention. In contrast, religious communications that foster passivity and self-blame are likely to be detrimental.

Biological Factors

One of the most challenging aspects of counseling people who are ill is distinguishing the treatment side effects and somatic correlates of the disease from psychological states. Physical symptoms can be manifestations of the disease, of medical treatment, of psychological issues, or of some combination of the three. For example, fatigue may be attributed to depression or breathlessness to anxiety, when in fact they are the result of the disease or treatment. Changes in sexual functioning may be falsely attributed to psychological reactions to mastectomy, when in fact they are the effects of hormonal changes (Kaplan, 1992). On the other hand, psychological issues can be overlooked when symptoms are seen solely as a consequence of physical causes. The seriousness of a client's depression may be underestimated because the counselor rightly sees depression as an appropriate reaction to a cancer diagnosis. However, where she may go wrong is in failing to assess the client's prior psychiatric history; in some cases, had she assessed premorbid functioning, she would have identified fairly serious chronic depression.

Psychological and physical health are inextricably intertwined. On the one hand, evidence is mounting that psychosocial factors affect physical health; for example, when a woman is chronically stressed, her anxiety increases, her blood vessels constrict, and her blood pressure rises. On the other hand, physical symptoms can affect psychological well-being: When people suffer pain, fatigue, nausea, and other disease symptoms, their moods also suffer. For instance, a typically patient young mother who is undergoing chemotherapy and is tired and nauseated has little patience for her toddler's whining. Furthermore, bizarre behaviors, labile mood, and unusual delusions may be indications that the cancer has metastasized to the brain, rather than being symptoms of stress-induced decompensation. Mental health professionals must neither negate the powerful impact of physical status on psychological well-being nor overemphasize physical symptoms as the sole cause of psychological distress and dysfunctional behavior. To achieve an accurate understanding of one's clients, premorbid and current psychological and physical functioning must be assessed.

Stage of the cancer. Although mental health professionals should know the stage of the cancer so they can have a framework for understanding the emotions and situations their clients will be experiencing, research has shown that the stage of the cancer has more impact on the psychological adjustment of family members than it does on cancer patients (Ell, Nishimoto, Mantell, & Hamovitch, 1988). Patients are more likely to respond to their actual physical symptoms.

Type of medical treatment. The nature and extent of women's psychological symptoms depend partly on the type of medical treatment they receive. Although the research results are mixed, many women with mastectomies do have concerns about their body image and femininity, and these concerns are likely to be greater than for women who have had breast-conserving surgery (Fallowfield, 1990). One study found that women who had mastectomies with adjuvant medical treatment (radiation or chemotherapy) felt less feminine and had poorer body images than did women treated by mastectomy alone, women who had lumpectomies, and women who had no surgery at all (Penman et al., 1987). A meta-analytic review of 40 investigations of psychosocial outcomes for women treated with breast-conserving surgery versus mastectomy confirmed more favorable body images for women who retained their breasts (Moyer, 1997). Prior empirical investigations of psychological adjustment (e.g., depression, anxiety, or anger) in women who had different types of breast surgery (e.g., lumpectomy, modified radical mastectomy) found no differences (Glanz & Lerman, 1992) or contradictory findings. The meta-analysis revealed small but significant benefits for women who had breast-conserving surgery. These benefits were more pronounced for women assessed 12 months or longer after surgery (perhaps because some women were receiving adjuvant chemotherapy or radiotherapy during the 12 months following surgery). Fear of recurrence was also found to be greater in women with mastectomies versus those having breast-conserving treatment (Kiebert, de Haes, & van de Velde, 1991; Moyer, 1997).

Proper preparation prior to surgery can reduce a woman's postoperative pain and promote faster recovery. Counselors who assess type of medical treatment can encourage women to seek this preparation from physicians or operating room personnel.

Time in medical treatment process. Different time periods in the breast cancer experience pose different challenges. Dysfunctional family interactions, for example, tend to be greatest in the first several months postsurgery, whereas reactions regarding body image are often delayed for several months or even longer (Penman et al., 1987). The ending of medical treatment may provoke strong emotional reactions in some women (Ward, Viergutz, Tormey, DeMuth, & Paulen, 1992): While the woman with breast cancer is undergoing medical treatment, she may feel that the disease is being controlled, but once medical intervention ceases, fear of recurrence looms large. Simultaneously, her denial is breaking down, and her sense of loss and feelings that her body betrayed her become prominent. Many professionals may assume that upon completion of successful medical treatment women would be relieved and even exhilarated; paradoxically, however, women are quite vulnerable at this time.

Medication. Counselors should inquire about the medications the patient is taking and be familiar with their side effects. Some medications alter moods, making the patient tearful and weepy, and others may result in the patient's feeling even more fatigued. Some chemotherapy agents affect sexual functioning and desire. Counselors who are unfamiliar with medications' side effects are likely to misinterpret their client's behavior or psychological state.

Pain. The counselor must assess the level of pain, if any, that the client is experiencing, because pain adversely affects a person's physical, social, and emotional well-being. Pain may persist after the woman has ostensibly recovered from surgery and appears to be in better physical health. Her partner and others, therefore, may not understand her pain and in fact may believe that she is exaggerating.

Physicians are generally conscientious about pain management, but when they are not, a counselor can be instrumental in helping clients describe their pain—whether it is continuous or intermittent, sharp or dull, and where it is located—and report discomfort to their physicians. The way pain is perceived, discussed, and responded to is a function of one's culture (Garro, 1990).

Personality Factors

Various personality characteristics have been associated with psychological distress. Many of these variables are strongly intercorrelated. Most recently, optimism has emerged as a critical predictor of emotional well-being for individuals with health problems in general and more specifically for women with early-stage breast cancer (Carver et al., 1993). Dispositional optimism, a tendency to expect positive outcomes in life, has been negatively correlated with psychological distress in numerous studies. Optimists are more likely to accept their illness and participate in activities to promote their health, whereas pessimists are more likely to feel hopeless and give up. Neuroticism, not surprisingly, has also been associated with psychological distress in past studies of individuals experiencing health problems.

Counselors must question clients regarding their expectations for a positive outcome: "Women who hold expectancies for bad outcomes in general (i.e., low optimism) as they approach breast biopsy are likely to attempt disengagement (e.g., cognitive avoidance), resulting in distress. On the other hand, those high in optimism are likely to cope through approaching the stressor (e.g., maintaining a positive focus), contributing to more positive mood" (Stanton & Snider, 1993, p. 21).

Cognitive Factors

Counselors should assess their clients' general intelligence, educational level, specific knowledge about breast cancer and its treatments, and attitudes toward health care providers. It is also critical to assess how clients view their illness (Lazarus and Folkman, 1984, refer to this as cognitive appraisal) and how they think about their bodies. Different racial-ethnic groups have been found to differ with respect to their beliefs about cancer. For example, Bloom and Kessler (1994) cite other researchers' reports that 65% of African Americans and 30% of Latin Americans believe that cancer is a death sentence, whereas their own primarily White sample did not hold this belief.

Cognitive appraisal. The objective severity of the disease does not affect psychological distress as much as individuals' perceptions of their disease (Compas et al., 1994; Given et al., 1993). A woman who is diagnosed with Stage II breast cancer may perceive that her life is over, whereas another woman with the same diagnosis will perceive that in a short period of time with some minor treatment she will again enjoy good health. In general, people who are optimistic tend to experience less psychological distress (Carver et al., 1993; Scheir & Carver, 1985, 1987).

Lazarus and Folkman (1984), in their transactional model of stress and coping, discuss how the level of psychological distress individuals experience depends in part on how they cognitively appraise the situation. It is therefore important that counselors ask clients questions such as, "To what extent do you see this illness as a threat?" "Do you believe that you have the resources to cope with breast cancer?" "How much control do you have over your physical health?" "Do you believe others (e.g., physicians) control your health?" or "Do you believe chance or fate determines whether you get sick or stay healthy?"

The more women perceive their cancer as a threat rather than as a challenge, the more distressed they will be. The more women believe that they do not have the resources or skills they need to cope with the disease, the higher their psychological distress will be. The more women perceive their life outcomes as under their own personal control and less dependent on more-powerful others, the better their self-esteem, body image, and functioning in daily life activities, intimacy, and social interactions will be (Penman et al., 1987).

Causal attributions. How patients attribute cause affects their level of distress. Not all patients with cancer ask "Why me?" but research suggests that patients who do ask that question are likely to be more distressed. Lowery, Jacobsen, and DuCette (1993) found that half of their sample of 195 breast cancer patients wondered why they had gotten breast cancer. These women felt less control since their diagnosis, believed that they and others could have done something about the cause of their cancer had they foreseen the diagnosis, and were more psychologically distressed.

Taylor, Lichtman, and Wood (1984) found that 65% of their sample of breast cancer patients had a hunch about the cause of their disease, and when pressed, 95% offered a theory, but their causal attributions were not related to their adjustment. When they believed they had personal control over the illness or that others had control, they were better adjusted.

Similarly, the extent to which people believe they have control over their health influences their health behaviors. We have a greater tendency to engage in health-promoting behaviors when we believe we can influence our health status. Causal attributions regarding an illness have also been found to affect health behavior (De Valle & Norman, 1992). If a woman believes that she caused her breast cancer, she may not have faith that medical interventions can cure her.

A recent study by Glinder and Compas (1999) found that women who blamed themselves for behaviors they had engaged in or failed to engage in (behavioral self-blame) were more distressed at the time of their breast cancer diagnosis, but these negative effects did not last. Women who blamed themselves for their breast cancer because of the kind of person they were (characterological self-blame), however, experienced more distress for up to a year following the diagnosis. The kinds of attributions women make about their cancer are clearly related to their psychological adjustment.

Behavioral Factors

Coping styles and behaviors. There is no one way to cope with breast cancer. Although the research may show that certain strategies, on average, are more effective than others, the mental health professional should not force a client to use specific coping mechanisms just because they have been empirically validated. A woman who does not cope through prayer should not be told that prayer is healing and given a schedule for religious services at a local church or synagogue. Yes, religion and spirituality have generally been associated with less psychological distress, but women who were not religious prior to diagnosis should not be pushed toward God and prayer as a way to alleviate their stress. On the other hand, women who depend on religion as a way to cope with crises should be encouraged to continue.

Some women who are coping with breast cancer rely on one set of coping strategies throughout the course of the illness, but others implement different strategies depending on the particular challenges they are facing (Heim, Augustiny, Schaffner, & Valach, 1993). It is critical, therefore, that psychologists assess a woman's customary approach to dealing with crises and problems. The kinds of questions the therapist might ask the client during the assessment phase include: "What are you doing now to feel better?" "Can you think about a stressful event that you went through prior to being diagnosed? Whom did you talk to? What did you do?"

Denial shields women from fully confronting the panic and terror they might experience without this defense. At least one researcher (Meyerowitz, 1980) suggests that only if the denial is interfering with the pursuit of medical treatment should the psychologist or other mental health professional directly intervene. However, the findings of Carver et al. (1993) contradict this and suggest that denial is never adaptive. One way to address issues without directly confronting the client's denial is by asking "What if" questions. For example, "What if the cancer did spread to your lymph nodes? Would you opt for follow-up treatment like chemotherapy or radiation?" These questions allow for some denial while still helping the woman to sort out her options (Haber et al., 1995).

Other research on coping with cancer indicates that avoidance coping (i.e., denying or avoiding the illness and its ramifications) negatively affects psychological and medical outcomes for cancer patients (Epping-Jordan, Compas, & Howell, 1994). There is also preliminary information that women fare better who do not avoid their cancer and its impact but who also do not dwell on it and instead look toward the future (Greer, 1991).

Kahane (1990) identified many common coping mechanisms in her study of 10 women who successfully dealt with breast cancer. These women sought information, found doctors they could trust, participated in their medical decision making, and did not shy away from interpersonal relationships. They shared their diagnosis, sought emotional support from others while avoiding or minimizing contact with people who were not supportive, and joined support groups or helped other women with cancer. These women nurtured their bodies and gave themselves time to heal—they started exercising, eating well, getting massages, and generally pampering their bodies more than they had prior to their cancer. They also put their cancer experience in perspective, realizing that others were worse off than themselves, and they made plans for the future and maintained a sense of humor, taking one day at a time and trying to plan pleasurable and fulfilling activities. Each had confronted her own mortality, had made a decision to survive, and tried to make each day count.

Interpersonal Factors

Social support. Social support is important to the psychological adjustment of women diagnosed with breast cancer, and research support is growing to indicate that it is important to survival as well (e.g., Spiegel, Bloom, Kraemer, & Gottheil, 1989). One study (Waxler-Morrison, Hislop, Mears, & Kan, 1991) found that women who had supportive friends and relatives, socialized, were married, and had a job tended to survive longer. Mental health professionals should assess their clients' satisfaction with the social support they are receiving from spouses, family, friends, and medical personnel. A recent study (Bloom & Kessler, 1994) found that breast cancer patients reported more emotional support in the 3 months following surgery than did women having other types of surgery; however, social support declined over time as the result of diminished social interactions and impairment in daily life activities.

Social support can be separated into several categories, for example, emotional, tangible or instrumental, and informational (House, 1981). These categories may guide the questions asked. For example, to assess satisfaction with emotional support, the counselor can ask "Whom do you talk to when you are anxious or down in the dumps?" or "How satisfied are you that your feelings are being heard and understood?" Tangible support can be assessed by asking questions such as "How do you get to your medical appointments, and does anyone accompany you?" or "Who watches the children when you are too tired to do so?" Satisfaction with informational support may be assessed by asking "How comfortable are you with the amount of information you have about breast cancer and its treatments?"

Support can come from various sources, such as friends, spouses, other family members, and medical personnel. The helpfulness of the support depends in part on who offers it and the type of support given. For example, medical advice given by doctors and nurses is seen as helpful, whereas the same type of information or advice offered by friends is not perceived as helpful (Dunkel-Schetter, 1984). Friends and relatives, on the other hand, can show their support by helping with child care, housework, and transportation to medical appointments.

Family functioning. Open communication between partners and among family members has been found to improve women's adjustment to breast cancer (Spiegel, Bloom, & Gottheil, 1983). In contrast, women who experienced poor communication in their marriages or dysfunctional family relationships tended to adjust less well to breast cancer. It is important, therefore, to assess relationship functioning prior to the diagnosis. Heterosexual couples whose marriages were conflictual prior to the diagnosis of breast cancer may find that their relationships deteriorate quickly postdiagnosis.

It is critical that the counselor have an understanding of the division of household tasks prior to the diagnosis. If the partner had assumed little or no responsibility for the functioning of the home, as that partner assumes more domestic responsibility in addition to a full-time job, he or she may become resentful and then guilty. Even in those situations where both partners previously shared the household duties, resentment and guilt may develop as the partner begins to feel the hardship of the added responsibilities.

The counselor should also assess the primary concerns of the client in relation to her children. Naturally mothers worry about the impact the disease will have on their children, regardless of their ages. Of course, the issues change according to the ages and developmental stages of her children. This topic cannot be sufficiently addressed in this chapter except to say that family functioning has a profound effect on the well-being and perhaps health status of women with breast cancer. Partners, children, siblings and parents are significantly affected by a cancer diagnosis, and their concerns are highlighted in detail in Chapter 8.

SUMMARY

This chapter identified the many factors mental health professionals need to consider when assessing women with breast cancer. In addition to psychosocial functioning, the often-overlooked areas of biological-medical factors and cultural influences must be assessed. The clinical interview was recommended as the preferred mode of gathering information, because it allows the counselor to interact with the client in a respectful and therapeutic fashion, but counselors can also gather client information from family and friends, nurses and doctors, and psychometrically sound and relevant instruments.

CASE STUDY ILLUSTRATION

The following case illustrates a psychosocial assessment interview conducted with Mrs. Letitia Smith, a middle-aged black woman, who is in the prediagnosis stage. "Mrs. Smith" is a composite of many clients. All identifying information has been changed.

Client Summary

At the suggestion of her work supervisor, Mrs. Smith decided to take advantage of her company's employee assistance program. The referral from her managed care company indicated that the presenting problem was acute anxiety and depression and that she was 63 years old and divorced. No other information was available prior to the first counseling session.

The Assessment Session

When Mrs. Smith arrived at the office, a receptionist asked her to complete a standard intake form that included much of the background information requested by the client's managed care company. When first meeting Mrs. Smith, the counselor noticed her client was uneasy, so she made sure that she introduced herself using her title and first and last names; this freed Mrs. Smith to address her in any way she felt comfortable. She also recognized that her client, being an older African American woman, might appreciate being addressed as "Mrs. Smith" rather than as "Letitia." To further establish rapport, the counselor made a short comment about the rainy weather; after engaging in small talk, Mrs. Smith visibly relaxed. The counselor then asked if she had ever been in counseling and what her expectations were. Mrs. Smith had never been in counseling and didn't really know what she was supposed to do. The counselor explained that "this is a place to talk about anything that is bothering you and I will ask you questions that are intended to help you to better understand your thoughts and feelings. Once we understand your situation more clearly, we can work together on some positive changes you might make." The client agreed that that seemed OK with her, and so the counselor asked what prompted her to come to counseling this morning. Mrs. Smith explained that she had been preoccupied and unable to concentrate; also, the client reported difficulty in sleeping and said she found herself snapping at her elderly mother, with whom she resided. Again, the counselor observed that her client appeared nervous and uneasy. After some time, Mrs. Smith disclosed that she recently had a "suspicious" mammogram and was scheduled to meet with a surgeon in a couple of weeks. Upon learning of the health issue, the counselor asked if anything else unusual had occurred recently that might contribute to her feeling worried or blue. The client reported no other unusual events, although she allowed that she had the usual stressors in her life—she has a lot of responsibility in her job as a secretary at a major corporation, and her elderly mother requires a lot of care. She complained that she is just too busy to be seeing a surgeon. Because there did not appear to be anything unusual in the client's report, the counselor began to zero in on the client's health issues. Using good reflective listening skills, the counselor allowed that it is difficult for many people to squeeze in time to go to the dentist or the doctor, but "you seem particularly stretched thin—as if you have no time for yourself." The client agreed, and the counselor continued with her assessment by asking, "How do you feel about having to see the surgeon when you have so many competing things in your life?"

Client: I just don't have time—but I want to get it over with, too.

Counselor: Two weeks is a long time to wait.

Client: Yes, it is. I've been having trouble sleeping ever since this began.

Counselor: Are there other times when you have trouble sleeping?

Client: Well sometimes, but not like this—I'm up and down all night . . . or else I just toss and turn. And then in the morning, I'm exhausted and can't get up for work.

Counselor: You seem very worried about what the surgeon will tell you.

Client: I'm worried about who will take care of Ma if something is really wrong.

Counselor: Really wrong?

Client: If I have cancer.

Counselor: You seem more concerned about your mother than yourself.

Client: Well, I am worried about myself, but I have good health insurance at work, and what will be will be; I can't change that; I put myself in God's hands. But I am worried about Ma; she is 87 and just doesn't get around well. I take her everywhere—she doesn't see well, so she can't drive anymore. If I am away, who will help her?

Counselor: I can see how concerned you are. Maybe it's premature to worry. Tell me what the doctor said when he referred you to the surgeon.

Client: That the mammogram was—I don't know, showed something.

Counselor: Do you have any idea what the surgeon will talk to you about?

Client: No, I'm just supposed to see him and take my mammogram with me.

Counselor: Oh.

Client: I'm afraid they will put me right in the hospital and I won't have time to make arrangements to take care of my mother.

Counselor: You're really concerned that because of this situation you may not be able to take care of your mother. Tell me what you know about breast cancer.

Client: My friend's mother died of breast cancer when we were in high school. One day she went to the hospital and I never saw her again. I know that a lot of people get it and that it is a horrible disease. I don't know why people get it, but it happens, so—so be it, I guess it is just bad luck.

Counselor: So if it turns out that you have breast cancer, you'd attribute it to bad luck. . . .

Client: Yes, that is pretty much it.

Counselor: I'm wondering if you are thinking that if you have breast cancer you will die as a result of it.

Client: Well, I don't know, I mean, I know that people get treatment and all, but it seems like a lot of people do die of it. I will pray about it and I know that whatever happens it will be for the best—except for Ma. I don't know.

Counselor: I'm wondering if you have ever had to deal with a situation like this before?

Client: What do you mean?

Counselor: Well, I guess I wonder if you have ever had something happen to you that caused you so much worry about your mom.

Client: Well, there was the time I fell and broke my ankle. That was hard.

Counselor: How did you deal with that?

Client: Well, I prayed a lot. And people at church helped me out cause they knew I couldn't get around and that my mother would need help, too. They were so nice. They came and helped with cooking and cleaning, and they also came just to talk to me. They were really kind. And, of course, my daughter helped out, too.

Counselor: How did people at church know that you needed help?

Client: Well, I let my friend at church know that I had fallen. We go to Wednesday night Bible study together, and she let people there know why I couldn't come.

Counselor: So they volunteered to help you and your mother out?

Client: Yes.

Counselor: You said they came and talked to you, too. . . .

Client: Yes, if they hadn't been there to talk to I think I would have gone nuts. Some days, I thought I would scream after spending the entire day with my mother—you know, she is a little senile and she keeps repeating her same stories. Sometimes it is hard for me to continue listening.

Counselor: Your friends from church seem like they offer you a lot of support. They listen to your problems and volunteer to help out with housework when you need it.

Client: Yes, they do.

Counselor: Are there other people who help you out or that you talk to?

Client: Not really. Most of my friends have died. My daughter is so busy with her own life. She tries to help me out, and she calls me or comes by when she can, but it is hard. She has a family and a job.

Counselor: But, you have your friends at church. Have you told them about what is going on with you now?

Client: No.

Counselor: Because . . . ?

Client: I don't know . . . I guess I don't want to tell anyone.

Counselor: You told me.

Client: You're different. It is OK to talk to you about this, but I'm afraid to talk to—you know—just people, about something so personal.

Counselor: You don't think people should talk about breast cancer.

Client: Well, not just to anyone.

Comments

The counselor gleaned a lot of background information from Mrs. Smith's intake form, including prior psychiatric history (there was none), current and past drug and alcohol use and abuse (client denied any use of substances), and prior medical conditions (the client reported no previous major illness).

Through the interview, the counselor was able to assess the client's beliefs about cancer. Mrs. Smith's comment about not being able to do anything about the cancer and that bad luck is why people get cancer in the first place, suggest that she believes she has very little control over her health. Her knowledge of the illness seems to be based on her experiences with friends or relatives who have had cancer, and her inability to articulate in any detail why she was being sent to a surgeon suggests that her knowledge of the disease is unsophisticated.

The counselor assessed Mrs. Smith's coping strategies by asking her about any situation that she had previously encountered in which she was worried about her mother. Although Mrs. Smith did not ask directly for the help she needed, clearly she was able to mobilize her support system, and they volunteered tangible as well as emotional support.

The counselor assessed Mrs. Smith's support system by asking directly about who helps her out and listens to her problems. Mrs. Smith seems to have a support system in place, albeit a limited one, but she is reluctant to tap them in this situation. Although she seems resigned to her fate, Mrs. Smith is anxious about her health situation. She has little knowledge about breast cancer and its diagnosis and treatment, and this is complicated by her concern about her elderly mother.

The counselor was able to utilize the information obtained in the assessment to formulate a treatment plan that included helping Mrs. Smith to mobilize her support system. Once she knew that her mother would be taken care of, her anxiety was substantially reduced. She then was able to focus on her own medical situation.

6

Intervening With the Individual

Evidence is mounting that psychological interventions for women with breast cancer can result in not only better quality of life but also, in some cases, better management of the disease and longer survival times. Psychoeducational interventions for promoting early detection of breast cancer are also proving to be effective. Counselors can play a crucial role in this endeavor by encouraging all their female clients to actively maintain their health, understand their health insurance coverage, and know how to navigate their health care system.

UNDERSTANDING HEALTH INSURANCE COVERAGE

Historically, the quality of health care people received was dependent on the availability of financial resources. If a family did not have the money to pay for a doctor's visit, the family simply did not go to the doctor. Minority group members, the poor, and the elderly typically have not had sufficient financial resources to obtain medical care; the situation continues to worsen because advances in medical technology have increased costs dramatically. Today the quality of health care received is still tied to the availability of financial resources, but most often in the form of health insurance. Individuals need to understand their health care options and be familiar with their health coverage when they are healthy. In this way, they can avoid unpleasant surprises and delays when they are going through the stress of diagnosis and treatment. Unfortunately, too often people are unaware of their rights and responsibilities and the limitations their insurance policies place on their treatment options and access to treatment. It is difficult to navigate the insurance company bureaucracy when one is healthy. When one is ill, the process may seem completely unmanageable. Counselors can assist their clients who are in need of assistance in dealing with their insurance companies and can alert them to possible pitfalls in their contracts.

Health Maintenance Organizations Ration Treatment

By 1996, it was estimated that 139 million Americans were enrolled in some type of managed care organization (Freudenheim, 1996). These organizations manage health care costs by negotiating capitation contracts with health care providers. What this means is that providers (e.g., physicians, psychologists, etc.) agree to treat a specified number of individuals for a certain gross amount of money each year. Then the organizations manage the enrollees' health care costs by determining whether an ordered or received service is medically appropriate or necessary and by authorizing (or denying) the provision of service. For example, suppose a woman sees her primary care physician (PCP) because she has found a lump in her breast. Her PCP, who is responsible for "managing" her health care, obtains authorization from the managed care company, and a referral for a mammogram is given to the woman. The mammogram indeed shows something "suspicious," but the PCP suggests that the woman wait 6 months and then have another mammogram to see if there is any change. However, suppose the woman is not comfortable with this and requests a referral for a second opinion. Again the PCP would have to get authorization, this time for her to see a physician for a second opinion. The managed care company does not see that the second opinion is medically necessary and denies her authorization. By rationing care, the managed care company limits costs.

Ostensibly, the goal of these organizations is to keep the cost of medical care low while still delivering adequate medical care. And the cost of care has remained low, as is evidenced by the median compensation provided to chief executive officers (CEOs) of managed care organizations: $3.5 million in 1997; in 1997 the highest paid HMO executive—the chairman and CEO of Oxford Health Plans, Inc.—earned $30,735,093 exclusive of unexercised stock options (FamiliesUSA Foundation, 1997). Yet these same managed health care organizations have (a) refused to pay for treatments, maintaining that patients did not receive proper referrals in advance of receiving treatment; (b) denied treatment altogether or allowed a less preferred treatment; or (c) delayed treatment until it was virtually too late.

Although state governments have resorted to writing and passing legislation to protect the millions of Americans who are the consumers of these health insurance plans, and the federal government has been urged to develop legislation to protect consumers, consumers cannot rely on the legal system to protect their rights in the area of health care; they must be vigilant and knowledgeable about their medical coverage.

Individuals should understand their insurance coverage before they need costly medical treatment. It takes time to receive member booklets and contracts that explain coverage from medical insurance companies, and it is difficult to read and understand these documents. Even when individuals have read their health care contracts, it is likely that they will be unprepared for the process that insurance companies use to deny coverage. For example, at least one insurance company's employee trainers teach case managers to identify claims that are likely to come under the protection of the Employee Retirement Security Act (ERISA).

Currently, when consumers sue health plans that are sponsored by their employers, ERISA prevents individuals from holding their health plans and the health plan administrators accountable for decisions that limit care and result in harm to the patient. At the time of this writing, only the cost of the procedure or the procedure itself can be recovered. Legal costs must be borne by the patient. For example, if a patient is denied a biopsy, but advanced breast cancer is diagnosed later, only the cost of the biopsy can be recovered by the patient. Because patients who have health plans sponsored by their employers do not have the right to sue for health problems that result from denied diagnostic tests or treatment, some consumer groups maintain that insurance companies handle claims that fall under the protection of ERISA differently from those claims that can result in expensive awards from juries. Legislation that limits the protection of ERISA claims is being debated in the House and Senate.

Counselors can help clients by explaining the following operating procedures of most managed care companies and urging women to check their contracts and policies; they can empower women to query their insurance representatives for answers to questions they do not understand.

1. Subscribers to HMOs and PPOs must comply with rules and regulations in order to obtain medical treatment. Such rules often prohibit individuals from seeking care from physicians and hospitals without a referral from their primary care physician. In the event an individual seeks treatment without the requisite referral, the insurance company will not cover the treatment provided, and the individual is responsible for costs incurred. For example, one individual did not understand that she needed a referral for every radiation treatment she received. Because her treatments occurred daily, she assumed that the initial referral applied to all treatments she received. However, the insurance company disagreed and denied her claim, saying she had not received the appropriate referral prior to receiving treatment.

2. Restrictions often prohibit patients from seeing the specialist of their choice if that specialist is not a provider in the network. However, if there is not a specialist in the provider network, a case can be made for going outside the network. The primary care physician must request permission for the patient to do so.

3. When prescription plans are included, HMOs often restrict the drugs that patients may be given. *Drug formularies* is the term used to refer to a specific list of drugs that the plan has selected. The physician can only prescribe drugs that appear on the list. If a physician wishes to prescribe medication that does not appear on the list, the physician or provider must have permission from the health plan.

4. Patients must understand when receiving treatment information from their physicians that some physicians may interpret a patient's request for information about treatment options as only referring to those that are paid for by the patient's plan. The patient may also want to know what treatments are available that are not covered by her plan. It is important that the patient make clear what she wants to know.

Counselors can also help women who wish to appeal if their claim has been denied. Member handbooks outline the process for appealing an unfavorable decision. A typical process requires that patients file their appeal through a telephone discussion. If this does not yield favorable results, then they must file a formal written grievance with the insurance company's grievance committee. If the consumer is dissatisfied with the decision of the grievance committee, then an appeal may be filed. An appeals committee decides if the determinations of the grievance committee will be reversed, amended, or upheld. The Internet is replete with people's stories of how they fought their managed care organization—some successfully. Unfortunately, state regulations make it difficult to detail a process that is exact and that is appropriate for every state. Some individuals who have appealed decisions give the following tips.

1. Detail all contacts with physicians in triplicate: Give a copy to your primary care physician, keep one for your records, and if necessary use the third to submit to your insurance company.

2. Keep a diary of all phone calls, enter the dates each was made, the name of the contact person from the insurance company, the questions asked, and the responses received. Keep copies of all written materials, including faxes, letters, bills, and so forth. Date any material that does not have a date on it.

3. Review your insurance contract and identify any statement that leads you to believe that your claim is legitimate.

4. Enlist the help of your primary care physician. Ask him or her to contact your insurance company on your behalf.

5. Find evidence in journals that supports your contention that the requested treatment is appropriate. Show this evidence to your primary care physician. Document the adverse consequences that may result from denying the requested treatment. Demonstrate that denial may lead to increased costs over the long run. If the insurance company has denied treatment by claiming that the treatment is experimental, submit evidence that medication or treatment is approved by the FDA and argue that therefore it is not experimental.

6. Contact your state and federal representatives and tell them about your problem. Ask them to intervene on your behalf.

7. Contact your state insurance commission. Find out whom you can forward your complaint to, then send that person a letter detailing your problem and include copies of all information you have collected regarding your case.

8. Contact your employer and tell him or her about your problem. Enlist the company's help. One consumer told of contacting the chairman of the board of his company, who was irate that the premiums the company was paying were not buying the coverage he thought they were. The chairman of the company pledged the cost of legal counsel to sue the insurance company.

9. If you go to an appeals hearing, be sure to know who will be present at the hearing. All names of individuals should be listed on a witness list from your insurance company. Bring all the documentation you have collected about your case. Make copies for those individuals who will be present, and distribute a folder containing the materials to each. Be prepared to explain why you think you deserve to have the denial of treatment reversed. Bring an advocate or physician to help you

with your hearing. Know that an attorney is not likely to represent you if your insurance is provided through your employer because of ERISA.

10. Always be courteous when talking to the insurance company. Be polite but firm. Do not lose your temper. When a woman is going through diagnosis and treatment, not only does she have to deal with her illness, but she also often has to deal with her insurance company to ensure that she gets the best possible treatment. Generally, the patient does not have the emotional energy necessary to do so. If a patient has a support system, she can tap these individuals to help her with insurance claims, or private advocates can be hired to help patients with their appeals and even to represent them at hearings. It is important that consumers recognize that their behavior may influence the outcome of their case. One former insurance company employee has commented that claims have been denied when consumers were less than cordial to company representatives, and at least one member handbook states that insurance policies can be terminated if the consumer is "being verbally or physically abusive to participating physicians or their staff, or employees of" the insurance company.

Medicaid Managed Care

A large number of health care insurance policies are sponsored by employers; however, not all individuals are employed, and even many who are employed do not have access to health insurance. In 1965, Medicaid was created by the U.S. Congress to fill this gap. However, Medicaid was not successful in providing the services needed by the poor, the elderly, or the disabled. Low physician payment rates coupled with increasing medical costs resulted in providers who were unwilling to serve individuals who depended on Medicaid to cover the cost of service.

As the managed care movement has gained strength, Medicaid has also undergone a transformation, and today 46 states have instituted Medicaid managed care programs. In fact, 11.6 million individuals are enrolled in Medicaid managed care (Bettering the Health of Minority Americans, 1996). Not all states have instituted adequate Medicaid programs, and exorbitant administrative costs have provided HMO administrators with luxury cars at the expense of the health of the Medicaid population (Dallek, 1996).

Counselors can help their clients by lobbying congresspersons for enforcement of legislation designed to ensure quality health care through Medicaid; they can help clients to understand what medical care they are entitled to and can assist with appeals when claims are denied. Counselors can also help by educating women about breast cancer, by encouraging them to seek preventive care, and by promoting the use of medical care at the first sign of symptoms. Long (1993) suggested multiple interventions to empower lower socioeconomic status African American women to combat the fear and fatalism associated with a diagnosis of breast cancer, but these strategies can be applied to all disenfranchised groups. As advocates for women, counselors can help communities provide health education and community outreach programs, motivate clients to make desired behavioral changes, and aggressively recruit women for breast cancer screening who are hospitalized for other conditions. Mobile mammography also may make possible widespread breast cancer screening in less affluent communities.

OUR APPROACH TO INTERVENTION

Given the empirical support for a wide range of psychological interventions and individual differences in client preference for techniques, mental health professionals need to be flexible in their treatment approaches. We agree with Arnold Lazarus's contention that all clients do not benefit from the same techniques and that individuals are multidimensional (Lazarus, 1989). Because individuals are affected by their thoughts, feelings, biology, behaviors, and other modalities, addressing any one of these to the exclusion of the others is not optimally effective.

Interventions are likely to be more beneficial when applied in the context of a strong therapeutic alliance. Counselors can be empathic listeners and provide an environment that is safe, thereby allowing clients to release pent-up tensions and anxieties. Once a strong therapeutic relationship has been established, counselors can use interventions from various theoretical perspectives to address clients' specific concerns.

"Amanda" was referred to counseling by her oncologist because she was ready to terminate medical treatment. Despite an excellent prognosis, she could no longer tolerate her chemotherapy protocols, the fatigue, the nausea, and the pain. She was tired of being a cancer patient. She wanted her old identity back. Amanda felt hopeless and disgusted. At this point she could not envision a better future. The counselor first empathized with Amanda and worked on developing a strong therapeutic alliance. She didn't try to talk Amanda out of her feelings and let her know that ultimately she had the freedom to continue or discontinue treatment. It was her choice and no one else's. From that base of respect for the client's autonomy, the counselor explained that her role was to help Amanda to make her own decision. Once a trusting relationship was developed, the counselor helped Amanda identify specifically what was making the experience intolerable. Amanda focused primarily on the side effects of chemotherapy. Very systematically, the counselor gave Amanda concrete tools to combat these side effects (e.g., relaxation training to address chemotherapy side effects, distraction techniques to reduce pain, assertiveness training to help Amanda communicate more effectively with her physicians). This tangible assistance allowed Amanda to continue with medical treatment, and ultimately she achieved a full recovery.

Although most of the techniques we review have established research support, use of these techniques with any individual client will not necessarily be beneficial. In some cases, the client may experience increased emotional difficulty and relationship conflicts as a result of the counseling. Consequently, it is imperative that counselors remember to inform their clients about the potential negative and positive consequences of psychological interventions prior to treatment. Choice of interventions must be guided by the results of a thorough psychosocial assessment, must be responsive to the challenges presented by the different phases of the illness, and must be tailored to the needs of the specific client. Such techniques should not be applied without consideration for the client's personality, educational level, culture, and intellectual and emotional resources.

We find that beginning with interventions that are comfortable for the client before moving to other areas that are potentially more threatening but also more beneficial increases our effectiveness as counselors. Lazarus refers to this as bridging: One begins with the modality in which the client is most comfortable, thus developing and increasing rapport. Then the counselor moves to other modalities that ultimately may be more helpful to the client.

For example, Linda, a 35-year-old, well-educated Chinese woman, had moved to the United States 1 year ago and was not acculturated to Western society. She was restrained in her expression of feelings about her breast cancer diagnosis, but her distress was evident in somatic complaints of headaches and gastrointestinal problems. Through consultation with her physician, organic causes for her complaints were ruled out. Although mental health professionals are trained to help clients process their feelings in order to reduce psychosomatic complaints, the counselor decided not to press Linda to divulge her feelings during counseling sessions. After establishing trust with Linda by empathetically paraphrasing the concerns she expressed, the counselor educated her about behavioral interventions. Hypnosis and relaxation training were conducted and helped to relieve stress. The success of these interventions increased Linda's trust in the counselor, and she was eventually able to express some of her emotional concerns. However, this might not have occurred had the counselor focused solely on affective techniques.

HOW THE COUNSELOR CAN
HELP THE WORRIED WELL

Even though heart disease is more common than breast cancer and kills more people, there is greater apprehension about cancer. In fact, breast cancer is the disease that women fear most; this fear is heightened in women with a family history of breast cancer. The majority of women with such histories overestimate their chances of developing breast cancer (Lerman et al., 1995). In one study, over half of such women reported intrusive thoughts and worries about the disease, and in one third, these concerns actually impaired daily functioning (Lerman et al., 1993). Valdimarsdotter and Bovbjerg (cited in Clay, 1996) found that women with family histories of breast cancer demonstrated high levels of distress prior to their mammograms in comparison with a control group. Both groups were less distressed after receiving normal test results, but a month later the women in the high-risk group were still more distressed and had more intrusive thoughts about breast cancer than did the comparison group. This suggests that negative test results do not by themselves have a lasting effect in calming the anxieties of high-risk women. Clearly, these women need help in coping with their increased risk.

Counselors can help them directly or refer them to professionally led support groups for women at high risk for developing breast cancer. These groups tend to be psychoeducational, in that actual risk information is presented, and women are taught to relax using progressive muscle relaxation techniques. Preliminary data suggest that support group participants have a more realistic and less anxiety-provoking picture of their actual risk, engage in more frequent mammography and clinical breast exams, and do monthly self-exams more regularly than do women who do not participate in support groups (Kash, Holland, Halper, & Miller, 1992).

It may be helpful for counselors to use cognitive restructuring processes to help women reduce their anxiety. These techniques are useful in both group and individual counseling. As we have discussed repeatedly throughout the book, the counselor must first acknowledge and empathize with fears expressed by the worried well. Once these fears are acknowledged, women are better able to work on reducing them. The next step is to teach clients that emotions are not automatic; they are a consequence of thoughts. Clients are asked to imagine a negative situation and to note the feelings that ensue. Then they are asked to imagine a positive event and note their feelings. Alternating between positive and negative imagined events reinforces how feelings are created. Once clients recognize that their feelings are not automatic, they may begin a cognitive restructuring process. First, clients are asked to identify the underlying belief that creates anxiety. For example, "Because my mother had breast cancer I know I will get it too." The counselor can then ask three questions. Where is the evidence for the belief? Does the belief serve some useful purpose? Does the belief make you feel good? Exploration of the first question allows the client to adopt a more realistic perception of her situation; anxiety will be reduced but not necessarily eliminated. Evaluating whether the belief serves a useful purpose helps to identify consequences of holding that belief. If the belief motivates her to get regular mammograms and do breast self-exams, it is serving a useful purpose. On the other hand, if her anxiety is so high that she is compulsively checking for lumps or avoiding screenings, the belief is not serving a useful purpose. When a woman recognizes that the belief is interfering with her quality of life, she can more easily make a decision to change it.

It may be helpful for women to keep a daily log of their anxiety levels in order to discover potential triggers. For example, anniversary dates of loved ones' deaths from breast cancer, driving by hospitals, and being around certain people can all trigger anxiety. Once these cues are recognized, counselors can help women develop techniques to cope with these events. There are workbooks available that a woman can use individually or in conjunction with a counselor to help relieve her anxiety and apprehension (e.g., Benson & Stuart, 1993).

Educational approaches can also be useful. Lerman et al. (1996) compared the efficacy of individualized breast cancer risk counseling to that of a general health education program for women with family histories of breast cancer. The breast cancer risk counseling that included personalized risk information for participants was more effective than was a general education program in reducing

breast-cancer-specific distress for the group participants with less formal education. Because in general, less educated women are not as likely to follow national
creening guidelines, it is critical that they receive this more personalized risk
information.

This study also compared the responses to the two treatments in women who
tend to focus on or magnify health threats (*monitors*) and in those who tend to
avoid and thus diminish the effects of threatening cues (*blunters*). Monitors in both
treatments tended to increase their general distress from baseline to the 3-month
follow-up, which may indicate that even general health information caused them
to ruminate about their personal risk. Monitors and blunters typically do not differ
in their distress levels until they are confronted with psychologically threatening
information; then, the monitors are likely to be more distressed. However, certain
types of information in some medical settings have been found to decrease distress
in monitors (Gattuso, Litt, & Fitzgerald, 1992). This area is still rather murky, and
more research is needed to ascertain what conditions and what types of information would enhance the functioning of monitors.

Women who are at high risk for breast cancer because of their family history
or because they carry the *BRCA* genes may consider having a prophylactic mastectomy or a preventive course of tamoxifen. In making a decision about which if
either course to follow, many issues need to be considered, such as what is the best
estimate of the woman's actual risk and how debilitating is the anxiety about getting breast cancer. Because highly anxious women tend to overestimate their risk
even after receiving lower objective risk figures, counselors must make sure that
women are not basing their decisions to engage in prophylactic measures on erroneous risk beliefs.

For those women considering a prophylactic mastectomy, a number of additional questions arise: How uncomfortable is the woman with the idea of wearing a
prosthesis, or how bothered would she be by the imbalance of her breasts if she
decided against reconstruction (a particularly pertinent issue for heavy-breasted
women)? How much are the woman's breasts tied to her self-image and sexuality,
and how would she feel about losing the ability to breastfeed? In any case, a substantial amount of time should elapse between the initial consideration and the
decision to have this controversial procedure. Ideally, multiple visits with the physician, the high-risk woman's partner (if she chooses), and a mental health professional should be scheduled to allow the woman sufficient time to carefully evaluate the physical and emotional consequences of the surgery.

For women considering tamoxifen, questions arise regarding side effects and
contraindications due to existing health factors. Although tamoxifen seems to
reduce the incidence of bone fractures, women over the age of 50 taking tamoxifen
have an increased risk of endometrial cancer and a higher risk of blood clots in the
veins and lungs. In addition, potential side effects such as hot flashes, nausea, or
vaginal dryness can compromise one's quality of life.

Training women in structured decision making has been found to facilitate
difficult decisions about surgery for breast cancer and to increase feelings of well-
being (Owens, Ashcroft, Leinster, & Slade, 1987). Although no information

currently exists regarding the impact of decision-making counseling on the use of tamoxifen, using formal decision-making skills may help women to make more effective decisions regarding prophylactic measures.

Too often, people have difficulties because they have not developed their decision-making skills. They may find themselves in conflict with significant others because they cannot come to a mutually satisfying agreement about whether to engage in prophylactic treatment. Or they may feel tormented because they are unable to decide whether to proceed with surgery or tamoxifen or to take no exceptional action. Counselors can help by teaching clients to list all possible options— surgery without reconstruction, surgery with reconstruction, tamoxifen, lifestyle changes such as diet and exercise, increased screening, clinical trials for new drugs, and no exceptional measures. After all options have been identified, each is examined, and objections can be raised. Options that are unacceptable are eliminated, and only the remaining ones are considered. Clients are reminded to focus on choosing the least toxic option that can help them achieve comfort. One woman might feel that prophylactic surgery would be the only option that would give her peace of mind, whereas another may be comfortable making lifestyle changes and doing monthly breast exams. Counselors can help clients to find their own solutions.

HOW THE COUNSELOR CAN HELP DURING PREDIAGNOSIS AND THE EARLY PHASES OF THE DISEASE

When a lump is discovered or a suspicious image is seen on a mammogram, most women experience some anxiety. Women who are diagnosed with breast cancer typically experience high levels of anxiety and depression—symptoms typical of reactions to severe stress. Anticipatory anxiety prior to an invasive procedure such as biopsy or surgery may also be high, and even higher when the woman is facing adjuvant treatment. Clearly, this time presents a crisis for women and their significant others, though generally symptoms tend to dissipate after surgery and hospitalization.

Denial of the symptoms or diagnosis of breast cancer can result in serious physical consequences and can also affect one's psychological adjustment. Women who deny initial symptoms and either don't pursue diagnostic testing or significantly delay it or women who deny the diagnosis and postpone or fail to pursue treatment altogether are putting their lives on the line.

Counselors can be quite helpful to women during the prediagnosis and early phases of breast cancer. For women who are reluctant to seek diagnostic testing or medical treatment, counselors may gently break through their clients' denial by emphasizing that the lump is most likely to be benign (as is true in 80% of the cases) while also asking them to recognize the outcome of no testing if indeed the lump is cancerous. We recommend breaking through denial only when a woman's life is dependent on it. Among techniques that are helpful, assertiveness training may improve clients' communication with significant others and medical personnel, with the result that their needs are more likely to be met; also, training in problem solving and decision making can empower women to be more involved in their own treatment planning. Counselors can also teach clients how to use cognitive restructuring techniques, how to identify when they are catastrophizing or limiting the number of possible solutions to their problem, and how to change their thoughts to more productive ones. Additionally, counselors may instruct clients to write down their thoughts and feelings during this stressful period, because this has been found to promote better adjustment in some women. Not everyone benefits from the writing process (Pennebaker, 1995), however. One study suggested that pessimists do not benefit from writing about feelings alone but that they do benefit from writing feelings in conjunction with coping plans (Cameron & Nicholls, 1998). Finally, counselors can help by empowering women to ask questions of their physicians, research medical care options, and actively participate in the treatment process (see Table 6.1).

Assertiveness Training and Communications Skills Training

Women who are ill encounter numerous situations in which they may benefit from being more assertive. They may feel too intimidated by their physicians to ask questions or to insist on straight answers. Surgeons can be condescending to their patients or pressure them to have procedures performed immediately (before they have had an opportunity to make an informed decision). Women who are not assertive may feel forced to undergo diagnostic procedures or treatments.

Out of misguided loyalty, women may be reluctant to seek a second opinion or to change to another physician who is more experienced and knowledgeable about their disease. This reluctance can actually be detrimental to women's health or even their survival. Sometimes when individuals seek a second opinion or consider changing physicians, they feel guilty, as if they had betrayed their doctor in some way.

Women may also feel misunderstood because they have not directly communicated their wishes. They may have a hard time asking for what they need, whether that be tangible assistance, emotional support, or space and time to deal with their own reactions. A valuable technique for empowering women in such situations is assertiveness training that includes education as to (a) the rights people have to self-respect and to respect from others, as well as the right to communicate their needs and desires to others; (b) the differences between passive, assertive, and aggressive behaviors; (c) modeling by the therapist of assertive statements; (d) training in communication skills; and (e) opportunities for behavioral rehearsal.

For women to be assertive, they must first understand what constitutes assertive behavior (i.e., responses that allow women to express their feelings, thoughts, and reactions in a way that doesn't infringe on the rights and feelings of others). Norms in many cultures and societies encourage passive behavior in women.

TABLE 6.1 Helpful Hints for the Early Phases of the Breast Cancer Experience

Questions You Should Consider Asking Your Physicians

What type of cancer do I have?

What stage and cell type is my cancer?

What is my prognosis? What are the odds that this cancer will be cured?

What are all the treatments that are available (including experimental treatments and clinical trials)? What are the side effects—long- and short-term—of these treatments? Exactly how is each of these procedures performed, and how invasive are they? How long is the recuperation period? What do outcome studies say about the efficacy of each of these treatments? What are the risks and benefits of each?

How many times have you performed this procedure? How many times during the last month have you performed this procedure?

How many of your patients have died as the result of this procedure?

Do you work with a team of specialists?

Where did you get your training?

What percentage of your patients have breast cancer?

Will other preexisting health conditions that I have be affected by the treatment? What about medication I am currently taking—will there be interactions? Must I discontinue them prior to treatment?

How can I prepare for these treatments? Are there lifestyle changes I need to make (e.g., diet, exercise, rest)?

During recovery, what can I do to reduce my recovery time (e.g., diet, exercise, rest) and enhance my quality of life?

What kind of follow-up care will I need? How often will I need to see a physician for checkups?

How can I participate in clinical trials?

Where are the closest major cancer centers, and how do I gain access to them?

What insurance do you accept, and are these procedures covered?

Once You Have Chosen a Physician

Tape-record your medical consultations.

Bring a close friend or family member with you to take notes during a doctor's visit.

Write down your concerns and questions for the doctor before you go for a visit. Keep a notebook with you so that as questions occur to you, you can jot them down.

(continued)

TABLE 6.1 Continued

Make sure you consult the list during your visits with the doctor and do not rely upon your memory. Take notes on the doctor's responses.

Seek a second opinion or even a third on your diagnosis, treatment options, and so forth.

Before agreeing to surgery, for example, explore all alternatives thoroughly. Know if biopsies will be performed in a physician's office or a hospital. Note that offices are not necessarily equipped as well as hospitals.

Research your choice of doctors. Know if their training occurred at a major cancer center, whether they are affiliated with the National Cancer Institute, the number of procedures they routinely perform, and whether they are board certified.

Research your choice of hospitals. Check the number of procedures performed at the hospital, the presence of high-technology equipment for diagnosis and treatment, and participation in clinical trials. It is important to know the background of the anesthesiologist who will be present at your surgery.

When hospitalized, it is helpful to have a family member or friend present as much as possible to advocate for you and to make sure you are receiving quality care.

Consequently, many women may dichotomize communications as either being passive or aggressive. Too often, because they misunderstand what appropriate assertive behavior is, they do not realize that it is permissible to be assertive. Once clients can differentiate between passive, assertive, and aggressive responses, communication skills training can help them understand how to design and deliver assertive statements. The counselor can model assertive statements that use "I statements" rather than blaming others. Women can be taught how not expressing oneself (passive behavior) often results in a build-up of tension that is likely to be released in an aggressive manner once the situation reaches a "boiling point," leading to a negative outcome rather than promoting intimacy. Finally, role playing can be used to increase a client's confidence before she attempts her new skills outside of the session. For example, the counselor can model assertive responses to be used with the client's physicians. Then, in a role play, the client can ask questions or communicate dissatisfaction with her medical treatment to the counselor, who plays the role of the oncologist or breast surgeon.

Counselors also can encourage women to "support their own magnificence." This concept is related to assertiveness training in that women learn that they have rights and needs and that supporting others is not their sole mission in life. They can learn to view themselves and their needs and desires as important, be urged to rest when their bodies require it, fit exercise into their lives, allow others to care for them without feeling guilty or as if they are a burden, and treat themselves to pleasures that in the past they may have denied themselves.

Women can also be taught other skills that may enhance their communication with significant others. For example, women can learn to use reflective listening skills, to identify and express their own feelings, and to express their needs and desires in ways that others can hear without becoming defensive. Using statements beginning with "I hear you saying," "I feel," or "I would like" are examples.

Diagnostic and Treatment Decision Making and Problem-Solving Skills

Having a choice of treatments can be advantageous. Studies suggest that women who have a choice have better outcomes than those who do not, regardless of the treatment chosen (Dean, 1988; Maguire, 1989; Morris & Ingham, 1988; Morris & Royle, 1988). Some women, however, become more anxious with increased choices. At the time women have to make decisions about diagnosis and treatment, they are already highly anxious, and as a result, their reasoning and concentration are likely to be impaired (Holland & Rowland, 1987). In addition to the pressure of making a decision, they often feel compelled to justify the decision to their physicians, significant others, and concerned friends. Counselors may feel a pull to be particularly active during the decision-making process in an effort to ensure that their clients get the best possible medical care, but they must monitor whether they are taking too much responsibility for what should be client decisions.

In order to help clients who are making decisions about diagnostic procedures and treatments, counselors must assess how their clients generally make decisions and how much involvement their clients want to have in the process. The counselor may ask clients to describe "a time when you made a really important decision; how did you go about making that decision? Did anyone help you to make the decision? How did you feel after you made your decision? If you had to do it again, would you use the same process? What elements from that experience can you use in your decision making about breast cancer diagnosis and treatments?" As clients respond, counselors should listen for the extent to which clients typically gather information and consult with others as well as for the type of information they gather. Understanding how a client has made an important decision may guide a counselor's interventions during the decision-making process. Note that a description of one instance of decision making does not indicate a typical decision-making style.

Counselors can help individuals identify how much involvement they want in treatment decision making and can help them to feel comfortable about their level of participation. Not all want to be actively involved in treatment planning; some prefer to defer decisions to their physicians. The counselor might ask: "On a scale of 1 to 10, how certain are you that your doctor will make the best possible treatment recommendation—where 1 means that you are not at all certain and 10 means you are completely certain? What are the reasons for your rating? What other information, if any, do you need in order to make this decision? Is there anybody else you want to talk to—other doctors, family members, friends, clergy?"

As discussed in Chapter 4, there are three types of decision makers: deferrers, delayers, and deliberators. The individual who prefers to defer to her physicians is likely to respond with high levels of anxiety or to "shut down" completely if the counselor attempts to encourage her to seek additional information or to list the possible treatment options in order to discuss the pros and cons of each. It may be more productive for the counselor to process the client's feelings of trust for her physicians and why she feels confident. The counselor may help her deal with her feelings toward significant others who are prompting her to get more information, additional tests, or another medical opinion. Counselors should not urge individuals to seek information that they neither need nor want, because that may contribute to clients' feelings of anxiety and of being overwhelmed. However, this does not mean that counselors should not appropriately challenge their clients as they make decisions about diagnosis and treatment.

Delayers, who are not interested in seeking additional information but need help in distinguishing between or among treatment options, can benefit when counselors help them evaluate each option, eliminate those that are clearly unacceptable, and identify how the remaining choices differ. Questions can be posed that focus on identifying what is objectionable about each remaining option so that clients can decide which is best for them.

Deliberators, those women who have a high need for information prior to making a decision, can be helped by the counselor in various ways. Counselors can start by helping these women to identify what decision they are actually trying to make. Some women, for example, may be interested in evaluating medical procedures, quality of hospital care, and physicians' expertise, whereas others may be content to evaluate doctors' credentials and experience until they find a physician in whom they have confidence. These individuals may benefit from instruction in the decision-making process if they are not already familiar with the procedure. Counselors may also be able to provide additional information or sources for information about physicians, hospitals, or treatment. Once all relevant information is identified, counselors can focus discussions on evaluating the pros and cons of each possible option. Because these women are likely to be highly distressed as they mull over the possible options and to express doubts once they make a decision, counselors can provide them with a place to release their feelings. Further, counselors can be a sounding board for clients' doubts once they make a decision.

Although women may be any one of these three types of decision makers, they face similar issues when negotiating decisions associated with breast cancer diagnosis and treatment. For example, women deciding between lumpectomy and mastectomy may not perceive this as a choice regarding the more effective treatment, but rather as a choice between their appearance and their survival. Interested and concerned friends and family members may be adamant about which option the woman with breast cancer should choose, resulting in her feeling guilty or confused if she prefers a different option. Some will offer technical information whether or not the woman wants it or is able to understand it. Clients may resist the decision-making process, or parts of it, and counselors must be sensitive to this resistance. At the same time, they should gently challenge clients' reasons for resisting additional information, diagnostic testing, a second opinion, or treatment. For example, the decision not to get a second opinion may be motivated by various factors, such as loyalty to the physician, the increased anxiety that goes with being assessed once again, or fear that a different opinion may complicate the situation. Rather than directly telling someone to get a second opinion, it is more effective to help the client come to her own conclusion by identifying what is preventing her from getting a second opinion and working through her feelings. Counselors need to encourage clients to process whether the decisions they are making are in their own best interest, rather than alienating clients by giving them direct and unwanted advice or information.

Logistics concerning medical treatment are not the only problems women with breast cancer need to solve. These logistics can so overwhelm a woman that they cloud her ability to concretely identify problems that, if solved, would reduce her distress. Some women may need to learn how to systematically problem-solve, whereas others know how but are too distressed to think clearly. Sometimes the biggest problem is identifying the problems. Once they are identified, a decision-making process can be implemented.

For example, Brenda had three small children and a full-time job when she learned that she had breast cancer. The time she needed to obtain information about various physicians needed to be worked into her current schedule. The counselor helped her brainstorm ways to "add" time to her day. Together they identified ways she could delegate responsibilities and identified household chores that could go undone. Brenda was encouraged to tap into her creativity and identify all options, no matter how far-fetched she perceived them to be. Then, working with the counselor, Brenda identified those options that were unacceptable to her. A plan was made that incorporated all workable solutions.

For more information about problem-solving training, the reader is urged to consult a book by Nezu, Nezu, and Houts (1999) that outlines a 10-session program to teach problem-solving skills to cancer patients. This approach can be adapted for use in individual, group, and family counseling; it provides excellent illustrations, session transcripts, and instructions for teaching problem solving from problem formulation through solution implementation.

HOW THE COUNSELOR CAN HELP DURING THE MIDDLE PHASES OF THE ILLNESS

The adaptation stage of the cancer experience can be conceptualized as a time when some women feel forgotten or mistreated. Counselors may need to be particularly aware of the issues that occur at this time so that they do not fall into the same behavior as friends, relatives, and medical personnel do. It is easy for all women who are in this phase of the illness to feel as if no one understands or cares about them. Women who have had lumpectomies have complained that others view them as no longer ill or as never having been seriously ill because they still have their breast. These women may feel particularly isolated and abandoned. Friends and relatives may withdraw support prematurely, but women cannot put the cancer experience firmly behind them because it isn't over. They may still experience physical pain and need to adapt to their surgical scars. They may be nauseated from adjuvant treatments. Even when all the treatments have ended, they will continue to have checkups just to make sure that the cancer hasn't recurred or metastasized. Nearly all women with breast cancer fear the possibility of recurrence, and each anniversary date or checkup brings back thoughts of the initial diagnosis. Anxiety mounts as appointment times near.

If the cancer recurs, then women once again face the crisis of a devastating illness. They frequently feel depressed, hopeless, and betrayed. Their confidence in their body and in medicine is deeply shaken. They feel as if they must confront their own mortality, and they worry that they will experience intense pain followed by death. Women who experience recurrence must deal with the whole process all over again, and yet they may feel that their physicians are minimizing the seriousness of their cancer if it is not metastatic.

Women confront social and financial issues in addition to psychological and physical ones. Recent studies demonstrate that individuals diagnosed with cancer may have their job duties drastically cut back, and in some cases, individuals have even lost their jobs. Even those who are still employed may feel that they can not change jobs because they are afraid they will lose their health benefits at a time when they can ill afford to do so.

The woman who is adapting to the cancer experience can achieve emotional and physical benefit from counseling that provides the support and understanding that she may not be receiving from family and friends. For many women, recurrence is the most difficult aspect of the entire experience. Women will particularly benefit from an empathic counselor who will help them manage their fears, doubts, and disappointments. The stress, pain, nausea, and fatigue that result from the treatment of breast cancer can be managed through cognitive and behavioral interventions such as relaxation training, hypnosis, and systematic desensitization; several techniques are discussed in the next section.

Stress Management and Coping Skills Training

Coping skills training can prevent or reduce stress in all aspects of the breast cancer experience. This training can help women to identify whether their problem situation can be changed or whether they need to learn to accept the situation and find ways to reduce their distress. They can be asked to identify present situations that are causing them anxiety as well as events that they anticipate will be stressful. With the help of a counselor, the client can then describe what specifically about the situation creates stress and systematically identify the coping skills that can be

TABLE 6.2 Helpful Hints for the Middle Phases of the Breast Cancer Experience

---

Simplify your life as much as possible while undergoing adjuvant treatments. Allow time for rest and relaxation by delegating responsibilities. Rely on loved ones for tangible support.

Discuss with your physician ways to prevent or treat nausea and vomiting associated with chemotherapy and pain associated with surgery.

Join a support group for women with breast cancer so you can help and be helped by others.

You have the right to your feelings—acknowledge them.

Overcome your reluctance to burden others by revealing your feelings; seek emotional or spiritual support.

Openly communicate with your partner (discuss sexual issues, fears, and hopes), allow your partner to help, and instruct him or her on how to be helpful. Partners can't read minds.

Support your own magnificence (get a massage, take a bubble bath, buy yourself something nice).

Eat well and exercise.

Maintain a sense of humor.

Avoid or minimize contact with people who make you feel bad.

Fill your life with pleasurable activities, and don't make cancer your whole life.

---

applied in that situation. Finally, she can practice those responses through cognitive rehearsal and role plays with the counselor.

For example, one client, Melissa, identified an upcoming family event, a wedding, at which she was going to see many relatives she feared would be insensitive to her. Melissa had had a double mastectomy followed by chemotherapy. She had decided to forgo reconstruction and chose not to wear a prosthesis; she had also decided against wearing a wig, choosing instead to wear a turban. She anticipated that several of her relatives would disapprove, make insensitive remarks regarding her decisions, and respond to her with pity. After empathizing with Melissa's feelings, the counselor asked whether, in fact, Melissa needed to attend the wedding. She replied that she indeed wanted to go to the wedding, and the counselor helped her brainstorm ways to reduce her stress. Melissa came up with several workable options, and the counselor reminded her that she could always leave if she became uncomfortable. The counselor also suggested that she contact the hostess and ask to be seated only with individuals whom she perceived would be sensitive to her. Melissa decided to do that. The counselor then helped Melissa to restructure her cognitions, in particular to dispel her irrational belief that she must be accepted by everyone and to replace that belief with positive self-talk. She was reminded to focus on the joy of the occasion and what she could do to have fun while at the wedding.

Treatment for Aversive Reactions to Chemotherapy

Some patients on chemotherapy develop anticipatory nausea as their chemotherapy session approaches. Stress management, including breathing and muscle relaxation techniques, can prevent conditioned responses from developing. Although not all patients respond to chemotherapy with nausea and vomiting, there is no effective way of identifying those individuals who are at risk. We do know that individuals who experience nausea and vomiting postchemotherapy are more likely to develop anticipatory nausea and to experience more severe reactions after subsequent treatments. Instead of using antiemetic drugs to relieve their nausea and vomiting once they occur, it would be more effective if these drugs were taken prior to the chemotherapy treatment. Although improvements have been made in pharmacological agents, the prophylactic use of antiemetic drugs is more likely to prevent the development of anticipatory nausea and vomiting than when these drugs are used only after the patient has already experienced the symptoms following chemotherapy.

Various cognitive-behavioral interventions have been developed that have successfully alleviated aversive reactions to chemotherapy, and outcome studies have produced strong empirical support for their efficacy. Clients can be taught to use positive self-talk and relaxation training including breathing techniques, such as breathing deeply from the diaphragm and slowly through the nose, prior to undergoing chemotherapy (Golden, Gersh, & Robbins, 1992). Also, progressive muscle relaxation training and guided relaxation imagery have been used successfully for cancer chemotherapy patients (Burish & Lyles, 1981; Lyles, Burish, Krozely, & Oldham, 1982). Some studies suggest that relaxation training in combination with imagery may be better than imagery techniques alone (Redd et al., 1987). Finally, hypnosis has also been found to be successful in alleviating aversive reactions to chemotherapy (Redd, Andersen, & Minagawa, 1982).

Deep breathing, relaxation training, and guided imagery. How is relaxation training conducted? In a quiet, dimly lit room, the counselor directs the client to get as comfortable as possible, ideally in a reclining chair or sofa. Clients may remove their shoes and glasses or contact lenses and loosen their belts, watchbands, or collars. The client is asked to take several deep, cleansing breaths, as this is the body's natural way to slow down pulse rate and lower blood pressure. Then the counselor directs the client to contract and then relax each muscle group until all the muscle groups in the body have been tensed and relaxed. Clients learn to observe the difference in how they feel when their muscles are relaxed and when they are tense. After much practice, clients are able to scan or monitor all their muscle groups in order to identify sites of tension. Ultimately, clients can spontaneously induce states of relaxation when they recognize that they are tense.

For patients who because of their illness are physically unable to tense and relax their muscles, other relaxation training methods may be used. For example, when practiced regularly, yoga can heighten the relaxation response because it teaches individuals to concentrate on their breathing. Goldfried and Davison (1976) discuss "letting go" relaxation, in which clients are taught to focus their attention on the various muscle groups and are instructed to "let go" of the tension without the initial physical contraction of their muscles.

Relaxation can be deepened by the use of guided imagery. The counselor first asks the client to describe a scene that is relaxing for her. Many women find beach or lake scenes relaxing; others enjoy mountains or a favorite room. The counselor teaches progressive relaxation methods first and then asks the client to imagine the chosen scene. The counselor guides the experience by asking the client to use her senses to imagine the scene; for example, "Notice how the air smells and feels on your skin. Listen to the sounds and take note of your surroundings." This helps the client to become fully immersed in the relaxing scene.

Systematic desensitization. Empirical support for the use of systematic desensitization to reduce the incidence of anticipatory nausea and vomiting is found in studies by Morrow and Morrell (1982) and Morrow (1986). Systematic desensitization operates on the premise that one cannot simultaneously experience relaxation and anxiety. Consequently, the counselor pairs relaxation with a noxious event. The first step in systematic desensitization is to teach clients relaxation techniques. Once clients are proficient, they, in conjunction with the counselor, can develop a hierarchy of events that are likely to provoke either nausea or anxiety, for example, anticipating chemotherapy treatment the day prior to the appointment, getting dressed to go to the clinic where chemotherapy is administered, or entering the treatment room. The counselor then works with the client during each therapy session, addressing each item in the hierarchy from the least to most noxious while the client attempts to maintain a state of relaxation. At any point that the client begins to feel anxious or nauseated, she signals the counselor by lifting her finger. The counselor then abandons the hierarchy and returns to the relaxation training. Working in this manner, most clients eventually can overcome each event in the hierarchy and can confront their chemotherapy without resultant nausea and vomiting.

Distraction. Preliminary research evidence suggests that distraction can reduce nausea and anticipatory nausea and vomiting (ANV). A study (Redd et al., 1987) with pediatric cancer patients indicated that the use of video games could reduce postchemotherapy nausea. A second study (Greene, Seime, & Smith, 1985) used the same technique with an adult patient with stomach cancer. In this multiple baseline study, at least initially, occurrences of ANV were reduced; however, results were not lasting. More studies need to be conducted with adults, specifically with women with breast cancer, before conclusions can be reached regarding the efficacy of this technique. Although some treatment centers might offer patients headphones so that they can listen to music or watch videotapes, patients might consider bringing their own videotapes or audiotapes and players so that they can listen to books or music of their choosing; patients might also bring hand-held video games. We suggest that women not bring their favorite music or books on tape in the event that a conditioned response develops as a result of pairing the tape with the chemotherapy treatment.

Pain Management

Hypnosis, imagery and other cognitive distraction methods, and engagement in diversionary activities can be used to help control pain. Pain may be acute—less than 6 months in duration—or chronic—longer than 6 months. Pain may also be progressive, worsening as time goes by. According to Golden et al. (1992), those individuals who request hypnosis or are enthusiastic about using hypnosis as a way to control their pain will respond most positively. Further, Turk, Meichenbaum, and Genest (1983) report that people who do not catastrophize about their pain are better able to manage it (cited in Golden et al., 1992). Chronic pain or progressive pain, however, is more difficult to control with pain-reducing techniques, although individuals who have the emotional and physical strength to persevere may be successful.

Women with breast cancer may experience pain as a result of the treatments they have received. If the pain worsens over time, these women may worry that their cancer has spread or that the disease is worsening and that they may soon die. Pain tends to lead to anxiety, and anxiety tends to increase the levels of pain. Ultimately, this cycle can lead to feelings of depression and hopelessness. Counselors may need to simultaneously help women reduce their anxiety and to instruct them on pain management, for example, by participating in diversionary activities to manage the pain and as a consequence reduce the anxiety and depression that accompanies the pain.

Women whose breast cancer has metastasized may experience intense pain, sometimes from fractures if the cancer has metastasized to the bones, that can be reduced through palliative medical care and psychological interventions. Clearly, women with breast cancer should be encouraged to consult their physicians regarding the use of pain medications. Those who are physically able can be encouraged to engage in diversionary activities; if they are physically unable to participate in activities, women can be encouraged to use imagery or other cognitive distractions. Such psychological interventions are not intended to replace palliative medical care, but rather are used as an adjuvant treatment. Physicians might not prescribe adequate pain medication, and some women are reluctant to ask for more. In such cases, assertiveness training can empower women to request increased pain medication (Golden et al., 1992).

Women can also be taught to self-monitor in an effort to understand when their pain increases or decreases. They can be taught to identify events, thoughts, feelings, or behaviors that preceded the pain or that decrease the pain. Although patients who are in the late stages of the disease may not be physically able to self-monitor independently, they may be able to participate in consort with the therapist. Because patients expect pain management techniques to quickly reduce pain, they may get discouraged when the pain does not immediately disappear or lessen. The counselor can intervene by encouraging clients to persist with the pain management techniques.

Hypnosis. Hypnosis is similar to relaxation training and has been used effectively to treat cancer pain (Spiegel, 1985; Spiegel & Bloom, 1983). The goal is to distract the individual from her pain by having her imagine pleasing scenes, thereby generating anesthesia "by imagining competing sensations as cold numbness or warm tingling" (cited in Suinn, 1997, p. 17), inducing amnesia for the pain experience, or distorting time. Using deep breathing and methods similar to relaxation training and guided imagery, clinicians can induce a hypnotic trance in their clients. While the client is in a trance, the clinician suggests that painful areas feel cold or numb. Clients learn to induce trances themselves so that they can access these posthypnotic suggestions of cold or numbness when they feel pain. Spiegel and Bloom (1983) used this procedure for 5 to 10 minutes during weekly breast cancer support group sessions with good effect.

Hypnosis has also been used to treat postchemotherapy as well as anticipatory nausea and vomiting (Redd et al., 1982) in women who have breast cancer. Protocols for trance inductions and an extensive discussion of the use of hypnosis can be found in *Trance and Treatment* (Spiegel & Spiegel, 1978).

Visualization

Once a woman is diagnosed with breast cancer, she may use healing imagery, such as visualizing her immune system becoming stronger or more powerful, whenever and as often as she chooses. During treatment, women can be instructed to visualize the chemotherapy drugs or the radiation attacking or eating the cancer cells. Simonton, Simonton, and Creighton (1978), who theorized that psychological factors caused the disease, also reasoned that visualization could then control cancer. However, no scientific evidence exists that supports the use of this technique in cancer management. On the other hand, the use of visualization may instill hope and a sense of control for some women, particularly those who feel a need to be actively involved in their medical treatment. Unfortunately, it may induce guilt and increase depression in those who do not experience remission. The implication that the mind has the power to cure the body is a double-edged sword: It motivates women to utilize their psychological resources to combat the disease, but it also results in some women feeling like they failed if the disease continues to progress.

Treatment for Weight Gain

Approximately 50% of women are likely to gain significant amounts of weight in the year following breast cancer surgery (Schag et al., 1993). Although physical activity and good nutrition may result in weight loss or may at least stop further weight gain, the practitioner can also intervene by exploring how these women interpret their weight gain. Do they feel responsible? Do they blame themselves for having a lack of control? Do they seem to gain weight despite their best efforts and then throw in the towel, thinking nothing will work? For these women, it may be helpful for the counselor to normalize the weight gain, explaining that it is not unusual to gain weight during the year after surgery. Some weight gain may be due to fluid retention, a possible side effect of chemotherapy. In addition, the counselor can refer clients to a nutritionist, provide behavioral counseling for weight loss, and encourage them to maintain an exercise schedule and a healthy low-fat diet that includes foods associated with reduced rates of cancer.

HOW THE COUNSELOR CAN HELP
WHEN THE DISEASE IS TERMINAL

Keeping people comfortable as they face death includes helping them to process the psychological conflicts and anxieties they experience as they confront the knowledge of their own death. The counselor is not engaged in problem solving, but rather is concerned mostly with empathizing with the woman in an effort to help her achieve a peaceful death. Ideally, this work should begin as soon as the individual becomes aware that her disease is terminal, even if she has few symptoms. It is preferable for individuals to confront issues instigated by a terminal diagnosis when they have the physical energy to do so, and so counselors can help clients to prioritize their struggles. However, the *client* must identify the issues to be addressed, because counselors can no more know what is right for a client who is dying than they can for one who has not been diagnosed with a terminal illness.

One issue commonly faced by people in terminal phases of disease is isolation. Counselors can help by actively listening, empathizing, and giving clients permission to express their deepest and most anxiety-provoking concerns; providing empty reassurances is not helpful. They can also help clients to discover ways they may unconsciously be contributing to their own isolation and to examine what feelings may be prompting their loved ones' withdrawal. It is not unusual for people who are dying to have increased conflict with the people they are closest to, because it makes separation easier for all involved parties. Insight into such dynamics gives clients an opportunity to change the patterns should they desire to do so. Other options are arranging family counseling sessions, consulting independently with family members to help them process their feelings so they are more available to their ill relative, and referring women to support groups. Finally, pet therapy has been found to reduce isolation and foster adaptation in dying cancer patients. Animals, unlike people, "never avoid the dying patient. They do not intrude, moreover, upon the patient's attempts to come to terms with mortality. The animal's quiet, accepting, and nurturing presence strengthens and frees the patient to resolve his or her final experience successfully" (Muschel, 1984, p. 457).

Many women with breast cancer also experience a sense of a loss of control throughout the cancer experience; however, when the cancer is classified as terminal, these issues of loss of control become dominant. Strong feelings of powerlessness can be instigated by a terminal prognosis. Consequently, the dying patient attempts to regain control as much as possible. Counselors can help the woman with breast cancer regain control by supporting and encouraging her to have input in decision making. For example, women can be active in determining their palliative medical care, and if they desire, the counselor can support them as they consider alternative treatments such as massage therapy, homeopathy, or unusual physical treatments. The counselor's support is particularly important because often women may be reluctant to reveal to their physicians that they are pursuing other treatments (Downer et al., 1994).

Further, counselors can help clients make decisions about how they will spend their remaining time. Often women who are dying are treated as if they are no longer able to function or are already dead. In fact, palliative medical treatment may make it possible for them to carry on with their routines or participate in other activities in which they are interested. Counselors can help by supporting women in their decisions and encouraging them to follow through on their plans. In fact, anecdotal evidence suggests that when women have a goal they wish to achieve, they often can achieve it before they die. For example, one woman known to us wanted to prepare a birthday celebration for her 6-year-old child before she died from her metastatic breast cancer. She bought and wrapped gifts, decorated her home, cooked food, and invited many people to the elaborate party. The party was a huge success and that evening, after the party was over, she died in her sleep. Rather than discouraging her from her plans, her ability to carry out the preparations for this event may have helped her to feel ready to die.

Counselors can assist women with terminal breast cancer to achieve a "dignified death." It is important that women have the opportunity to determine how they would like to live the remainder of their life and to do so with little internal conflict, while maintaining their ideal self, maintaining or restoring important relationships, and achieving any remaining wishes or attending to remaining concerns (Rando, 1984). Counselors can ask these women to explore questions related to these topics so that they are not robbed of the time they have left.

Such care can focus on two areas: (a) helping women address issues that they identify as unfinished or that are sources of stress for them, and (b) helping women find meaning in their death so that they can continue to grow in their final phase of existence. Unfinished business from her past may reemerge, but she may not be interested in resolving it now, having time and energy only for preparing for her death. Counselors can be most helpful by inviting but not pushing a client to deal with this unfinished business, unless the woman decides she wants to do so. Similarly, counselors can help women identify relationships that are still troublesome to them and can inquire about their need to resolve these conflicts, but if the woman is not interested in alleviating conflicts, forcing confrontations may serve to heighten psychological distress.

TABLE 6.3 Helpful Hints for the Terminal Phases of Breast Cancer

---

Decide what, if any, unfinished business you want to complete, but should you decide not to attend to unresolved conflicts, that's OK.

Plan how you want to spend the rest of your days, whether it's doing the things you've postponed or continuing in your regular activities.

Decide how and where you want to die.

Don't be afraid to discuss your fears and other feelings about dying with significant others, including partners, parents, and children.

Don't be afraid to make your needs known to doctors and family members regarding palliative care and other decisions.

Remember that you have the right to request or refuse additional treatment.

Speak up if your pain medication is not adequately controlling your pain.

Seek spiritual support if you want or need to.

NOTE: See Arnot (1992) for more extensive information.

In summary, counselors can help a woman with terminal breast cancer to put her "experience into a religious, philosophical, or personally meaningful perspective . . . or lend it a transcendental frame of reference that will give it some meaning and allow it to be better tolerated" (Rando, 1984, p. 207). They can help her to talk openly about her feelings if she wishes to do so, and they can help her to decide how she wants to live as well as how she wants to die. Finally, counselors can be instrumental in empowering women to advocate for themselves with respect to pain medication and other palliative care issues, and, should women become too ill to advocate on their own behalf, counselors can serve as their advocates and encourage family member participation.

A FRAMEWORK FOR INDIVIDUAL COUNSELING

Seligman (1996) provides a six-session counseling framework that can be adapted; sessions can be added or eliminated depending on the needs of the client. The framework is intended for adults who come to counseling soon after diagnosis. The general framework is as follows: Session 1, Understanding the person with cancer; Session 2, Introduction of cognitive and behavioral strategies; Session 3, Facilitating the use of support systems; Session 4, Solidifying coping skills; Session 5, Dealing with medical treatments; and Session 6, Reinforcing and building on gains. Seligman includes worksheets in the framework's appendix to facilitate psychotherapy with cancer patients. These include instructions to help clients (a) write about the diagnosis, (b) identify ways to cope with cancer, (c) facilitate difficult conversations about cancer with other adults and children, (d) promote qualities and behaviors that are associated with a better prognosis, and (e) cope with the fear of recurrence or treatment failure.

SUMMARY

Breast cancer is not a singular event but a process that involves ever-changing challenges. Mental health professionals can facilitate their clients' emotional adjustment from the prediagnostic stages all the way through diagnosis; treatment; and for many women, remission; and for some others, death. They can also help to reduce aversive physical reactions to the treatment such as pain, nausea and vomiting, and fatigue. This chapter has described strategies for individual intervention and provided illustrations of their application.

CASE STUDY ILLUSTRATION

The following case study illustrates the results of the assessment interview and the intervention with a Latina with early-stage breast cancer. "Rosa" was based on a number of past clients. All identifying information was changed.

Client Summary

Rosa sought counseling at the urging of her husband, Carlos, to whom she's been happily married for 10 years. She reports having functioned well in her family and career up until now and has never participated in psychological counseling. Rosa is a 32-year-old Puerto Rican American woman, married with two children (Elsa, 7 years old, and Felix, 4 years old), who has recently been diagnosed with early-stage breast cancer with no lymph node involvement. She is in otherwise excellent physical condition. Rosa is a moderately attractive, neatly dressed woman.

She and Carlos are college educated and are employed as schoolteachers. Consequently, they have good medical insurance and maintain a middle-class lifestyle. They are nonpracticing Catholics. Rosa's parents live nearby, as does her younger sister, Ana, and her family. Ana is godmother to Rosa's children and frequently baby-sits for them. Rosa's family came to the United States when Rosa was 5 years old. Carlos was born in the United States to parents who had emigrated from Puerto Rico a few years prior to his birth. Carlos's parents live out of state, and as a result, Rosa and Carlos seldom see them.

Rosa had a modified radical mastectomy 8 weeks ago. Although the doctor told her that a lumpectomy with follow-up radiation would be just as effective as the mastectomy, Rosa and Carlos, after consulting with Rosa's family, decided Rosa would have the entire breast removed. She did not want to extend her

TABLE 6.4 Interventions To Address Concerns of Women With Breast Cancer

Problem	Phase of Illness	Intervention
Fear/Anxiety; Death anxiety	Early, middle, late	Psychotropic medications, problem solving, decision-making counseling, empathy and support, relaxation training, systematic desensitization, cognitive restructuring, education, stress management
Anger	Early, middle, late	Communication training, empathy and support, problem-solving training, decision-making counseling, anger-management training
Depression	Early, late	Psychotropic medications, cognitive restructuring, empathy and support, behavior therapy
Fatigue	Early, middle, late	Lifestyle changes in sleep, exercise, diet, social and work schedules
Interpersonal conflict	Early, middle, late	Assertiveness training, communications training, referral for couples or family counseling
Role changes	Middle, late	Assertiveness training, communication training, referral for couples or family counseling
Body image concerns	Early, middle	Cognitive restructuring, communication training
Perceived loss of femininity	Early, middle, late	Cognitive behavior therapy
Diminished self-worth	Middle, late	Cognitive behavior therapy
Difficulties in sexual functioning	Middle, late	Behavior therapy, medication, sex therapy, relaxation and communication training, couples counseling
Vaginal dryness	Middle, late	Education, empathy and support, medication
Hot flashes	Middle, late	Education, empathy and support
Nausea and anticipatory nausea	Middle, late	Systematic desensitization, relaxation training, guided imagery, hypnosis, cognitive distraction
Alienation/ Loneliness	Middle, late	Social skills training, referral to group counseling or support groups
Job or career concerns	Middle, late	Career assessment and counseling
Reduced arm mobility and lymphedema	Middle, late	Empathy and support, physical therapy
Pain	Middle, late	Biofeedback, relaxation training, guided imagery, hypnosis, cognitive-behavioral therapy, education, stress-inoculation training

treatment because she believed that radiation, chemotherapy, or both would have impeded her from caring for her children and fulfilling her teaching responsibilities. She opted not to have breast reconstruction at the time of the surgery, but she is still considering this option.

Rosa's physical recuperation from surgery was excellent. Her physical discomfort has dissipated, and what little pain she does experience is managed with over-the-counter analgesics. Rosa and Carlos are well-informed about health issues. They easily read, understood, and digested information regarding medical treatment for breast cancer.

Rosa was prone to "tearful fits" both in her oncologist's office and at home. Her husband and her doctor were disturbed and perplexed by her reaction, because her prognosis was excellent. Rosa and Carlos enjoyed a healthy and active sexual relationship prior to the diagnosis. Since her recovery from the mastectomy, they have not had sex. Rosa reports that their lack of a sexual relationship is becoming increasingly problematic.

Case Conceptualization

Seeking counseling was particularly difficult for Rosa, because in Hispanic American families, a distressed individual is expected to work out problems within the family (Grieger & Ponterotto, 1995). However, Carlos, as head of the family, urged her to seek the help of a professional. Being highly acculturated, he felt comfortable getting outside help. Despite her reluctance, Rosa agreed to see a counselor.

Information gathered during the assessment phase enabled Rosa's counselor to identify her client's concerns and to formulate ways to intervene. Several factors indicated the potential for a good outcome for Rosa, including good financial resources and adequate medical insurance, lack of pain, no complications from medication, a strong marital relationship, good tangible social supports, successful medical treatment, and an excellent prognosis. Further, she functioned very well prior to her diagnosis of breast cancer and demonstrated good coping skills.

Nevertheless, Rosa and Carlos had to cope with the shock of the diagnosis, treatment planning, the mastectomy, and recovery. They had little time to experience and work through their feelings. Once surgery was over and no other medical interventions were needed, Rosa felt overwhelmed by her emotions.

At first, Rosa coped by denying the implications of her diagnosis and focusing entirely on seeking information and participating actively in her treatment decision making. Her emotions went underground as she tried to digest all the medical information, learn new terminology, and see several doctors. Problem-solving coping methods helped her to successfully negotiate the presurgery period. However, once her recovery from surgery was well underway, Rosa was unable to handle the flood of emotions she experienced. Her problem-solving style was not as effective at reducing her distress after the mastectomy, because there were fewer concrete problems to address. Having been socialized to take care of others, Rosa felt uncomfortable asking others for assistance. Similarly, like many women in Puerto Rican culture, she tended neither to express her anger directly nor to communicate about sexual matters. Although her usual coping repertoire had been adequate in the past, she now needed to develop new coping behaviors to manage her feelings about the mastectomy.

Rosa is unaware of some of her feelings and is unwilling to discuss others. She feels hurt and confused because her friends seem to avoid her. At times she feels angry and resentful toward friends and family members for not providing the emotional support she craves. She is sad about the loss of her breast. She is afraid that she is no longer attractive, and she wonders if she will ever want to have sex again. These feelings coexist with her fear that the disease will recur and concerns that she is not pulling her weight when it comes to family responsibilities. Finally, she feels guilty because she is sick and unable to control her emotions. It appears that Rosa's denial may be breaking down, and she may be at a particularly vulnerable point because treatment has ended.

Rosa's interactions with her husband, mother, sister, and children have been affected adversely by her breast cancer experience. Her tearful outbursts, self-blame, and depression may be explained by her inability to directly express her anger about her disease to her family. Cultural demands to remain stoic and in control further constrain Rosa's emotional expression. She does not perceive that her family has given her adequate emotional support, but the considerable tangible support they have provided make it difficult for her to acknowledge her anger.

Rosa's family role is strongly influenced by culture. She believes that it is primarily her responsibility to care for and nurture her young children; since her illness has been diagnosed, she has been unable to fulfill this role to her satisfaction. Because of her fatigue, she is often too tired to spend time with her children. Because of her operation, she is currently unable to lift Felix. On top of this, she fears that her emotional outbursts are deeply disturbing to Elsa and Felix. In an effort to protect them, she hides in her bedroom to avoid crying in front of them. She feels inadequate as a parent and guilty for introducing such stress into her family.

Rosa, although a nonpracticing Catholic, is quite spiritual. Despite a high level of acculturation and the attainment of a college degree and middle-class status, she is still influenced by the belief that evil spirits cause illness. Rosa sees her breast cancer as a punishment for past deeds, for not being a "good enough person."

Aside from culture, other factors have contributed to Rosa's psychological distress. Carlos's anxiety and concern about losing Rosa have led him to minimize Rosa's fears and anxieties. By reassuring her that everything will be fine, he is, in effect, reassuring himself. Her mother's and sister's anxiety about Rosa's disease, as well as their fears that they too someday may be diagnosed with breast cancer, have strained their relationship. In the past, Rosa's mother and Ana were emotionally available to her, but since she became ill, they have withdrawn. When Rosa attempted to disclose her feelings, they minimized her concerns and then changed the topic. As a result of her family members' behavior, she feels increasingly confused and isolated.

Intervention

Beginning stage of counseling. Why was Rosa anxious and tearful when "everything was going to be OK?" As Rosa talked with her counselor, it became clear that any time Rosa attempted to express her feelings, her husband and friends responded by saying things such as "What are you upset about? Everything's going to be fine"; "Don't worry, the doctor said she got all the cancer"; and "Honey, I love you. Please don't harp on the negative; it will only make you sick." Rosa could not find anyone to acknowledge her feelings about her mastectomy and her fears about recurrence.

For 30 min. of a 45-min. session, the tensions, fears, and concerns that Rosa had bottled up spilled out of her. When she was finished, her body was less tense, her speech was less pressured, and she reported a sense of calm. The counselor listened to Rosa without judging her and empathized with her fears about a possible recurrence of her illness. Rosa had been literally crying out for someone to acknowledge her concerns. The more others tried to reassure her, the more isolated, confused, and self-doubting she became. Her husband and doctor had intended to reduce her distress and paradoxically had increased it with their reassurances.

The counselor provided a safe environment for Rosa to express her feelings and fears, even if these fears were largely unfounded, and as a result, Rosa felt tremendous relief. When feelings are accepted, many women begin to feel more in control and less isolated. Of course Rosa had concerns about her experience with breast cancer. What woman wouldn't? When the counselor normalized her feelings and let her know that they were appropriate despite an excellent prognosis, Rosa was freed to release her bottled-up feelings.

Rosa readily acknowledged that she felt self-conscious about her physical appearance. It was difficult for her to even look at herself in the mirror. She thought her scar was ugly and shuddered at the thought of even washing that area. She felt repulsive and couldn't understand how Carlos could want to be sexual with her. She avoided undressing in front of Carlos despite his reassurances and sexual overtures. Lack of sexual desire due to feelings of depression, fatigue, and anxiety also led Rosa to reject Carlos.

As a result of a trusting relationship with her counselor, Rosa came to recognize that in addition to her fear, grief, and inability to accept her own body, she was very angry at Carlos for not giving her the emotional support she needed. In the past, Carlos had always understood what she needed without her having to express it directly. One way her anger was manifested was in her withholding sex from Carlos. This passive-aggressive behavior may have been due in part to culture. It was surprising to her that she was withholding sex to punish Carlos for not understanding and meeting her emotional needs.

The counselor also helped Rosa to recognize that she was blaming herself for her illness. Through the counselor's probing and reflection, Rosa came to realize that her belief in spirits made her feel responsible for being ill. At this stage, Rosa expressed a great deal of conflict as she explored the impact of her spiritual beliefs.

Working stage of counseling. During the beginning stage of counseling, the counselor focused on understanding and empathizing with Rosa's feelings. During the working stage, the counselor, understanding those feelings, continued to help Rosa to identify and express them. The counselor asked her to set aside a specific time each day to get in touch with her feelings and to express them, whether through crying, yelling, hitting a pillow, and so forth. In this way, Rosa had an emotional outlet, and she felt more in control. No longer afraid of having emotional outbursts, she felt more comfortable spending time with her children. This increased quality time with Felix and Elsa reduced her guilt about her parenting role.

The counselor also assisted Rosa to identify and then communicate her needs to her husband and friends. In order to give Rosa a sense of control, the counselor, rather than suggesting, asked Rosa if she would find it helpful to rehearse new behaviors. For example, instead of having Carlos try to reassure her, she preferred that he hug her and acknowledge her feelings. Instead of his trying to "fix it" by giving advice about how she could feel better, she wanted him to be with her and accept her feelings. In session, Rosa rehearsed telling Carlos that she knows that he means well when he tells her not to worry or cry. By actively practicing within the therapy sessions, Rosa became more confident about communicating with her husband and family members. By learning to express her needs directly, she was able to get the emotional support she needed for recovery, and Carlos felt included by her. Once Rosa and Carlos communicated better, the overall quality of their marriage improved, and Rosa was able to participate in sex.

The counselor sensitively challenged Rosa's self-blame during the working stage. Although the counselor did not dismiss her belief in spirits, when Rosa heard the counselor restating her belief that she was being punished for being a bad person, she herself questioned its validity. Consequently, she began to feel less responsible for her illness. Because Rosa was not immersed in traditional Puerto Rican culture, and because she was highly educated, she was able to effectively challenge this belief, and the counselor did not refer her to a Puerto Rican folk healer.

Another issue for Rosa was whether to pursue reconstruction. The counselor helped her to draw upon her preferred coping style, which was to systematically evaluate all the options and attendant risks. The counselor asked Rosa to voice concerns regarding each possibility, so that she was able to better understand which option was best for her. The counselor was careful not to impose her own opinion regarding reconstruction.

Termination of individual counseling. After the fourth session, Rosa indicated that she was feeling much better. The counselor suggested they meet two more times in order to review their progress together and to determine whether Rosa wanted to continue participating in counseling. During these sessions, Rosa discussed feeling more confident that she could ask for support from her significant others. Her relationships with Carlos and with other family members had improved, but it was also clear that many issues remained unresolved. No matter how much people who were close to her tried to understand her experience, she always sensed a gap. She frequently thought that her friends without breast cancer were silently saying, "Thank God it is not me." These feelings of being misunderstood by her friends resulted in Rosa's feeling suspicious, distrustful, and isolated. She still had many issues regarding her body image and seemed unwilling to discuss them in depth. It was hard for her to believe that friends with two healthy breasts, or even her counselor, could understand how she felt. Rosa and her counselor decided together that for additional support, Rosa would attend a breast cancer support group co-led by her counselor and a social worker. In a group of other women with breast cancer, she might feel less isolated.

The counselor and Rosa discussed how group counseling differs from individual counseling and how Rosa would now have to share session time with other women. They shared their sadness at ending their current relationship and anticipated working together in a group context.

Books detailing other women's personal accounts of breast cancer were recommended to Rosa. Not all women are appropriate for or have the time, energy, or inclination to join support groups, yet they could benefit from hearing the stories of other women with breast cancer.

Comments

Counselors need to respect the choices women make and not impose their own value system. For example, a feminist counselor may reject reconstruction because in her view it promotes the image of a woman as a sexual object. A counselor with more traditional values may try to encourage a woman to have reconstruction. Any imposition by the counselor is likely to instigate feelings of confusion, insecurity, or doubt about the decision. Although some women are clear about their decision regarding reconstruction, others will need the counselor's help. As with any decision making, it is critical that the counselor only help the client to identify and understand all the options and then to critically weigh each one before she makes her own decision.

7

Group Interventions

Many of the concerns faced by women with breast cancer can be effectively addressed through participation in professionally led support groups. Although groups can provide psychological, spiritual, and perhaps even physical healing that may not be possible to the same extent via individual therapy, many women are reluctant to join a group. Possible obstacles are fear of burdening or being burdened by other group members, shame about exposing themselves to others, concern about making an additional time commitment when they are already feeling so overwhelmed, and confusion about how the group can be helpful to them. It is imperative for mental health professionals to communicate to their primary referral sources, in effect managed care companies and medical personnel, the demonstrated benefits and cost-effectiveness of group work. If the group is planned for a hospital or clinic setting, request input from key personnel such as doctors, nurse practitioners, nurses, and administrative staff who, as a result of your consultation, are more likely to support the group.

THERAPEUTIC FACTORS

Yalom (1985), a renowned group therapist, discussed 11 therapeutic factors that exist in groups. We list some of these here, showing how they are particularly relevant to women with breast cancer.

1. Universality is the recognition that others are in the same boat. Most women are comforted to know that they are not the only ones who are struggling to meet the challenges presented by the disease and its treatments; in fact, women often feel that other women with breast cancer are the only ones who truly understand them. Some women fear that even their best friends may be thinking "Thank God it's not me," silently pitying them, or distancing themselves. Sharing their stories with other women with breast cancer reduces feelings of isolation.

2. Altruism, the experience of helping others, is therapeutic for women with breast cancer because they have an opportunity to feel useful through their contributions to the group. Tangibly helping others by offering advice, emotional support, information, and reassurance provides a sense of purpose and meaning to their lives. This factor can be especially important for women whose illness has robbed them of other avenues and functions from which they have derived meaning or defined themselves. For example, a woman who can no longer fulfill her job or household duties but has always seen herself as a "doer" can "do" in the group by providing support to others.

3. Instillation of hope occurs when group members can see and hear how other women have coped with similar emotions and physical side effects and moved past them. Seeing other women recover also gives women hope that breast cancer can go into remission and potentially be cured permanently. Similarly, seeing other women die with dignity offers hope that they can also "depart" honorably.

4. Identification occurs when group members model effective behavior for other group members. There are typically some group members who are excellent role models—optimistic, sensitive, and empathic to others. They have a "fighting spirit" that, if modeled by others, might increase others' chances for survival. These role models also find effective ways to negotiate interpersonal interactions with physicians, family members, and friends. Finally, they are comfortable with the fact that death is inevitable, but they focus on living and on making each day count. Women in the group can clearly benefit by their exposure to positive role models.

5. Catharsis is the emotional release people experience when they express their innermost, and often pent-up, feelings in the safe environment of the group. For some women, the group may be the only place they feel permitted and even encouraged to fully express their feelings. Loved ones may not be able to tolerate an honest expression of emotions because it makes them too anxious; consequently, they may cut off any genuine communication by changing the subject, offering empty reassurances, and reminding the patient to focus on the positive. Paradoxically, providing individuals the time and space to express their concerns is what frees women to "fight" the disease. Denial and repression sap energy that could be productively directed toward health-promoting behaviors.

6. Group cohesiveness, a "sense of unconditional acceptance and belonging, is important to offset the dreadful isolation so many terminal patients experience" (Spiegel & Yalom, 1978, p. 234). Women look forward to the group, attendance is more stable, and the bond among members grows stronger. The group may become one of the most important experiences in the lives of its members.

7. Existential factors can promote significant growth in support group participants. Women with breast cancer are encouraged to confront their own mortality and to make choices about how they want to live out the remainder of their days. As their self-awareness increases, they can give up ungratifying behaviors and live more authentically rather than responding to the expectations of others. Even women who are not dying from breast cancer are forced to acknowledge the potential seriousness of their disease and to make more conscious decisions about what

is important to them. In fact, many women report being more able to trivialize that which is actually trivial and to focus more clearly than ever on what they want and the steps they need to take to get there. Frankl (1963) noted that it is not how long we live but how we live that decides the value and purpose of our life. A support group can help each woman find meaning and help to make each day count.

RESEARCH SUPPORT FOR
GROUP EFFECTIVENESS

There is considerable research to support the efficacy of group therapy. In the 1970s, Irvin Yalom and David Spiegel, the latter a Stanford University psychiatrist, ran weekly 90-min support groups for women with advanced metastatic breast cancer. The support group was founded on the following assumptions: that "sympathetic and direct confrontation with life and death issues results in mastery rather than demoralization and that the group setting provides emotional support, enhances the patients' repertoire of coping strategies, and diminishes the sense of isolation, helplessness, and worthlessness" (Spiegel, Bloom, & Yalom, 1981, p. 528). Spiegel and Yalom found that 1 year after the initiation of the groups, participants were less anxious, fearful, fatigued, and confused and used fewer maladaptive methods of coping with stress, such as overeating, smoking, or drinking, than did members of the control group. It is particularly noteworthy that despite significant physical deterioration over the year, treatment group members did not experience increases in fatigue and declines in energy. The control group members, on the other hand, were more tired and less energetic. No differences were found on measures of self-esteem, denial about their illness, health locus of control, and depression, although treatment group members tended to be less depressed.

Spiegel and Yalom (1978) believed the group would psychologically benefit members but did not expect their survival to be affected. Ten years after the groups were conducted, however, Spiegel and Bloom (1983) reviewed the records of the patients in the treatment and control groups and found that the support group participants survived, on average, twice as many years as the women in the control group. Because Spiegel and Yalom's study was methodologically rigorous, the results are enormously exciting and provide further support for the notion of a mind-body connection. Growing evidence from research in psychoneuroimmunology supports the ideas that stress compromises immune system functioning (e.g., Kiecolt-Glaser et al., 1987) and that psychotherapeutic group treatment enhances the functioning of the immune system (Fawzy et al., 1990).

Geoffrey Reed, the assistant executive director of development for the Practice Directorate of the American Psychological Association, is collaborating with Blue Cross and Blue Shield of Massachusetts on a study that will evaluate outcomes for women who were diagnosed with breast cancer within the last year (as opposed to Spiegel and Yalom's sample of metastatic cancer patients). Women in the treatment group are receiving 16 weeks of group psychotherapy as an integrated part of their medical treatment, as compared with a control group of women with breast cancer who are receiving standard medical care augmented by patient education as well as referrals for psychological services. Although women in the control group may elect to avail themselves of psychological services, the help they receive will not be a systematic part of their medical treatment. After the 16 weeks, researchers will measure psychological adjustment and quality of life, compliance with treatment regimens, participation in healthy lifestyle behaviors, immune functioning, work and social functioning, satisfaction with care, and medical outcomes and costs. The groups primarily focus on allowing women to express their feelings about the illness and treatment in a safe, supportive environment, but the groups also incorporate patient information and relaxation training. The outcome of this study has significant implications for insurance coverage for psychological services for women with breast cancer.

A recent study showed that breast cancer patients who participated in social support groups that included training in progressive muscle relaxation and encouragement to exercise regularly and improve their diets had lower levels of cortisol, a stress hormone, and higher levels of an antibody that fights breast tumors than did patients who did not participate. Further, women who participated in the intervention were more likely to adhere to their chemotherapy regimens, and they reported less depression, increased energy, and increased social support from friends (Kass, 1999).

GUIDELINES FOR CONDUCTING BREAST CANCER SUPPORT GROUPS

Support groups for women with breast cancer tend to be more focused on content than on process. (See Table 7.1 for recommendations for leading a support group.) Exploration of intrapsychic and interpersonal dynamics are deemphasized relative to discussions of very immediate concerns such as death and dying, family-related problems, difficulties communicating with medical personnel, coping with treatment side effects, sharing information about traditional medical and alternative treatments, and issues related to reconstruction. In other words, leaders are less likely to process here-and-now interactions as they relate to members' current behavior outside of group or historical dynamics. We refer readers to Spiegel and Spira's (1991) excellent treatment manual on conducting supportive-expressive therapy groups for women with recurrent breast cancer.

GROUP LEADERSHIP

Typically, professionally led support groups have two leaders. One is a psychologist, social worker, or other mental health professional who is skilled in group process, and the other is a health professional, typically a nurse or nurse practitioner, who is well-informed about the medical issues. Sometimes one of the coleaders is a breast cancer survivor, a nutritionist, or a chaplain. Continuity must be provided so that the coleaders are present at each session. As with any group, it is important for the coleaders to have good communication, recognize if territoriality is developing, and process the group sessions together to ensure quality. Coleading also minimizes counselor burnout because it allows one leader who may be feeling overwhelmed at any particular moment to remain quiet for a period and observe the group while his or her partner takes a more active role. Leaders can also seek support from other colleagues, who can help them troubleshoot or problem-solve when or if the group is not flourishing.

Group Composition

Ideally, support groups for women with breast cancer should be heterogeneous with respect to ego strength, but otherwise they should be fairly homogeneous. We recommend that groups be developed for women at similar phases of the breast cancer experience (e.g., newly diagnosed, following mastectomy or lumpectomy, during chemotherapy or radiation, following active treatment) and also who are in similar stages of breast cancer (e.g., Stages I and II, Stage III, or potentially terminal patients in Stage IV of the disease). The phase and stage of the disease determine to a large extent the particular themes that will be most important to group members, and as much as possible, the members should be homogeneous so they can benefit optimally from the information shared. The type of treatment may also affect how cohesive the group becomes; for example, women who had lumpectomies have reported feeling that their experiences have been minimized by those women in the group who had mastectomies (Oktay & Walter, 1991). Although it may not be realistic to convene a group that is homogeneous on all these factors, there are clearly benefits to homogeneity: Information can be specialized, the structure of the group can be tailored to meet the needs of the participants, cohesiveness may develop more quickly, and women may feel safer discussing delicate issues.

Size of the Group

The optimal size of a support group is approximately seven members (Baker, 1977; Yalom & Greaves, 1977). If more than seven women show up for the group, the coleaders might consider splitting the group in half for a period of time and then reuniting toward the end of each session. This process allows more clients to get "air time." Of course, more structured psychoeducational groups could probably tolerate more members, but it is helpful even in these groups for leaders to divide the groups in half for smaller discussion sections after the informational portion of the session.

TABLE 7.1 Recommendations for Leading a Support Group

1. Promote cohesion: The strongest tool for promoting cohesion is the group members' preexisting homogeneity. Thus, leaders can emphasize this universal, all-in-the-same-boat phenomenon by
   - encouraging interactions that are conducive to cohesion by being attentive to group process while nipping destructive processes in the bud,
   - attempting to minimize social distance between themselves and members as well as between members and members, and
   - using consensus in decision making whenever possible.

2. Develop a safe climate: Group leaders can develop a safe climate by
   - avoiding premature or excessive demands for self-disclosure;
   - helping members accept one another's differences;
   - avoiding a focus on personal change—the goal is support;
   - avoiding interpretation, unless it involves the entire group;
   - using a cotherapist to avoid intense transference;
   - maintaining sufficient control to prevent group casualties and destructive interactions; and
   - using humor to help the group modulate its intensity.

3. Help support evolve: Group leaders can help support evolve by
   - introducing the concept of mutual aid and educating the group about the role of such aid,
   - highlighting empowerment of the individual and the group in an effort to reduce passivity and helplessness,
   - showing empathy both as a role model for others and as a support-building process, and
   - modeling support through interactions with the group.

4. Be generous with reinforcement: Leaders can reinforce the group by
   - focusing on positive and productive behaviors, and
   - promoting the building of members' self-esteem.

5. Foster reduction of stress: Leaders can foster the reduction of group members' stress by
   - providing refreshments and snacks to help foster comfort;
   - providing a structure that gives the group comfort and support; and
   - planning for enjoyment, laughter, and fun to balance the seriousness.

6. Give information: Leaders can impart information to group members by
   - being well-informed or having well-informed coleaders, and
   - exploring ideas as a group (leaders do not always have to be the experts).

SOURCE: Adapted with permission from Vugia, 1991, pp. 102-103.

PLANNING THE GROUP

Although groups can be open or closed, the great majority of cancer support groups are open-ended such that new members can join at any time. There may be days when members are too ill to attend, and some patients will inevitably die during the course of the group. In any case, it is more realistic when counseling groups of women with breast cancer to acknowledge that a commitment to attend every session for the duration of the group is unreasonable. Whether the cofacilitators decide that the group will be open or closed will depend on a careful examination of the advantages and disadvantages of open and closed groups. For example, when a patient dies, it can be more devastating to the members of a closed group who witness a continuous decline in group size. On the other hand, closed groups have the advantage of developing greater cohesiveness as members come to know and trust each other. Open groups can be advantageous in that members can mourn other members and can take comfort that when they die they will also be mourned, but at the same time, group size doesn't dwindle as new members infuse life and energy into the group.

Screening Potential Members

Formal screening is not necessary for one- or two-session educational groups, but it is necessary for longer-term and less structured groups. Potentially destructive members such as very needy, angry, withdrawn, or excessively dominant women should be excluded, as should active drug or alcohol abusers. One can assess a client's potential suitability for a group, in part, by inquiring about their histories in group situations such as school, work, and family.

Location

Where should support groups be held? Typically they are held in conference rooms at cancer centers; ideally these should be warm and comfortable, rather than cold, sterile, and businesslike, and the rooms should invite people to relax. Further, the group room should not be next to a chemotherapy waiting room or another location with which there might be unpleasant or even noxious associations (Vugia, 1991). The group might also rotate to different members' homes or occasionally take place in a hospital room if one of the members is hospitalized.

Length of Group Sessions

Most support groups are scheduled for 90 min. once a week, but they can range from 1 to 2 hr. Some inpatient groups meet more regularly because of forced time constrictions related to hospital discharge (Ferlic, Goldman, & Kennedy, 1979). For example, if patients are hospitalized for 1 week, the group might meet three times. Shorter group meetings are preferable for women who are fatigued or suffering from other side effects from the disease or treatments.

Structure

The degree of structure leaders impose generally depends on the purpose and duration of the group. Ongoing support groups tend to be less structured, allowing topics to be introduced by group members. Open discussion gives members more control of the group and ensures attention to concerns immediately relevant to group members. Affording women this control during a time in which they generally perceive minimal control may be therapeutic. On the other hand, research shows that information and skill development are also valuable (Telch & Telch, 1986). Consequently, some groups are very formally structured, with specific topics addressed at each session by expert speakers such as nutritionists, medical experts, and religious leaders. If a group is structured, it is preferable to have part of the session devoted to a specific topic and then to have a follow-up period of unstructured discussion.

STRUCTURED GROUPS FOR WOMEN NEWLY DIAGNOSED WITH BREAST CANCER

A structured support group may be instrumental in helping women cope with the initial crisis instigated by a breast cancer diagnosis. Newly diagnosed women barely have time to recover from the initial shock before they are asked to choose among multiple diagnostic and treatment options. They need to assess how much medical information they want and to what extent they want to participate in medical decision making. At a time when these women are asked to make decisions about treatment options, the group provides access to information and time to ask questions of knowledgeable coleaders. At a time when they feel very much alone, the group provides the opportunity to share their experiences with others in the same boat. At a time when they need good communication with physicians for optimal treatment of their disease, the group affords them the chance to learn assertiveness and communication skills. At a time when their anxiety is skyrocketing, the group provides training in relaxation skills to help them cope with the stress. At a time when their family is thrown into chaos, they can learn methods for negotiating temporary role change. Perhaps most important, at a time when their usual support system may fail to fully listen because of its members' own fears and anxieties, the group allows women with breast cancer to express the complex feelings they have without the fear of frightening, burdening, or alienating their friends and loved ones. The group can also teach women how to reach out to friends and family and to ask for what they need. This type of brief structured group for women who are newly diagnosed could potentially prevent them from developing more serious intrapsychic, interpersonal, and physical difficulties.

Correcting misconceptions by providing state-of-the-art information and enhancing coping and communication skills can go a long way to reduce psychosocial morbidity.

A Six-Session Group Program

Ferlic et al. (1979) conducted a 2-week structured, interdisciplinary group counseling program for 30 recently diagnosed hospitalized adults with advanced cancer of various types. The group met three times per week for 90-min sessions. The first half hour of each group session was devoted to patient and staff introductions, the second half hour to didactic presentations by the leaders on predetermined topics, and the final half hour to group discussion. Members of the group were fairly homogeneous in regards to the phase and stage of the illness, although the site of the tumor differed. The group was primarily educational, based on the assumption that the more informed patients are about their disease, the better able they are to cope effectively with their problems. Group members were, in fact, found to improve their self-concepts in comparison to control group members. Consequently, we have adapted this six-session structured group for women newly diagnosed with breast cancer. We like the structured psychoeducational approach for these women because it provides needed information and promotes a greater sense of order and control. Educational groups are also more likely to attract members because little stigma is attached to such groups in contrast to psychotherapy groups. The following is the adapted outline of group sessions.

In Session 1, leaders provide medical information about breast cancer. Women are acquainted with cancer terminology, the hospital and insurance systems, and various organizations that can provide additional support. General descriptions of breast cancer and its major treatments and their side effects are provided to reduce feelings of confusion. Although physicians may have offered this information when the diagnosis was made, it is unlikely that women can absorb it at that time, given their initial shock at first hearing the word *cancer*. This session may be particularly helpful because it follows the office visit when the diagnosis was first presented. With time, women are better able to absorb the information. Also, the fact that the group is structured minimizes anxiety.

In Session 2, leaders provide more detailed information on the medical aspects of breast cancer. Topics include cancer etiology; treatments and their side effects; alternative treatments; and the importance of good nutrition and physical activity in controlling anxiety, maintaining strength and a positive self-concept, and minimizing side effects through diet. Another major focus of this session is to help women establish clear communication with their physicians. Assertiveness training skills are taught and practiced so that women who historically found it intimidating to ask questions about their diagnosis and treatments or who wanted more time to speak with their doctors can learn to communicate their needs clearly.

Session 3 is devoted to the psychological aspects of breast cancer. The leaders present common emotional reactions in order to normalize these reactions, and leaders explain how the crisis diminishes over time. They also examine reactions of family and friends and provide a context for why people who love the patient very much may behave in ways that feel unsupportive. Participants examine their feelings about death, pain, and suffering and are taught problem-solving skills that help in treatment planning as well as in professional and personal relationships. Leaders emphasize the importance of expressing feelings verbally so they aren't acted out in ways that are personally destructive or destructive to relationships, and they discuss research findings about the connections among optimism, a fighting spirit, and survival.

Session 4 focuses on the exploration of religion and faith as ways to cope with cancer and mortality—particularly emphasizing faith as "ever available and nonjudgmental" (Ferlic et al., 1979, p. 761). Some women might experience a loss of faith because they feel their cancer must be a punishment: They lived their lives in a positive way and served others and now they ask, "Why must I suffer? Is there a just God?" Suggested readings such as *When Bad Things Happen to Good People* (Kushner, 1981) can help to reduce self-blame and may prevent abandonment of spiritual or religious support that could facilitate coping. Nonbelievers can be invited to explore or reexplore their beliefs about spirituality as well as other avenues that may provide comfort.

Session 5 is devoted to issues of sexuality and self-image. Group members explore physical changes resulting from the cancer or its treatments; body image and self-concept; problems or fears about reactions of partners or their own feelings about sex; and the importance of touching, physical closeness, and nurturing to reestablish positive sexuality.

Session 6 focuses on a diverse group of topics: relationship strains with spouse, family, and friends; fears that cancer is contagious; fear of genetic aspects such as transmission of genes to daughters; and fear of how breast cancer might prevent women from forming new intimate relationships.

SUPPORTIVE-EXPRESSIVE GROUPS FOR WOMEN WITH ADVANCED CANCER

Supportive-expressive groups provide a safe place for women to express their feelings. The purpose is not to restructure personality, as in therapy groups, but to deal with immediate life issues. These groups differ from therapy groups in other ways as well. In therapy groups, the leader aims for heterogeneity in problem situations but homogeneity in ego strength. In supportive-expressive groups the opposite is true. In therapy groups, outside interaction among members is discouraged, whereas in supportive-expressive groups members are encouraged to telephone and visit one another between sessions (Haber et al., 1995).

The focus of a group for advanced cancer patients is not dying but living. That said, allowing women to directly discuss issues of death and dying does not sap energy, reduce hope, and promote withdrawal, as many people believe; rather, it invigorates members to take control by actively choosing how they want to live out their remaining weeks, months, or years. Many women with cancer and many health professionals who are in the position to refer women to groups worry that the impact of watching other women deteriorate and ultimately die from breast cancer would be devastating and would significantly exaggerate women's own fears of death. Clinical and research evidence challenges that view. For example, Gibbs and Achterberg-Lawlis (1978) found that prior experience with death of a loved one decreased death anxiety. It shouldn't surprise us that exposure to death decreases our fears. It is firmly established that avoidance perpetuates phobias, and the same process appears to hold in the case of death; encountering another's death is really not as bad as one's fantasies about death. The group members in Spiegel, Bloom, and Yalom's group of women with metastatic cancer also found that exposure to death and the free and honest discussion of it somehow demystified and detoxified it. Furthermore, mourning the death of group members provided the members with the comfort that they too would be mourned.

To overcome common initial reactions to a terminal diagnosis, such as feeling victimized, helpless, and permanently cheated, a group can help women realize their unfulfilled dreams or focus on what will make them happy. Frequently, we heard our clients with cancer say things like "I was waiting until all the kids had finished college before my husband and I took that trip to Europe" or "I've always wanted to write, but the needs of the children, my husband, my parents, and the responsibilities of running the house took precedence. I always waited for the demands to lessen so I could have time to focus on myself; now I don't have that time." These scenarios are particularly common for women who were socialized to put the needs of others ahead of their own. A breast cancer diagnosis often catapults women into a head-on confrontation with their own mortality. They are faced with a choice: to die as helpless victims of an unfortunate and undeserved fate or to summon their energies and concentrate on living as fully as possible with the time they have left.

The Counselor's Role

We see the counselor primarily as a group facilitator who encourages interactions among group members and gradually takes more and more of a back seat as the group becomes more cohesive. For example, in the initial stages of the group, the leader may share medical information while empowering members to participate. It is typical for women to discuss safer, informational topics at the beginning of the group, and even these shared experiences are likely to foster cohesiveness. Members offer one another information about alternative treatments and chemoprevention trials and advice about ways to handle interactions with doctors or family members. It is not unusual for patients to trade war stories about physicians who have been insensitive or disrespectful or who have withdrawn from them when the cancer was no longer controlled. As the group becomes more familiar, the leaders can elicit more frequent and specific sharing of feelings and experiences, as opposed to external generalities (Spiegel & Spira, 1991). For example, instead of saying, "Doctors don't give a damn about their patients," members may say, "I am very upset with my doctor for the way he treated me today."

Anger toward the medical establishment and managed care companies is usually not entirely deserved. It is virtually impossible for physicians to live up to the unrealistic standards to which patients hold them (Yalom & Greaves, 1977). When initially diagnosed, many women find it comforting to believe that their doctors are saviors and all-knowing, an image some physicians promote. When their cancer has recurred or metastasized, however, the fantasy collapses, and they displace their anger onto their physicians. The consensus of terminal patients is that physicians tend to withdraw when patients' prognosis worsens. Some withdraw because they feel that they failed the patient; others withdraw because it is painful to confront the terminal status of a patient. In any case, leaders can help women to understand the various sources of their anger and allow the group to progress to a more intimate level. The shared resentment toward physicians and managed care serves to foster a bond among women in the initial stages of the group.

Group leaders who provide a lot of direction and structured exercises may be evaluated by members as more competent and as better leaders, but those favorable evaluations are not necessarily associated with better outcomes for members (Yalom, 1985). In other words, members of groups with active leaders do not grow as much or make as many positive changes as do those with leaders who are less prominent (Yalom, 1985). Group leaders who are more experienced, and typically more confident, tend to trust in the group process more, don't need the glory of being admired or seen as an expert, and are more likely to empower group members to take more responsibility for their own growth.

One aspect of a leader's role is to instill hope, but counselors may be confused about what type of hope can be offered to women who are terminally ill with breast cancer. Clearly, giving false hope is detrimental; the recipients are likely to feel betrayed and robbed of the opportunity to say their good-byes or to wrap up unfinished business. Yet hope is essential to maintaining well-being. Without hope, women are likely to die more quickly and to have a poorer quality of life. Perhaps one answer to this dilemma is to focus on areas where hope exists, such as gaining more effective control over pain, deciding how and where one wants to die, and so on.

Handling Difficult Issues in the Group

When a group is not progressing satisfactorily, the coleaders must first ask themselves whether they are doing anything to contribute to the problem. For example, coleaders might consider whether silences in the group or superficial discussion are occurring because the leaders have subtly communicated that they cannot tolerate direct and honest discussions about very anxiety-provoking issues such as death, pain, isolation, and grief. Being an effective leader for a group of terminally ill women requires that the group leader share in the triumphs but also the pain and anxiety of the group. Leaders must confront their own mortality, be able to tolerate being the target of members' anger toward healthy individuals, recognize survivor guilt, and tolerate the anxiety that comes with not having answers to the big questions that emerge for people who are diagnosed with a potentially life-threatening illness. Leaders must be able to acknowledge that they don't know why their clients are sick and they are not, that it isn't fair that they get to go home and be with their families at the end of a day and their hospitalized clients do not. Leaders must be able to resist the instinct to minimize what their clients are enduring and focus on life and living while actively confronting the inevitability of death for all—even for "healthy" support group leaders. Training, including observation and then participation in support groups, and good supervision help group leaders to work through countertransference feelings so they do not stymie the group.

However, countertransference issues are not the only reasons groups do not progress. As in any group, members will be resistant to discussing painful issues. Members may never deepen their communications in the group. When this happens, it may be because the leaders or members are avoiding specific topics. The leader can use immediacy, in effect disclosing his or her feelings and wondering aloud if others might be feeling the same way or making a process comment. When a member dies, other members may unconsciously collude to avoid discussing the death. The leader also may collude because the absence of the group member is keenly felt and painful. When that happens, bickering and scapegoating, superficiality of discussion, or silence may occur. It is critical that the coleaders point out what is happening and free up discussion.

Monopolizers; silent members; or competitive group members, who want others to know either that they have the most tragic stories in the group (sometimes called "Queen for a Day") or how much healthier they are than the others, can seriously impede the progress of the group. We refer readers to *The Theory and Practice of Group Psychotherapy* (Yalom, 1985) for guidelines on handling interpersonally difficult group members.

SUMMARY

Empirical research supports the efficacy of group treatment in various forms, such as time-limited structured psychoeducational groups and ongoing longer-term supportive-expressive groups. Therapeutic factors in groups that are particularly relevant for women with breast cancer are catharsis, altruism, identification, interpersonal learning, instillation of hope, and existential factors. We recommend structured psychoeducational groups for newly diagnosed women because of their needs for information and more perceived control. They are also more likely to attend an educational group rather than a psychotherapy group and will feel less isolated and better understood by women in the same boat. These structured groups are generally short-term. Supportive-expressive groups for women with advanced cancer, on the other hand, tend to be open-ended and longer-term. They have been found to increase not only quality of life but survival time as well. In these groups, women have the opportunity to confront their mortality in a safe and supportive environment and to make choices about how they want to live out their remaining weeks, months, or years. Open discussions of death seem to reduce women's fears and feelings of isolation and help them to focus on living. The group may become one of the most valued aspects of the lives of women with terminal breast cancer.

8

Family Issues

"How will I ever take care of the children by myself?" asks the partner of a woman with breast cancer. "Will I get breast cancer too?" wonders the sister of a woman who was recently diagnosed. "Is Mommy going to die?" thinks a young child who learns that his mother is ill. Breast cancer has a significant impact on family members of women who have been diagnosed.

People who love a woman with breast cancer are likely to feel anxiety and deep sadness at the possibility of losing her, helplessness because there is nothing they can do to take away the cancer, pain at seeing the woman with metastatic breast cancer suffer the indignities of the treatment, and relief when death rescues her from these indignities. On the other hand, individuals who are angry at the woman before she is diagnosed often have more complex reactions. If, for example, an angry son had fantasies about some harm befalling his mother, he may be tormented by the belief that he, in some way, is responsible for his mother's illness. This type of magical thinking is especially common in younger children.

The feelings of family members fluctuate during the course of the treatment and illness, depending in part on the physical status of the patient or news from the doctor. The ambiguity and unpredictability of cancer is unsettling for family members.

Feelings of elation when the news is good turn to despair when the news is discouraging. After repeated cycles of positive and negative medical news, people tend to constrict the range of their emotions, avoiding the extremes of elation and despair and settling instead for moderate feelings of guarded optimism and disappointment. Similarly, many people find it difficult to sustain emotional involvement with the patient through the cycles of highs and lows. Eventually, they become numb and withdraw from the patient.

Family members may withdraw from the patient physically or psychologically in order to protect themselves from painful feelings. Most cancer patients have reported at least one instance in which people have avoided them or engaged in another type of rejecting behavior. This avoidance may be motivated by several factors (Wortman & Dunkel-Schetter, 1979).

- Family members are unsure how to react. They don't know what to say or what not to say. They fear saying something that would hurt the patient's feelings or invade her privacy.

- When someone has a potentially life-threatening illness, others become anxious because they are forced to confront their own mortality.

- Seeing the effects on the patient of the illness or the treatments shatters their denial of their loved one's illness. If they minimize contact with the ill person, they can pretend nothing has changed.

- They may be unsure about how they will react to the patient's changed appearance. Family members fear that they will be awkward or communicate disgust or pity in response to weight loss or gain, hair loss, or effects of the surgery.

- Some people will blame the victim. Because of a belief in a just world, family members may believe that the woman either deserved cancer or that she got breast cancer because she didn't do breast self-exams or go for a yearly mammography. If a "logical" cause can be found for why a woman developed breast cancer, then others can still feel safe—"This won't happen to me." Feelings of anger also manifest themselves in avoidance.

When a woman is diagnosed and treated for breast cancer, her family members are affected in complex ways. In turn, the reactions of family members have implications for the patient's own coping.

PARTNERS' REACTIONS TO BREAST CANCER

Spouses are clearly stressed by their partner's cancer diagnosis, regardless of the site of the primary tumor, and according to at least one study (Baider & Kaplan De-Nour, 1988), this is particularly true for male spouses of female patients. Men tend to be moderately distressed by their partners' breast cancer diagnosis and treatment (Northouse, 1988, 1989; Northouse & Swain, 1987; Zahlis & Shands, 1991), and at least one study suggests that up to one third of partners of cancer patients experience clinical levels of anxiety and depression (Compas et al., 1994). That study and others either report comparable distress levels for patients and spouses or find spouses to be more anxious and depressed than patients (e.g., Compas et al., 1994; Keitel, Zevon, Rounds, Petrelli, & Karakousis, 1990).

Most husbands are primarily concerned about their wives' physical and emotional well-being and express fears that their wives could die (Sabo, Brown, & Smith, 1986).[1] Many have difficulty dealing with their wife's emotions (Zahlis & Shands, 1991), particularly her feelings of depression and her concerns about her own femininity. Often they feel incapable of providing the emotional support their wives need (Sabo et al., 1986). Further, husbands report feelings of disbelief, alarm, isolation (Sabo et al., 1986), and guilt (e.g., if their financial resources are inadequate to provide for costly medical treatment).

Anger at the illness, at God, or at the unfairness of the situation are common reactions. Some husbands are angry at their wives for being ill and may feel betrayed by them. The illness has derailed their lives; things had been going well, and now they have to rearrange routines to accommodate their partner. They may feel burdened and exhausted from having to fulfill additional daily duties while dealing with their grief about their partners' illness.

Some men find their wives less attractive after they have undergone cancer treatments such as mastectomy and chemotherapy. Fearful that they are unable to cope with changes in their wives' physical appearance (Zahlis & Shands, 1991), they wonder if their sex life will suffer. Husbands may lose their sex drive, withhold physical affection, and fear that sexual behavior may injure their wives. Women who had mastectomies have, in fact, reported that their husbands have reacted in these ways (Vess, Moreland, Schwebel, & Kraut, 1989). Other men may be concerned that their wives will feel inhibited and shut them out both physically and emotionally. In one study of 31 spouses, about one third reported that the mastectomy had a negative impact on their sexual relationship; nearly one half reported that their ability to work and sleep had been affected, and one fourth had some problems with eating (Pfefferbaum, Pasnau, Jamison, & Wellisch, 1977-78).

At a time when husbands need support, given all the difficult feelings and reactions they experience, these men tend to feel unsupported and socially isolated as they cope with their wives' cancer and treatment. Many women serve as their spouses' primary emotional support, and consequently if men do not believe that they can ask their wives for support, then they have no one to help them emotionally (Ell, Nishimoto, Mantell, & Hamovitch, 1988). Some husbands ignore their feelings (Sabo et al., 1986), and as a result, their emotional and physical well-being is compromised. For example, Oberst and James (1985) found that husbands who concealed their health problems from their wives became increasingly maladjusted in the postsurgical period, while their wives' concerns decreased (Baider & Kaplan De-Nour, 1984).

In addition to reacting to the surgery, partners also report high levels of stress in response to the side effects of a woman's chemotherapy treatment. In fact, this stress was exceeded only by global concerns about whether their wives would survive the disease (Hart, 1986-1987; Hinds, 1985).

The psychological impact of cancer recurrence on partners and family members of women with breast cancer is likely to be greater than the impact of initial diagnosis. Given and Given (1992) found that family members of women with a recurrence of breast cancer felt more depressed than they did at initial diagnosis, and their levels of depression increased during the 6 months following the diagnosis of the recurrence.

These family members reported that their health and day-to-day schedules were affected much more than were those of family members of women who were newly diagnosed with breast cancer. Chekryn's (1984) interviews of 10 spouses of women whose cancer recurred also revealed that they were grief-stricken, angry, and fearful and that they experienced an acute sense of injustice. Many reported having difficulty relaxing because they were never certain that the cancer would completely remit. Northouse et al. (1995) found that although spouses experienced low to moderate levels of distress, their ability to fulfill their psychosocial roles was impaired, particularly if they had their own health problems.

Effects on the Marital Relationship

Seven percent of marriages end in the aftermath of a breast cancer diagnosis (Lichtman, 1982). The dissolution is usually initiated by women who recognize that their needs are not being met by their husbands. Heterosexual couples whose marriages were unhealthy prior to the diagnosis of breast cancer may find that their relationships deteriorate quickly postdiagnosis. However, many marriages remain the same or grow even stronger and more intimate after dealing with cancer (Hughes, 1987; Lichtman, Taylor, & Woods, 1987). In some instances, the threat of losing one's partner may lead to the partners' becoming overly interdependent (Carter, Carter, & Salunias, 1993).

Experience with illness in one's family of origin influences how partners cope with illness. Each partner comes into the relationship with a set of norms regarding behaviors that are appropriate when a family member is ill, for example, rules about how feelings are managed and expressed, whether or not outside resources are used, how the patient is treated, and how much secrecy or openness about illness is permitted (Rolland, 1994). These family norms influence the current dynamics between the cancer patient and her partner. For example, if a woman with breast cancer comes from a family where an ill person is coddled, but her partner comes from a family with a "stiff upper lip" mentality, conflict is almost inevitable. In such a case, the woman's need for nurturance would be frustrated, because her partner, believing that ill people should be independent and not let their illness get in the way of their responsibilities, would not pamper her. As a result, she might intensify her complaints about the illness in an attempt to get sympathy and caring. Her partner may become more disgusted by what he perceives to be whiny, unappealing behavior and further withdraw. A vicious cycle develops in which the woman grows more and more dependent and her partner becomes more and more angry and distant.

Partners' misperceptions regarding their roles as caregivers can lead to behaviors that are destructive to the relationship and to the well-being of both marital partners. Difficulties arise when a partner misunderstands the extent to which changes in role functions are warranted. Such a partner may feel compelled to stay at his wife's side even when she doesn't need him to be there or when another person could offer her companionship. He may not let his wife maintain the roles and responsibilities that she is capable of maintaining. "Overcaring" may be motivated by a husband's guilt about being healthy, in which case he tries to reduce his guilt by excessively pampering and catering to his wife; overcaring may also occur because the husband cannot control the cancer, and so he overfunctions in an attempt to regain control. Because the woman has already suffered the losses associated with breast cancer or its treatments, this stripping of her responsibilities is likely to do harm even though the spouse has good intentions. Eventually, such a "caregiver" will feel burned out, exploited, and angry. To prevent this cycle, the caregiver must recognize how his erroneous beliefs about his role and responsibilities create tension in his marriage.

The husband with traditionally masculine attitudes and behaviors may resent assuming the role of caregiver. After all, his wife always took care of their family's physical and emotional needs, and he doesn't believe that this work is his responsibility. In fact, he may believe that he is incapable of providing the nurturance his wife wants. His rigidity in turn angers her. At the same time, because she is unaccustomed to receiving help, she may unconsciously communicate her own ambivalence by feigning independence. She is uncomfortable being a "receiver" and feels more vulnerable when she depends on others. As a result she becomes angry at her husband and herself.

Even couples who had healthy relationships prior to the cancer diagnosis face serious challenges. Illness clearly interrupts a couple's natural harmony. For example, husbands and wives may have discrepant needs; one needs space while the other craves closeness. On the other hand, both partners may need space but for different reasons: A woman may need time to become comfortable with her body after a mastectomy, and her partner may need time alone to regain normalcy and rejuvenate. Yet each may feel guilty for wanting some time away from the other.

The patient's coping should not be examined in isolation. Rather, mental health practitioners must evaluate the reactions and psychological adjustment of partners, because these have significant implications for the patient's own mental health and marital satisfaction. Empirical research (Ptacek, Ptacek, & Dodge, 1994) suggests that women with breast cancer use a greater number of strategies and different strategies than do their husbands. Husbands tend to use more problem-focused coping strategies than do their wives, but this coping strategy is not related to better mental health. Also, husbands are likely to seek information from those in authority (Gotay, 1984). Similarities and differences in coping strategies used by husbands and wives can affect each partner's psychological distress and marital satisfaction (Keitel, Zevon, Rounds, & Schroder, 1990; Ptacek et al., 1994). More specifically, when spouses use similar coping strategies, they report higher marital satisfaction but greater psychological distress. Couples who use dissimilar coping strategies report lower marital satisfaction and lower psychological distress (Keitel, Zevon, Rounds, & Schroder, 1990).

OFFSPRING AND SIBLINGS OF WOMEN WITH BREAST CANCER

Family members typically feel frightened about losing their loved one to breast cancer. Young children wonder, "Who will take care of me?" They may be anxious about separation while their mother is in the hospital and confused about why she cannot play with them during recovery from surgery or when she is experiencing side effects from chemotherapy or radiation. Children and adolescents may feel alone, ashamed, embarrassed, and angered by their mother's illness. At a time when they so need to fit in, they are different from their peers. Adult children may feel overwhelmed by competing responsibilities and wonder, "How can I take care of my mother, my husband, my children, and my job?" For all offspring, the illusion of their parent's invulnerability is permanently shattered.

Although several research studies have examined the responses of offspring whose parents were diagnosed with cancer, much more research is needed. Lichtman and Taylor (1986) reported that daughters of women with breast cancer are negatively affected and suggested therefore that same-sex offspring may be more affected by a parent's cancer diagnosis. Compas et al. (1994) also found that female adolescents whose mothers have cancer were more anxious and depressed than were male adolescents or boys and girls mostly between 6 and 10 years old. Furthermore, adolescent daughters of cancer patients reported the highest levels of stress response symptoms, such as intrusive thoughts and emotions and avoidance, when compared to other adolescents and young adults. Although the young children reported lower anxiety and depression than adolescents did, they also tended to present themselves in a socially desirable light, so it is unclear whether they were in fact less distressed. In any case, children and adolescents were more distressed than were adult offspring.

Why are young children and adolescents, particularly female adolescents, more vulnerable than adults to feelings of distress in response to their mother's cancer? For young children, a lack of information about the disease and its treatments may be one factor that could cause confusion and anxiety. Adolescents, on the other hand, may be given as much information about their mother's cancer as are adult offspring, but because their coping resources are less well-developed, they become distressed. In addition, roles may be reversed, and offspring may be expected to become the nurturers instead of the nurtured. This role reversal is more difficult when it is out of sync with "normal" developmental patterns.

Finally, adolescent girls may be particularly vulnerable perhaps because they are more sensitive than boys to stress in other family members (Wagner & Compas, 1990). In comparison to sons, they may worry about the genetic aspects of the disease and fear developing breast cancer, and they may be assigned more caregiver duties. These hypotheses have some support but need to be further researched.

Sales, Schultz, and Biegel (1992) found that daughters of women with breast cancer were more supportive to their mothers than were sons. The authors hypothesized that the sexual and personal aspects of breast cancer made sons uncomfortable. Consequently, they tended not to initiate discussions with their mothers about the illness and did not provide as much support.

Adult Offspring of Women With Breast Cancer

Adult offspring have many of the same fears that younger children have when their mother is diagnosed and treated for breast cancer. They may fear that treatment will be unsuccessful and that their mother could die. They may feel vulnerable in ways that they have not felt since childhood. At the same time, they may be thrust into a caregiver role for the first time and may be expected to provide emotional or tangible support to their parents. A mother's relationship with adult children can be particularly challenging—they may have strong, competing demands for their time such as starting college, beginning a marriage, establishing a career, and raising their own young children. A mother may not want to burden her children so she may say "Don't come home from college—your education is your first priority" or "You have young children to take care of, don't worry about me." But her children may need to be there for her, and she may need to allow them to do that; otherwise, they may feel rejected and shut out. Conversely, a mother could demand support from her children without acknowledging the other important demands in their lives, with the result that they may feel resentful. This dynamic is especially true when the ill parent was not generous to or nurturing of her children and yet now expects total care and devotion from them.

The effects of their mother's cancer on the personal lives of daughters was studied by Wellisch, Gritz, Schain, Wang, and Siau (1991), who compared 60 adult daughters of mothers with breast cancer to a matched control group. The participants were white, relatively affluent, and well-educated. Their mothers had either died from breast cancer or were still alive. None of their mothers were very ill at the time of the study. The researchers found that

> Daughters of breast cancer patients showed significantly less frequent sexual intercourse, lower sexual satisfaction, and greater feelings of vulnerability to breast cancer, and they could identify a greater number of symptoms of breast cancer. No differences between groups were found in psychological symptoms, coping styles, breast self-examination practices, mammography practices, health knowledge, or body-image ratings. (p. 324)

The authors suggested two reasons why no differences in psychological symptoms were found: Their study participants were highly educated, and they had not sought counseling. In contrast, prior studies that highlighted coping difficulties in daughters of breast cancer patients used clinical samples, who would be expected to have more psychological symptoms.

Although the external validity of this study is limited, we maintain that the difficulties in sexual functioning reported by daughters of breast cancer patients in this study have potential clinical significance and suggest an area needing further investigation.

Adult daughters of women who have breast cancer may struggle with a variety of issues. Concern for their mothers may compete with feelings regarding their own vulnerability to the disease, and yet it may be difficult for them to openly reveal their fears for themselves and for their mothers. At times, they may secretly be glad that it is not they who were diagnosed, yet they may be apprehensive about the future and become overly preoccupied with their bodies, frequently checking and rechecking their breasts for lumps or other signs of cancer. Some daughters may focus on how breast cancer could influence their lives rather than attending to their mothers, and they may begin exploring the possibility of prophylactic surgery.

When a mother is diagnosed with this life-threatening illness, life continues for her healthy daughter. The daughter must continue to attend to her job and family obligations. She may feel pulled in many directions as she attempts to process her own feelings, respond to her mother's needs, and continue to attend to personal demands. She may feel guilt if she does not live geographically close enough to help her mother through the crisis and at the same time feel relief because she is "off the hook."

Such circumstances may adversely affect the relationship between mother and daughter. The woman with breast cancer may feel abandoned and may not know how to address this with her daughter. The healthy adult daughter may find it difficult to refuse her mother's requests for assistance with housework, attending medical appointments, or simply for companionship. There may be regret that she cannot do enough to help her ill mother, or she may feel angry at her mother for upsetting her life routine.

Sisters of women who have breast cancer may share many of the same strong feelings as adult daughters do. One difference is that sisters are less likely than daughters to view the woman with breast cancer as the protector. Sisters who tend to be competitive with each other may have complicated reactions. The healthy sister may feel that she is responsible for her sister's illness because of unconscious negative fantasies. These fantasies could be current or from the past. When their younger sisters are diagnosed, older sisters may experience survivor guilt or fear for their own future health.

HOW THE COUNSELOR CAN HELP

The support of spouses is critical to the adjustment of women who have undergone a mastectomy. Ideally, the partner should be included in some counseling sessions, and indeed some husbands are willing to fully participate with their wives in counseling, with the result that relationship issues have a better chance of being resolved. In some cultures, family members expect to be included in therapy, and multigenerational family groups may be beneficial. In these families, problems are viewed as a family rather than an individual concern. Counselors with training in family systems or couples counseling have a clear advantage in working with such families.

Open communication between partners and among family members has been found to improve women's adjustment to breast cancer (Spiegel, Bloom, & Gottheil, 1983). When each partner learns to recognize and understand the other's feelings and perspectives, they can begin to support each other through the crisis of breast cancer. Counselors can be instrumental in helping husbands and wives to express their thoughts and feelings to each other.

When couples are faced with a life-threatening illness, many issues need to be discussed. Counselors can challenge client assumptions that negative feelings about chronic or terminal illness should be avoided or denied. Openly airing feelings about potential or actual losses builds intimacy and helps to maintain well-being (Gottman & Levenson, 1992), which allows couples to then redirect their energies in more positive directions. The issue of communicating about the disease and treatment with a significant other is complex, however. Ward, Leventhal, Easterling, Luchterhand, and Love (1991) found that clear communication has positive effects but that poor communication can actually be detrimental. In their study, the self-esteem of women undergoing adjuvant chemotherapy for breast cancer actually decreased with greater communication about the disease and treatment. It is conceivable that the communication was perceived as unsupportive by the patient, perhaps because the partner was uninformed about the side effects of chemotherapy and somehow blamed the patient for her reactions. Another possibility is that the patient preferred directing her attention away from the cancer experience rather than discussing it. Ward et al. (1991) compared the effects of limited information presented to the patient, enhanced information about chemotherapy presented to the patient alone, or enhanced information presented to the patient and a significant other simultaneously. The enhanced information conditions included messages that chemotherapy was difficult, described side effects, and explained that failing to control side effects was not the patient's fault. Communicating about the disease and treatment was associated with decreased self-esteem for women in all conditions except for the condition in which enhanced information was presented to the woman and significant other simultaneously. For people in this condition, self-esteem was enhanced if communication occurred and diminished if communication did not occur. These findings suggest that open communication about the disease and treatment is not always desirable and that open communication is more likely to increase a woman's self-esteem if it occurs after both partners receive adequate information together. Of course, discussion may never be particularly helpful for women who prefer to distract themselves from, or altogether avoid, their illness. A good rule of thumb may be that partners of women with breast cancer not initiate discussions about the cancer but wait until they are approached.

Although the illness may not progress, it is generally beneficial for the counselor to pose "what if" questions to promote discussion about estate planning, including provisions for child care where relevant, wishes concerning life support, and funeral arrangements. These topics are often perceived to be taboo, and they prevent couples from engaging in conversations that can alleviate anxiety for both partners. Couples can write down the topics they believe are taboo as a way to identify issues they might decide to discuss (Rolland, 1994). Particular times and places for having these discussions can be set. However, couples should recognize that they need to be flexible about rearranging the time if one or both parties need a respite.

Counselors can promote a couple's awareness that over time the illness will affect their relationship and their behaviors toward one another. Frequent renegotiation of patient and caregiver roles is recommended. Specifically, counselors can ask what role changes the couple believes are currently necessary and whether they will be necessary in 3 months or 6 months or in 1 year. Counselors can help couples to recognize that old patterns eventually may be reestablished. Through open discussions of how family roles and tasks are affected and change over the course of the illness, the couple can establish "healthy boundaries, so that the inertia of the ill partner's dependency needs and fears and the well partner's sympathy do not take over" (Rolland, 1994, p. 246).

Conflict is unavoidable when couples face a life-threatening illness. Members of a couple will invariably vent their feelings of intense anger and frustration by attacking each other. To reduce shame and guilt, counselors can normalize angry thoughts clients have about their partners and can help both to recognize that the enemy is the cancer and not one another. Frank discussion can minimize feelings of anger, hurt, and disappointment.

Mental health professionals can identify relationship patterns that are detrimental to the healing process of the woman with breast cancer. For example, the illness could bring secondary gains to the patient, such as the husband's assuming a more fair share of the responsibilities for housework, child care, or both. Once this shift in responsibilities occurs, the patient may fear that if her health improves or she reports feeling better, the old unsatisfactory patterns will resume. The counselor could help identify such disincentives for the client to get well.

It is important that couples continue their usual activities and patterns as much as possible and that the breast cancer does not entirely dominate their relationship. They should preserve time to discuss not only self-care and caregiver issues, but also politics, movies, or other "normal" topics, and they should consider entertaining in their homes when they are ready. In the immediate aftermath of cancer surgery or other medical treatments, interruptions in sexual and social functioning may be warranted, but couples should be encouraged to resume normal activities as soon as possible. For example, it may be appropriate for a partner to refrain from sex right after surgery. If, however, a man is afraid to touch his wife after she is ready to be intimate, tension in the relationship is likely to occur.

Our clinical experience suggests that not all partners see a need for counseling. Some view breast cancer as the woman's problem, encouraging her to take care of it through professional counseling, and others simply cannot acknowledge that the illness has psychological ramifications. However, relationship issues can still be addressed in individual sessions with the cancer patient.

Helping Mothers With Breast Cancer

Mothers with breast cancer can help alleviate some of their children's concerns but cannot completely "make everything all right." Many mothers wonder how much, if anything, to disclose. Understandably, they want to protect their children. Counselors can help women to identify how they want to handle interactions with their children and how to evaluate whether their wishes are in the children's best interest. Counselors can share information about developmental stages that can help mothers understand their children's reactions. For instance, if an adolescent daughter doesn't want to be involved in caring for her mother and continues socializing with her friends, a mother may feel hurt, angry, and betrayed. Letting her know that her daughter's seeming indifference is developmentally appropriate and reframing this "indifference" as her daughter's attempt to normalize her life may decrease the mother's distress and help to improve her relationship with her daughter. After all, adolescence represents a natural transition period of separation from the parent. Adolescence is also a time when being "different" from peers is painful, and having a mother with breast cancer may intensify feelings of alienation and instigate anger toward the ill mother. To complicate matters further, this anger may quickly turn to guilt as the teen recognizes that it is not her mother's fault and thinks, "What right do I have to be angry? I must be a terrible person." Relationships between teen girls and their mothers tend to be complicated anyway, and breast cancer introduces additional stress.

A mother may also worry about the implications her breast cancer diagnosis has for her daughter or daughters. Is there a genetic component to her disease? Are her daughters vulnerable? What, if anything, should she tell them at this point? We believe mothers need to consider their daughters' ages in deciding what to disclose. Of course they should answer questions honestly and to the best of their ability. Daughters may be reassured by the fact that only 5% to 10% of women with breast cancer carry the gene. It is probably best for mothers to emphasize the more controllable risk factors and to encourage their daughters to develop healthy lifestyle patterns in general and to adhere to screening guidelines and do monthly breast self-examinations beginning at the recommended ages.

We advise mothers to take their cues from their children with respect to how much they want to know. They should answer their children's questions honestly, in language children can understand, and reassuringly if possible. There is no guidebook that details exactly what parents should say and do. It is best that mothers provide an environment that allows open discussion and expression of feelings, but they must understand and respect their children's wishes and ways of coping. In other words, discussion of feelings should not be forced. The point we wish to emphasize is that parents should be supportive of their offspring's coping behaviors unless they are destructive.

Parents may want to know about their children's cognitive understanding of death and illness. Counselors can educate parents that most children until age 5 view death as reversible. They do not see death as inevitable or as resulting from the cessation of bodily functions. From ages 5 to 9, children see death as avoidable but irreversible "once it gets you." After age 9, most children have a mature conception of death. Understanding cognitive development may guide parents in their discussions with young family members.

Children are more perceptive than most adults give them credit for, and they do recognize tension and unspoken fears. Their fantasies are often worse than reality, and they will feel distrustful and betrayed when their queries about what is happening are answered with platitudes such as "Don't worry, everything is fine." They know that everything is not fine. Children are better able to deal with the crisis of cancer when issues are out in the open. Greening (1992), for example, reported that children adjust better when they receive clear information, feel involved, are reassured, are given a chance to air their thoughts and feelings, and maintain regular routines and activities.

What do Greening's findings mean in concrete terms? Giving clear information means that when parents discuss the illness with children and adolescents, they should use the word cancer. If adults avoid labeling the disease, whisper, or stop speaking whenever a child enters the room, the child will be frightened. Open discussions allow misconceptions about cancer to be clarified. Furthermore, if children have only witnessed people dying from cancer, they need to hear about or meet cancer survivors.

In general, parents will be most helpful to their children if they are kind and encouraging. If a child asks his or her mother, "Are you going to die?" she could respond, "I am very sick but I'm getting the best medical treatment, and the doctors are working hard to help me." If the parent perceives that the child is worried, she should ask directly, "Are you afraid that I am going to die?" and help the child talk about his or her concerns. If the time should come when a woman knows she is dying, it may be most beneficial for her children if she prepares them by sharing how much she loves them and how she will miss them, allowing them to share their feelings, and by reassuring them about future arrangements such as who will take care of them. Religious perspectives on the afterlife, such as the idea that Mommy will be with God in heaven, may comfort some children. Children must be permitted to actively grieve if their mother is dying and to participate in death rituals such as wakes or funerals if they wish. Death rituals differ among cultural groups and should be understood by counselors and respected.

Parents may shield their children unnecessarily, for example, deciding that they should not make hospital visits or see their mom after chemotherapy. Most children and adolescents, however, feel less anxious when they can see their mom (even if her appearance has changed), particularly if adults explain that treatment effects are temporary. When children are isolated from Mom, they may start worrying that she is dead or sicker than she is. However, parents need not frighten young children by exposing them to situations that are overly disturbing or information that is highly technical and difficult to understand.

Because children often feel helpless in relation to their mother's cancer, exploring ways they can be involved, such as quietly keeping mom company when she needs to rest, reading her a book, and serving her drinks, can be beneficial. Ideally, kids should be asked whether, how, and how much they want to be involved.

If a mother with breast cancer does not have a strong support system (either because she is a single parent or because she is in a primary relationship with a partner who is emotionally, behaviorally, or geographically distanced), she may inappropriately look to her children for support. She may ask them to take on responsibilities that are developmentally inappropriate or may too openly disclose all of her fears and pain. Children will clearly be burdened if they are drawn into the primary caregiver role. It is important that the ill parent remain "the Parent," even if children have to temporarily take on new responsibilities. And if children do take on added tasks, those tasks should be fairly divided among the children so that one child (typically the oldest or a daughter) is not unduly burdened.

Even if parents create an atmosphere in which children can express themselves and ask questions, children may be uncomfortable doing so because they do not want to further burden their parents. Counselors can encourage a woman with breast cancer to provide other outlets for her children, such as the ear of another family member or a close friend. Peer support groups and individual or family therapy sessions are other alternatives. That said, children who do not wish to talk about their feelings should not be pressured to do so. Children, like adults, cope in various ways. For instance, some children pretend the illness is only a game that will end soon. Others distract themselves with activities and try not to think about it. Humor helps many kids cope, particularly if their Mom can find humor in the situation (e.g., taking her wig off at some inopportune time). Because hair loss can be quite disturbing to all family members, reframing it as funny and reassuring kids that hair will grow back can help. Having faith in God or in physicians' abilities to heal their mother also can be very comforting for children.

Johnson (1997) described a comprehensive, adaptation-based treatment plan for counseling well children in a family in which a parent or sibling has cancer. She emphasized the importance of facilitating emotional expression through journaling and play and activity therapy; providing information and promoting involvement through psychoeducational groups and peer support networks; and fostering coping skills through cognitive reframing, bibliotherapy, relaxation training, and guided imagery. She also described how counselors can become advocates for these children by discussing with parents, other relatives, and teachers how they can best be helpful. One point worth making here is that teachers should not announce the mother's diagnosis to classmates unless he or she has permission from the child first. Once a child is ready for others to know, teachers might suggest that the class make get-well cards and brainstorm other ways to show support. Johnson also includes an excellent bibliography of reading materials for children experiencing cancer in the family, a resource list for counselors working with well children, and an outline for a model group for working with well children.

UNDERSTANDING DIVERSE FAMILIES

Because early theories of family were developed on traditional white middle-class families, they are inadequate for understanding how many families function. In order for counselors to be effective, they must be aware of cultural factors that may influence how they work with individuals and families of diverse groups. Only within the last decade has the counseling profession begun to understand that diverse families are often different from traditional nuclear families, that is, a heterosexual couple raising their biological children. In fact, this family type constitutes less than half of all families today. Divorce, remarriage, death of a parent, intermarriage, gay and lesbian relationships, and adoption all change the nature of families today. Further, many cultural groups define families to include nonblood members, and many cultures tend to emphasize the importance of large extended families.

How families are structured may influence how counselors interact with their clients. In African American families, it may not be unusual for the client to bring an "aunt" or some other nonblood relative along with blood relatives to counseling sessions. In Hispanic families, a *comadre* or comother might attend the sessions.

Cultural beliefs also influence how families operate; for example, the gender roles in Hispanic American and Asian American families are often clearly delineated: The husband-father heads the family, and the wife-mother takes care of the household and children. Other cultural groups tend to be less concerned with traditional gender roles and have more role flexibility. For example, in African American families, it is common for someone other than the father to assume the role as head of the family. Clearly, for counselors to be effective, they must be knowledgeable of cultural beliefs about family functioning. However, we caution counselors against making judgments based solely on cultural beliefs. The level of acculturation of members of the family may influence how strongly each adheres to traditional cultural values. It is possible that some family members are more acculturated than others. When this happens, tensions among family members may develop.

We encourage practitioners to examine their own biases regarding nontraditional families and to become educated about families who challenge the mainstream culture. Several resources (e.g., Boyd-Franklin, 1989; Okun, 1996; Paniagua, 1994) exist that can help counselors understand how to work with diverse families.

SUMMARY

This chapter examined how breast cancer affects family members. Issues relevant to partners, siblings, and offspring of women who have breast cancer were discussed. Further, issues that influence how counselors intervene were also presented; for example, family structures and cultural values may influence how families operate and, consequently, how counselors can intervene.

More empirical research is needed so that mental health practitioners can predict which families are at risk. It is important for researchers to identify which stressors and family characteristics contribute to more adaptive behavior so that effective early intervention can be implemented. Finally, more outcome studies are needed, because family interventions that have been offered have not been sufficiently evaluated.

CASE STUDY ILLUSTRATION

The following case study illustrates how one counselor intervened with Lisa, a woman who was diagnosed with metastatic breast cancer. A very poor prognosis convinced her she would die soon, and she was concerned about what would happen to her child and partner after her death. "Lisa" is based on a composite of individuals. All identifying information has been changed.

Client Summary

On the suggestion of a close friend and neighbor, Lisa first sought counseling about 3 weeks after she had been diagnosed with metastatic breast cancer. Although Lisa had participated in counseling once before, when she divorced her husband, she does not have much psychological insight. However, she knows that counseling helped her to "feel better" before, so when her neighbor suggested it, she thought that it just might help. Lisa is a 42-year-old lesbian who has been in a committed relationship for 6 years. She and her partner, Anna, share a home with their 12-year-old daughter, Robin, who is the product of Lisa's first marriage. Ten years ago, Lisa divorced her husband and gained custody of their daughter. Lisa began seeing Anna about 2 years after her divorce and reports that, for the most part, their relationship has been quite harmonious.

Lisa has an undergraduate degree in history, and she recently began graduate school. It is her dream to complete a master's degree in urban planning. She has been working as a paralegal for a law firm. Lisa's parents and siblings live in the same town, and they see each other often. However, Lisa reported that her relationships with members of her family of origin tend to be difficult.

Prior to her diagnosis, Lisa had been feeling tired and had had flu-like symptoms for about 6 months. Despite her symptoms, she continued working at her full-time job and attending night school up until about 2 months ago, when she became too ill to carry on with her daily functioning. Although she had been seeing her physician, she was treated first for a respiratory infection and then for asthma. Her ill health had put a strain on her family relationships, but following her cancer diagnosis, relationships with her partner and her daughter have become even more conflicted. She is quite distressed about this because her parents, brothers, and sister have been critical of her lifestyle and her sexual orientation. Anna had always been supportive when Lisa had difficulty dealing with her family members of origin, but now she is angry about the way Lisa is treating her. Lisa acknowledges being almost habitually nasty to Anna; she had justified her behavior as symptomatic of the stress she was experiencing. But now that more time has elapsed, she just doesn't understand why she continues to behave like this.

Case Conceptualization

Lisa's presenting concern was her relationships with her family of origin; however, early on she revealed her terminal breast cancer diagnosis and her anger toward family members who continue to pretend she isn't dying. She is fed up with how they are treating her and incredulous that they continue to disparage her sexual orientation; she is beginning to think they are no longer deserving of her energy. Lisa believes that she will be in a "better place" after her death. Her diagnosis and prognosis have put things into perspective for her recently, and she now wants to begin putting her affairs in order.

Intervention

During the most recent session with Lisa, she was quite angry and began the session by telling the counselor what had transpired during the previous week. She wasted no time in getting to the issue that was foremost on her mind:

> My ex-husband and family members are saying that I have breast cancer because I am a lesbian. Have you ever heard anything so ridiculous? Apparently, they read an article that reported a higher incidence of breast cancer in gay women; of course, they didn't bother reading the whole article. They just assume that's it— that's the reason I have breast cancer. That's just another point to add on to their list of negative reactions to my sexuality. You know what? That's not even important anymore. It's taken a breast cancer diagnosis to put things in perspective for me. I can't believe I ever wasted time trying to get them to accept me, for what? I realized last night that my real problem is that I don't know what to do . . . I am so worried about what will happen to my daughter, Robin, after I die. My ex-husband will ask for custody, and he's an unfit parent. Besides, she's been living with Anna and me for the past 6 years, and she loves Anna. I'm nervous about Anna, too—I really worry. I'll be in a better place and I know I'll be OK, but they will have to carry on without me—and I just don't know how they will manage.

After hearing this, the counselor asked Lisa if she would feel better if she had some certainty that Robin and Anna could continue to live together. Lisa replied that she thought this might help and added that she would think about ways to clarify this issue, perhaps by drafting a letter to her ex-husband. This action plan reduced Lisa's immediate anxiety about the future. The counselor also responded to Lisa's desire to understand why she continues to snap at Anna and Robin. Through good reflective listening on the part of the counselor, Lisa recognized how being angry with the people she loved served two functions: It made it easier to say good-bye, and it protected her from the realization of her worst fear—that they would abandon her as her condition worsens. In effect, by rejecting them first she felt less vulnerable. The price for doing that was high, though: Lisa felt increasingly alone. The counselor also helped her to clarify which relationships were priorities for her at this time. Although she ideally wanted to repair the relationships with her family of origin, she did not think that was realistic. She decided that what was most important to her was reestablishing intimacy with Robin and Anna. The counselor arranged several family sessions to help Lisa achieve this goal.

Note

1. Although most of the literature has examined the reactions of husbands to their wives' breast cancer, we do not want to exclude lesbians, their partners, and family members. At times, for clarity, we will refer to the partner of the woman with breast cancer as the husband or spouse.

9

Therapeutic Issues

Counselor: I received the message that you want to cancel your next appointment, and I wondered if you want to reschedule.

Client: I don't think so—now is not a good time.

This is not an unusual exchange for a woman with breast cancer and her counselor. Family, household, social, and job commitments and numerous medical appointments all vie for the patient's time. Women may spend hours waiting to see an oncologist, waiting for results of blood work, or completing extensive insurance forms. Cancer treatments also are time consuming, and their side effects, such as nausea and fatigue, may impede daily functioning. Routine activities may become monumental tasks; even showering and dressing may make women feel as if they have completed a full day's work. Further, women tend to be the primary caregivers for their partners, their children, and their elderly parents. Is it any wonder that many women find it hard to take care of their mental health when so much of their time and energy is devoted to caring for their physical health and daily responsibilities?

There are many reasons besides busy schedules, fatigue, multiple medical appointments, and treatment side effects that deter women with breast cancer from seeking or maintaining a counseling relationship. Something as simple as the inconvenient location of the counselor's office may prevent a client from keeping an appointment. Appointments also may be canceled because the client may view the counselor as one more person to whom she has to repeat her story. Women from some cultural groups may prefer a priest or spiritual healer because they are suspicious of mental health professionals. Cost, a lack of understanding about how counseling can help, and not speaking the dominant language also influence the decision to seek mental health services.

Clients will often discontinue counseling when mental health practitioners misinterpret these barriers as resistance. Clearly, women with breast cancer, like most therapy clients, do experience resistance; however, they also confront realistic obstacles. Many mental health professionals are not sensitive to these difficulties. Is it any wonder then that most women with breast cancer do not seek or maintain counseling?

REACHING OUT TO WOMEN WITH BREAST CANCER

What can mental health professionals do to encourage women to participate in counseling? They can acquire specific knowledge about the disease and the unique issues of women who have breast cancer, and they can learn specific intervention skills that improve survival time and quality of life. They can loosen traditional psychotherapy boundaries and be willing to reschedule appointments because clients may be tired and ill. Phone sessions, home or hospital visits, and more frequent but shorter sessions can be arranged.

Mental health professionals also need to initiate and nurture relationships with physicians, who are likely to be their most effective source of referrals. They can discuss with physicians how psychological services can result in a better quality of life for their patients and, in some cases, better management of the disease and longer survival times. They can present empirical data on the effectiveness of psychological interventions. For instance, the use of support groups has been found to increase survival time and quality of life for women with breast cancer (Spiegel, Bloom, Kraemer, & Gottheil, 1989; Spiegel, Bloom, & Yalom, 1981). A structured psychoeducational counseling group was found to improve patient self-concept and confidence in medical staff (Ferlic et al., 1979). Cancer patients have also reported that stress management and coping skills training interventions have benefited them (Fawzy et al., 1993; Heinrich & Schag, 1985). For example, one study found that avoidance coping negatively affects psychological and medical outcomes for cancer patients (Epping-Jordan, Compas, & Howell, 1994). There is also preliminary evidence that women fare better when they do not avoid their cancer and its impact, but also do not dwell on it; focusing on the future is a more productive tactic (Greer, 1991).

Despite the substantial support for the efficacy of psychological interventions, physicians face obstacles in making referrals to mental health professionals. Physicians may have a bias against psychotherapy, and even when they embrace the value of psychological interventions, they might fear that their patients will respond negatively, perhaps believing that the physician is insinuating that they are crazy and need a "shrink." After all, many people still attach a stigma to receiving psychological assistance. Others are afraid that engaging in psychological counseling is tantamount to admitting that their personality caused the cancer. For still others, engaging in therapy is a sign of weakness or an invasion of privacy. Finally, strong family or cultural mandates against divulging family problems to strangers reduces participation in counseling.

Physicians who are willing to refer their patients to mental health professionals might need some suggestions on how to successfully frame referrals. Physicians should first explore how their patients feel about the use of psychological counseling in addition to medical intervention. They should be sensitive to the possibility that some patients view psychological services as helpful only if their "personality" somehow caused the illness. Physicians can clarify to their patients that psychotherapy and counseling can be beneficial regardless of the etiology of the disease. For patients who are still skeptical or reluctant, physicians can discuss the benefits of psychological interventions, such as reduced pain and stress, shorter postsurgical recovery periods, and decreased interpersonal tension. Further, psychological interventions can normalize the stress that cancer introduces for patients and their family members.

CHARACTERISTICS OF EFFECTIVE COUNSELORS

Certain counselor characteristics are particularly important in dealing sensitively with the life-and-death issues presented by the cancer patient. The courage to take interpersonal risks is essential. The counselor must be able to tolerate the physical and emotional pain of others, know when it is appropriate to use a comforting touch, and know how to put into words those feelings that a client may be afraid to utter. It is also important that the counselor be able to confront his or her own mortality, openly process feelings about death and dying, and be comfortable discussing issues related to sexuality and the physical consequences of the illness. Paradoxically, the sensitive use of humor can help clients get perspective on aspects of the illness or treatment.

COUNTERTRANSFERENCE

Issues that arise when counseling women with breast cancer can evoke strong countertransferential feelings. When clients with breast cancer express their fear, the counselor may also become afraid. When healthy clients wonder, "Will I get breast cancer?" the counselor may also anxiously ask, "Will I (or someone I love) get breast cancer?" When a terminal breast cancer patient reveals her intense sadness about having to say good-bye to her partner, the counselor's own unresolved issues of loss may surface. Sadness and helplessness may predominate, particularly when the client's disease is terminal. It is painful to watch a client for whom one has developed deep affection physically deteriorate. One result of countertransference is a feeling of inadequacy at comforting the client, which, when coupled with the realization that they can't change the course of the disease, may lead counselors to question their own competence. Further, fear of disease and death may make it difficult for the counselor to be fully present to her client. Finally, counselors may get angry at clients who evoke difficult feelings such as helplessness, inadequacy, intense sadness, guilt, and fear.

At times, clients may become angry at counselors who are healthy. To preserve the client-counselor relationship, counselors can acknowledge that they don't know why their clients are sick while they are healthy; it isn't fair that they get to go home and be with their families at the end of a day while their hospitalized clients don't. Of course, actively acknowledging that any woman can develop breast cancer is unnerving. Counselors, like most people, prefer to view life as more predictable and under control than it really is. We feel more vulnerable when we recognize that we too can become ill and will eventually die. Accepting the inevitability of death for all—even "healthy" counselors—while clearly emphasizing life and living is beneficial to clients.

Clients who overtly or covertly express anger toward their therapists may exacerbate survivor guilt. Inappropriate counselor responses to survivor guilt include minimizing what clients are enduring, getting angry at clients, or becoming overly solicitous of clients and meeting unreasonable demands. It is critical that counselors recognize these feelings so they do not negatively affect treatment.

Because early detection and effective treatment of breast cancer can be a matter of life and death, counselors may start feeling overly responsible for their clients' well-being; particularly at risk are those counselors who tend to take too much responsibility for client progress. Understanding that health can be jeopardized by engaging in certain lifestyle habits and that second opinions and the quality of health care providers may be the difference between life and death may cause counselors to be overzealous in their interventions. In other words, counselors may too forcefully encourage women to make healthy lifestyle changes, or they may strongly advise their clients to seek second opinions or a different physician or hospital for treatment. In an effort to care for their clients, counselors may inadvertently communicate that the woman is completely responsible for her health, when in fact, one's biology still plays a much greater part in who gets ill and who does not. Counselors who are emphatic about how women should manage their health care or treatment may instigate feelings of blame in their clients when what their clients may most need is to reduce feelings of self-blame. When clients are not doing all that they can do to promote their health, counselors must empathize with how difficult it can be to make these changes. Gentle suggestions will be more effective than passionate crusades.

Breast cancer evokes strong emotional reactions in counselors via several paths: They can feel what their clients are feeling but may or may not be expressing, they can respond in the same way other people respond toward their clients, or counselors can react based on their own unresolved issues. For example, the counselor may be angry, but the anger may be originating from different sources. To identify the source of the feeling, the counselor must always ask, "Why am I feeling this way?" After careful self-reflection, the counselor may realize that she has become the vehicle for the client's unexpressed anger, that her feelings of anger mirror those experienced by others in the client's life, or that she is angry because she has not resolved her anger about the loss of a loved one from breast cancer.

How might these feelings be manifested? Counselors may seek to "protect" themselves by avoiding or minimizing clients' feelings, problem-solving prematurely, administering tests, or using the session to process their own feelings and experiences. They can also act out by expressing inappropriate feelings toward their clients and blaming them for their disease or problems. They can be immobilized by becoming mired in their clients' feelings of hopelessness. Some counselors may experience a heightened awareness of their bodies and a heightened fear of the disease, causing them to repeatedly check their breasts for lumps. Countertransference is likely to be even more pronounced for counselors who are at risk for breast cancer or who perceive the client to be similar to themselves in sex, age and life stage, income, or education.

HOW SUPERVISION CAN HELP

Supervision can help counselors be sensitive to the types of behaviors that might indicate a need for consultation. Counselors who are self-aware and willing to self-reflect may be able to identify their feelings and the source of their feelings and to use that awareness productively with their clients, a difficult task to do alone. Supervisors or colleagues can help counselors process their feelings and gain new perspectives, thus enabling them to work much more effectively. Not every client with breast cancer will prompt a counselor to seek supervision or consultation, but some will. Counselors should recognize when they need assistance.

Supervision can also help prevent counselor burnout. Counselors who are truly empathic tend to experience the ups and downs of remission and disease progression. Remaining with a client through the terminal phase of the illness can be painful for counselors. It is hard to say goodbye to someone with whom you have worked closely. In watching a client die, you directly confront your own mortality as well as the ultimate mortality of everyone you love. A positive relationship with a supervisor can be a much-needed support and can provide counselors with an outlet for their emotional reactions.

Supervisors can help counselors take care of themselves by encouraging them to incorporate healthy habits into their lifestyles. Relaxation, exercise, recreation, a balanced diet, maintaining a sense of humor (tumor humor), and setting limits enable many oncology professionals to be effective in their work.

REWARDS FROM WORKING WITH
WOMEN WITH BREAST CANCER

Counselors are enriched by their work with terminally ill people or with people who have a potentially terminal illness. Direct experiences with women who are dying force professionals to acknowledge that death is inevitable and can come at any time. This realization provides an opportunity for professionals to examine their own lives and life choices. Questions such as "Am I living my life the way I want to?" "Is life fulfilling?" "What would I like to do before I die?" and "Are there unresolved issues in my relationships?" can facilitate life changes that may significantly alter one's life course.

Many people delay gratification. They live their lives as if there are endless tomorrows. They work nonstop and sacrifice their own desires for a period they see as temporary but that ends up being permanent. They postpone realizing their life dreams, waiting for a "better time." Often this better time never comes; instead, cancer strikes. Many of our terminally ill clients regretted that they did not travel or accomplish their personal goals because they were so busy attending to the needs of others. Others regretted that their relationships suffered because they focused so much on their professional responsibilities. Working with people who are dying can serve as a wake-up call to professionals. Confronting death helps one to find meaning, to make better choices, and to minimize regrets tomorrow by taking risks today.

It can be very gratifying to watch clients grapple with major life issues. Despite being physically weakened by illness, many women have inner strength that enables them to continue to be productive, to advocate for other women with breast cancer, to courageously confront the losses caused by their illness, to endure often barbaric traditional cancer treatments, and to participate in their own healing.

SUMMARY

By reaching out to potential clients, by intervening sensitively and effectively, and by understanding their own and their clients' feelings about the disease and treatments, mental health professionals can greatly benefit women with breast cancer. In turn, professionals can also benefit by working with breast cancer patients. It can be inspiring to see women who actively confront their illness, draw on their strengths, and cope effectively with the challenges of the disease. Participating in a woman's confrontation with death allows mental health professionals to confront their own eventual death and make new life choices.

Appendix A

Resources for Women
With Breast Cancer

THE BREAST CANCER RESOURCE LIST

The Breast Cancer Resource List, a comprehensive directory of services and information on breast cancer published by the National Alliance of Breast Cancer Organizations (NABCO; 1-800-719-9154 or www.nabco.org), is invaluable. It lists books and publications covering the myths and facts of breast cancer, various treatment options, personal stories of breast cancer survivors, and numerous resources regarding the following topics:

1. Breast examination: Information on breast exams include fact sheets and guides concerning breast self-exams, understanding changes in your breasts, finding low-cost exams, finding quality mammography exams, and locating breast specialists.

2. Risk factors: Includes risk factors for breast cancer. Genetic testing and risk-counseling resources are cited.

3. Breast cancer treatment: Includes information on treatment choices, including alternative therapies, breast reconstruction options, the management of lymphedema, and natural remedies for menopause. Information on chemotherapy covers topics such as where to obtain treatment, explanation of the chemotherapy process, and coping with side effects. In addition, hormonal therapy and bone marrow transplant information is also discussed. Guides and practical information regarding metastatic breast cancer, coping with pain, and treatment options are provided as well. Lists of resources detail diet, appearance, exercise, and financial and legal concerns during and after cancer treatment.

4. Adjustment: A variety of on-line chat sites, resource guides, magazines, support groups, counseling hotlines, and videos is listed for help with the adjustment of living with breast cancer. Printed guides, videos, support groups, and counseling resources for family members and partners are included to assist those whose loved one is diagnosed with breast cancer. Similar resources exist for children and friends of the breast cancer patient. Guides also exist for survivors, some of which deal with issues of breast cancer advocacy and volunteerism.

5. Other sources: Finally, a wide range of other sources is cited in NABCO's *Breast Cancer Resource List.* These include resources for medical information and support, listings of organizations and societies, support groups throughout the United States, on-line sites, journal databases, materials for health professionals, National Cancer Institute (NCI) designated cancer centers, resources available in Spanish, and an index to *NABCO News,* a quarterly newsletter devoted to discussing various breast cancer issues.

SELECTED RESOURCES

Information and Support

The Cancer Information Service of the NCI (1-800-4-CANCER)

This service provides information on all forms of cancer and refers callers to medical centers and clinical trial programs. Spanish-speaking information specialists are available.

American Cancer Society (1-800-227-2345 or www.cancer.org)

Provides current information regarding the diagnosis and treatment of cancer including breast cancer, and sponsors educational and support groups for patients.

Susan G. Komen Breast Cancer Information Helpline (800-IM-AWARE)

Provides lists of mammography and cancer treatment centers and information for talking to physicians.

Breast Cancer Information Clearinghouse (http.nyservnet.org/bcic/)

What you need to know about breast cancer.

Adjusting to Breast Cancer

Cancer Care (1-800-813-4673, or 1-800-813-HOPE)

Calling this toll-free number connects one to social workers who offer support, information, education, financial assistance, and referrals.

YWCA of the USA/Encore plus (1-800-953-7587)

Conducts an early detection program for breast cancer. Provides land and water exercise programs and peer group support for women recovering from breast cancer. These programs are available throughout the United States.

Reach to Recovery

Contact the American Cancer Society at 800-227-2345, and they will connect you to Reach to Recovery in your community. Trained volunteers who themselves are cancer survivors will visit newly diagnosed women and will provide information and support.

Bloch Cancer Foundation (1-800-433-0464)

Upon request, volunteers who are breast cancer survivors will contact cancer patients and provide support.

Y-ME, National Breast Cancer Organization (1-800-221-2141 CST; 312-986-8228, 1-800-986-9505 Spanish Language Hotline, Monday through Friday, 8:00 a.m. to 6:00 p.m.; www.Y-ME.org)

Breast cancer survivors provide information and hotline counseling 24 hr/day. Packets of information tailored to the individual caller's situation are mailed upon request. Y-ME has also started a hotline for men whose partners have breast cancer.

Appearance

tlc (Tender Loving Care; 1-800-850-9445)

This is a catalog that includes hats, hairpieces, mastectomy bras, and prostheses among other supplies that women with breast cancer may choose to purchase. The catalog is produced by the American Cancer Society.

Land's End (1-800-356-4444)

Catalog displays a line of mastectomy swimwear.

Look Good . . . Feel Better (1-800-395-LOOK or 1-800-ACS-2345)

A service that provides print and videotape materials (in Spanish and English) to help women recovering from cancer handle treatment-induced changes in their appearance. Instruction sessions may be available in which a licensed cosmetologist instructs women in small groups of 10 to 12 on how to apply makeup to skin and nails that have changed following cancer treatment.

Women's Health Boutiques (1-800-494-2374)

Medicare, Medicaid, and private insurance is accepted at these stores that sell prostheses, lingerie, wigs, and other products and services. Certified fitters and women's health specialists are available to help women make choices.

Y-ME Prosthesis and Wig Bank (1-800-221-2141)

If the appropriate size is available, the Bank will mail wigs and breast prostheses to women in financial need anywhere in the country for a small handling fee.

Videocassettes and Audiocassettes

Voices in the Night audiocassette series (1-800-268-0009)

Patient to Patient: Cancer Clinical Trials and You, 1995; (1-800-4-CANCER)

What I Wish I Knew (Amgen, makers of Neupogen, 1995). Amgen, Inc. (1-800-333-9777)

For On-line Information Seekers

Web Sites

NABCO web site (www. nabco.org)

The National Cancer Institute (www.nci.nih.gov)

Oncolink (cancer.med.upenn.edu)

Breast Cancer Answers (www.biostat.wisc.edu/bca/bca.html)

Breast Cancer Compendium (www.microweb.com/clg)

CancerGuide (cancerguide.org)

Can Search (www.access.digex.net/7Emkragen/index.htm)

Web Sites on Breast Cancer (darkwing.uoregon.edu/7Ejbonine/bc_sources.html)

For information about clinical trials: http://cancertrials.nci.nih.gov

For information about specific clinical trials: http://cancernet.nci.nih.gov/prot/patsrch.shtml

For summaries of research articles from scientific journals: http://igm.nlm.nih.gov

Computer Bulletin Boards and Listserves

America Online: Go to keyword GLENNA

Compuserve: Go to the Cancer Forum in the Health Professional section, or GO CANCER.

Prodigy: Go to the Medical Support Board under the Cancer topic.

E-mail users can subscribe to a breast cancer mailing list. To subscribe send e-mail to LISTSERV@morgan.ucs.mun.ca and write SUBSCRIBE BREAST-CANCER in the text of the message. For more information, see cure.medinfo.org/lists/cancer/bc-about.html.

References

Andersen, B. L., & Doyle-Mirzadeh, S. (1993). Breast disorders and breast cancer. In D. E. Steward & N. L. Stotland (Eds.), *Psychological aspects of women's healthcare* (pp. 425-446). Washington, DC: American Psychiatric Press.

Anderson, S. G., Rodin, J., & Ariyan, S. (1994). Treatment considerations in postmastectomy reconstruction: Their relative importance and relationship to patient satisfaction. *Annals of Plastic Surgery, 33,* 263-270.

Andrykowski, M. A., & Jacobsen, P. B. (1993). Anticipatory nausea and vomiting with cancer chemotherapy. In W. Breitbart & J. Holland (Eds.), *Psychiatric aspects of symptom management in cancer patients* (pp. 107-128). Washington, DC: American Psychiatric Press.

Arnot, B. (1998). *The breast cancer prevention diet.* Boston: Little, Brown.

Arnot, R. (1992). *The best medicine: How to choose the top doctors, the top hospitals, and the top treatments.* Reading, MA: Addison-Wesley.

Ashby, M. A., Kissane, D. W., Beadle, G. F., & Rodger, A. (1996). Psychosocial support, treatment of metastatic disease and palliative care. *Medical Journal of Australia, 164,* 43-49.

Ayres, A., Hoon, P. W., Franzoni, J. B., Matheny, K. B., Cotanch, P. H., & Takayanagi, S. (1994). Influence of mood and adjustment to cancer on compliance with chemotherapy among breast cancer patients. *Journal of Psychosomatic Research, 38,* 393-402.

Baider, L., & Kaplan De-Nour, A. (1984). Couples' reactions and adjustments to mastectomy. *International Journal of Psychiatry in Medicine, 14,* 265-276.

Baider, L., & Kaplan De-Nour, A. (1988). Adjustment to cancer: Who is the patient—the husband or the wife? *Israel Journal of Medical Science, 24,* 631-636.

Baker, K. (1977). Oncology support groups for outpatients. *Hospital Topics, 55,* 40-42.

Baumann, A. O., Deber, R. B., & Thompson, G. G. (1991). Overconfidence among physicians and nurses: The "micro-certainty, macro-uncertainty" phenomenon. *Social Science and Medicine, 32,* 167-174.

Belar, C. D., & Deardoff, W. W. (1995). *Clinical health psychology in medical settings.* Washington, DC: American Psychological Association.

Benson, H., & Stuart, E. M. (1993). *The wellness book: The comprehensive guide to maintaining health and treating stress-related illness.* New York: Fireside.

Bergner, M., Bobbit, R. A., Carter, W. B., & Gibson, B. S. (1981). The Sickness Impact Profile: Development and final revision of a health status measure. *Medical Care, 19,* 787-806.

Bettering the health of minority americans [On-line]. (1996, June). Available: http://www.cmwf.org/progsumm/betminor.html.

Black, W. C., & Fletcher, S. W. (1996). Effects of estrogen on screening mammography: Another complexity. *Journal of the National Cancer Institute, 88,* 627-628.

Bloom, J., & Kessler, L. (1994). Emotional support following cancer: A test of the stigma and social activity hypotheses. *Journal of Health and Social Behavior, 35,* 118-133.

Boyd-Franklin, N. (1989). *Black families in therapy: A multisystems approach.* New York: Guilford Press.

Bradford, J., & Ryan, C. (1988). *The national lesbian health care survey.* Washington, DC: National Lesbian and Gay Health Foundation.

Breast cancer network [On-line]. (1997). Available: http://www.breastcancer.net.

Brownworth, V. A. (1993, March). The other epidemic: Lesbians and breast cancer. *Out,* 60-63.

Burish, T. G., & Lyles, J. N. (1981). Effectiveness of relaxation training in reducing adverse reactions to cancer chemotherapy. *Journal of Behavioral Medicine, 4,* 65-78.

Butler, A. W., Damarin, F. L., Beaulieu, C., Schwebel, A. I., & Thorn, B. E. (1989). Assessing cognitive coping strategies for acute post-surgical pain. *Psychological Assessment, 1,* 41-45.

Cameron, L. D., & Nicholls, G. (1998). Expression of stressful experience through writing: Effects of self-regulation manipulation for pessimists and optimists. *Health Psychology, 17*(1), 84-92.

Carter, R. E., Carter, C. A., & Salunias, M. (1993). Marital adaptation and interaction of couples after a mastectomy. *Journal of Psychosocial Oncology, 11*(2), 69-82.

Carver, C. S., Pozo, C., Harris, S. D., Noriega, V., Scheier, M. F., Robinson, D. S., Ketcham, A. S., Moffat, F. L., & Clark, K. C. (1993). How coping mediates the effect of optimism on distress: A study of women with early stage breast cancer. *Journal of Personality and Social Psychology, 65,* 375-390.

Cawley, M., Kostic, J., & Cappello, C. (1990). Informational and psychosocial needs of women choosing conservative surgery/primary radiation for early stage breast cancer. *Cancer Nursing, 13,* 90-94.

Cella, D. F., Mahon, S. M., & Donovan, M. I. (1990). Cancer recurrence as a traumatic event. *Behavioral Medicine, 16*(1), 15-22.

Chekryn, D. (1984). Cancer recurrence: Personal meaning, communication, and marital adjustment. *Cancer Nursing, 7,* 491-498.

Cimprich, B. (1999). Pretreatment symptom distress in women newly diagnosed with breast cancer. *Cancer Nursing, 22,* 185-194.

Clay, R. A. (1996). *Should patients be told of their risk for cancer?* [On-line]. Available: www.apa.org/monitor/sep96/prevent.html.

Coates, R., Bransfield, D., Wesley, M., Hankey, B., Eley, J., Greenber, R., Flanders, D., Hunter, C., Edwards, B., Forman, M., Chen, V., Reynolds, P., Boyd, P., Austin, D., Muss, H., & Blacklow, R. (1992). Differences between black and white women with breast cancer in time from symptom recognition to medical consultation. *Journal of the National Cancer Institute, 84,* 938-950.

Colditz, G. A. (1990). A prospective assessment of moderate alcohol intake and major chronic diseases. *Annals of Epidemiology, 1,* 167-177.

Collaborative Group on Hormonal Factors in Breast Cancer (1996). Breast cancer and hormonal contraceptives: Collaborative reanalysis of individual data on 53,297 women with breast cancer and 100,239 women without breast cancer from 54 epidemiological studies. *Lancet, 347,* 1713-1727.

Compas, B. E., Worsham, N. L., Epping-Jordan, J. E., Grant, K. E., Mireault, G., Howell, D. C., & Malcarne, V. L. (1994). When mom or dad has cancer: Markers of psychological distress in cancer patients, spouses, and children. *Health Psychology, 13,* 507-515.

Corey, G. (1996). *Theory and practice of counseling and psychotherapy: An overview.* Pacific Grove, CA: Brooks/Cole.

Corrall, C. J., & Mustoe, T. A. (1996). Controversy in breast reconstruction. *Surgical Clinics of North America, 76,* 309-326.

Crown, J. (1998). Evolution in the treatment of advanced breast cancer: A prodigy comes of age. *Cancer Investigation, 17,* 121-136.

Cummings, S. R., Eckert, S., Krueger, K. A., Grady, D., Powles, T. J., Cauley, J. A., Norton, L., Nickelsen, T., Bjarnason, N. H., Morrow, M., Lippman, M. E., Black, D., Glusman, J. E., Costa, A., & Jordan, V. C. (1999). The effect of raloxifene on risk of breast cancer in postmenopausal women: Results from the MORE randomized trial. *Journal of the American Medical Association, 281,* 2189-2197.

Dallek, G. (1996). *Learning the lessons of Medicaid managed care* [On-line]. Available: http:/www.familiesusa.org/medaid.html.

Dean, C. (1988). The emotional impact of mastectomy. *British Journal of Hospital Medicine, 39,* 30-32, 36, 38-39.

DeAngelis, T. (1995, January). Research on breast cancer views: Psychosocial factors. *APA Monitor, 26,* p. 37.

De Valle, M. N., & Norman, P. (1992). Causal attributions, health locus of control beliefs and lifestyle changes among pre-operative coronary patients. *Psychology and Health, 7,* 201-211.

Derogatis, L. R., & Lopez, M. (1983). *Psychosocial Adjustment to Illness Scale (PAIS and PAIS-R) scoring, procedures and administration manual.* Baltimore: Clinical Psychometric Research.

Devlen, J., Maguire, P., Phillips, P., & Crowther, D. (1987). Psychological problems associated with diagnosis and treatment of lymphomas. *British Medical Journal/Clinical Research Edition, 295*(6604), 955-957.

Dickens, B. M., Pei, N., & Taylor, K. M. (1996). Legal and ethical issues in genetic testing and counselling for susceptibility to breast, ovarian and colon cancer. *Canadian Medical Association Journal, 154,* 813-818.

Diefenbach, M. A., Miller, S. M., & Daly, M. B. (1999). Specific worry about breast cancer predicts mammography use in women at risk for breast and ovarian cancer. *Health Psychology, 18,* 532-536.

Doka, K. J. (1997). When illness is prolonged: Implications for grief. In K. J. Doka & J. Davidson (Eds.), *Living with grief when illness is prolonged.* Bristol, PA: Taylor & Francis.

Downer, S. M., Cody, M. M., McCluskey, P., Wilson, P. D., Arnott, S. J., Lister, T. A., & Slevin, M. L. (1994). Pursuit and practice of complementary therapies by cancer patients receiving conventional treatment. *British Medical Journal/ Clinical Research Edition, 309*(6947), 86-89.

Dunkel-Schetter, C. (1984). Social support in cancer: Findings based on patient interviews and their implications. *Journal of Social Issues, 40*(4), 77-98.

Dura, E., & Ibanez, E. (1991). The psychosocial effects of an information program involving Spanish breast cancer patients. *Journal of Psychosocial Oncology, 9*(2), 45-65.

Egan, K. M., Newcomb, P. A., Longnecker, M. P., Trentham-Dietz, A., Baron, J. A., Trichopoulos, D., Stampfer, M. J., & Willett, W. C. (1996). Jewish religion and risk of breast cancer. *Lancet, 347,* 1645-1646.

Ell, K. O., Nishimoto, R. H., Mantell, J. E., & Hamovitch, M. B. (1988). Psychological adaptation to cancer: A comparison among patients, spouses, and non-spouses. *Family Systems Medicine, 6,* 335-348.

Epping-Jordan, J., Compas, B., & Howell, D. (1994). Psychological predictors of cancer progression. *Health Psychology, 13,* 539-547.

Faden, R. R., Becker, C., Lewis, C., Freeman, J., & Faden, A. I. (1981). Disclosure of information to patients in medical care. *Medical Care, 19,* 718-733.

Fallowfield, L. J. (1990). Psychosocial adjustment after treatment for early breast cancer. *Oncology, 4,* 89-96.

Fallowfied, L. J., Hall, A., Maguire, G. P., & Barum, M. (1990). Psychosocial outcomes of different treatment policies in women with early breast cancer outside a clinical trial. *British Medical Journal, 301,* 575.

FamiliesUSA Foundation. (1997). *Despite industry losses for 1997 average compensation of top HMO execs tops $2 million: Industry hypocritically wages advertising campaign about lawyers profiting from consumers and costs of protections* [On-line]. Available: familiesusa.org/97rel.htm.

Fawzy, F. I., Fawzy, N. W., Hyun, C. S., Elashoff, R., Guthrie, D., Fahey, J. L., & Morton, D. L. (1993). Malignant melanoma: Effects of an early structured psychiatric intervention, coping, and affective state on recurrences and survival 6 years later. *Archives of General Psychiatry, 50,* 681-689.

Fawzy, F., Kemeny, M., Fawzy, N., Elashoff, R., Morton, D., Cousins, N., & Fahey, J. (1990). A structured psychiatric intervention for cancer patients: II. Changes over time in immunological measures. *Archives of General Psychiatry, 47,* 729-735.

Ferlic M., Goldman, A., & Kennedy, B. J. (1979). Group counseling in adult patients with advanced cancer. *Cancer, 43,* 760-766.

Fisher, B., Brown, A., Mamounas, E., Wieand, S., Robidoux, A., Margolese, R. G., Cruz, A. B., Jr., Fisher, E. R., Wickerham, D. L., Wolmark, N., DeCillis, A., Hoehn, J. L., Lees, A. W., & Dimitrov, N. V. (1997). Effect of preoperative chemotherapy on local-regional disease in women with operable breast cancer: Findings from National Surgical Adjuvant Breast and Bowel Project B-18. *Journal of Clinical Oncology, 15,* 2483-2493.

Forte, D. A. (1995). Community-based breast cancer intervention program for older African American women in beauty salons. *Public Health Reports, 110,* 179-218.

Fox, S. S., & Stein, J. A. (1991). The effect of physician-patient communication on mammography utilization by different ethnic groups. *Medical Care, 29,* 1065-1082.

Franchelli, S., Leone, M. S., Berrino, P., Passarelli, B., Capelli, M., Baracco, G., Alberisio, A., Morasso, G., & Santi, P. L. (1995). Psychological evaluation of patients undergoing breast reconstruction using two different methods: Autologous tissues versus prostheses. *Plastic and Reconstructive Surgery, 95,* 1213-1218.

Frankl, V. (1963). *Man's search for meaning.* New York: Washington Square Press.

Freeman, H. P., & Wasfie, T. J. (1989). Cancer of the breast in poor black women. *Cancer, 64,* 324-334.

Freudenheim, M. (1996, April 2). Health care in the era of capitalism. *New York Times* "Week in Review," Column 4.

Fulton, J. P., Rakowski, W., & Jones, A. C. (1995). Determinants of breast cancer screening among inner-city Hispanic women in comparison with other inner-city women. *Public Health Reports, 110,* 476-482.

Ganz, P. A., Polinsky, M. L., Schag, C. C., & Heinrich, R. L. (1989). Rehabilitation of patients with primary breast cancer: Assessing the impact of adjuvant therapy. *Recent Results in Cancer Research, 115,* 244-254.

Garro, L. C. (1990). Culture, pain and cancer. *Journal of Palliative Care, 6*(3), 34-44.

Gattuso, S. M., Litt, M. D., & Fitzgerald, T. E. (1992). Coping with gastrointestinal endoscopy: Self-efficacy enhancement and coping style. *Journal of Consulting and Clinical Psychology, 60,* 133-139.

Gaus, C. R., & DeLeon, P. H. (1995). Thinking beyond the limitations of mental health care. *Professional Psychology: Research and Practice, 26,* 339-340.

Gibbs, H. W., & Achterberg-Lawlis, J. (1978). Spiritual values and death anxiety: Implications for counseling with terminal cancer patients. *Journal of Counseling Psychology, 25,* 563-569.

Gilligan, C. (1982). *In a different voice: Psychological theory and women's development.* Cambridge, MA: Harvard University Press.

Gillum, R. F. (1987). Overweight and obesity in black women: A review of published data from the National Center for Health. *Journal of the National Medical Association, 79,* 865-871.

Given, B., & Given, C. W. (1992). Patient and family caregiver reaction to new and recurrent breast cancer. *Journal of the American Medical Women's Association, 47,* 201-206.

Given, C. W., Stommel, M., Given, B., Osuch, J., Kurtz, M. E., & Kurtz, J. C. (1993). The influence of cancer patients' symptoms and functional status on patients' depression and family caregivers' reactions and depression. *Health Psychology, 12,* 277-285.

Glanz, K., & Lerman, C. (1992). Psychosocial impact of breast cancer: A critical review. *Annals of Behavioral Medicine, 14,* 204-212.

Glinder, J. G., & Compas, B. E. (1999). Self-blame attributions in women with newly diagnosed breast cancer: A prospective study of psychological adjustment. *Health Psychology, 18,* 475-481.

Golden, W. L., Gersh, W. D., & Robbins, D. M. (1992). *Psychological treatment of cancer patients: A cognitive-behavioral approach.* Boston: Allyn & Bacon.

Goldfried, M. R., & Davison, G. C. (1976). *Clinical behavior therapy.* New York: Holt, Rinehart & Winston.

Gotay, C. (1984). The experience of cancer during early and advanced stages: The view of patients and their mates. *Social Science and Medicine, 18,* 605-613.

Gottman, J. M., & Levenson, R. (1992). Marital processes predictive of later dissolution: Behavior, physiology, and health. *Journal of Personality and Social Psychology, 63,* 221-233.

Gradishar, W. J. (1999). High-dose chemotherapy and breast cancer. *Journal of the American Medical Association, 282,* 1378-1380.

Greene, P. G., Seime, R. J., & Smith, M. E. (1985). Distraction and relaxation training in the treatment of anticipatory nausea and vomiting: A single subject intervention. *Journal of Behavior Therapy and Experimental Psychiatry, 22,* 285-290.

Greening, K. (1992). The "Bear Essentials" program: Helping young children and their families cope when a parent has cancer. *Journal of Psychosocial Oncology, 10*(1), 47-61.

Greer, S. (1991). Psychological response to cancer and survival. *Psychological Medicine, 21*, 43-49.

Grieger, I., & Ponterotto, J. G. (1995). A framework for assessment in multicultural counseling. In J. G. Ponterotto, J. M. Casas, L. A. Suzuki, & C. M. Alexander (Eds.), *Handbook of multicultural counseling* (pp. 357-374). Thousand Oaks, CA: Sage.

Guidry, J. J., Aday, L. A., Zhang, D., & Winn, R. J. (1998). Information sources and barriers to cancer treatment by racial/ethnic minority status of patients. *Journal of Cancer Education, 13*(1), 43-48.

Haber, S., Ayers, L., Goodheart, C., Lubin, L. B., Siegel, M., Acuff, C., Freeman, E. L., Kieffer, C. C., Mikesell, S. G., & Wainrib, B. R. (1995). *Breast cancer: A psychological treatment manual.* New York: Springer.

Hack, T. F., Degner, L. F., & Dyck, D. G. (1994). Relationship between decisional control and illness information among women with breast cancer: A quantitative and qualitative analysis. *Social Science and Medicine, 39*, 279-289.

Hagopian, G. A. (1993). Cognitive strategies used in adapting to a cancer diagnosis. *Oncology Nursing Forum, 20*, 759-763.

Halbreich, U., Shen, J., & Panaro, V. (1996). Are chronic psychiatric patients at increased risk of developing breast cancer? *American Journal of Psychiatry, 153*, 559-560.

Hart, K. (1986-1987). Stress encountered by significant others of cancer patients receiving psychotherapy. *Omega Journal of Death and Dying, 17*, 151-169.

Harvard Medical School. (1998, June). *Harvard Women's Health Watch, 5*(10), 1, 3, 5, 7.

Heim, E., Augustiny, K. F., Schaffner, L., & Valach, L. (1993). Coping with breast cancer over time and situation. *Journal of Psychosomatic Research, 37*, 523-542.

Heinrich, R. L., & Schag, C. C. (1985). Stress and activity management: Group treatment for cancer patients and spouses. *Journal of Consulting and Clinical Psychology, 53*, 439-446.

Hinds, C. (1985). The needs of families who care for patients with cancer at home: Are we meeting them? *Journal of Advanced Nursing, 10*, 575-581.

Holland, J. C., & Rowland, J. H. (1987). Psychological reactions to breast cancer and its treatment. In J. R. Harris, S. Hellman, I. C. Henderson, & D. W. Kinne (Eds.), *Breast diseases* (pp. 632-647). Philadelphia: J. B. Lippincott.

Holmes, M. D., Hunter, D. J., Colditz, G. A., Stampfer, M. J., Hankinson, S. E., Speizer, F. E., Rosner, B., & Willett, W. C. (1999). Association of dietary intake of fat and fatty acids with risk of breast cancer. *Journal of the American Medical Association, 281*, 914-920.

Hortobagyi, G. N. (1998). Drug therapy: Treatment of breast cancer. *New England Journal of Medicine, 339*, 974-984.

House, J. (1981). *Work, stress, and social support.* Reading, MA: Addison-Wesley.

Huang, Z., Hankinson, S. E., Colditz, G. A., Stampfer, M. J., Hunter, D. J., Manson, J. E., Hennekens, C. H., Rosner, B., Speizer, F. E., & Willett, W. C. (1997). Dual effects of weight and weight gain on breast cancer risk. *Journal of the American Medical Association, 278*, 1407-1411.

Hughes, J. (1981). Emotional reactions to the diagnosis and treatment of early breast cancer. *Journal of Psychosomatic Research, 26*, 277-283.

Hughes, J. E. (1987). Psychological and social consequences of cancer. *Cancer Surveys, 6,* 455-475.

Jacobsen, P. B., & Butler, R. W. (1996). Relation of cognitive coping and catastrophizing to acute pain and analgesic use following breast cancer surgery. *Journal of Behavioral Medicine, 19,* 17-29.

Johnson, L. S. (1997). Developmental strategies for counseling the child whose parent or sibling has cancer. *Journal of Counseling and Development, 75,* 417-427.

Johnson, S. C., & Spilka, B. (1991). Coping with breast cancer: The roles of clergy and faith. *Journal of Religion and Health, 30,* 21-33.

Joyce, J. (1998). *Travails with HMO* [On-line]. Available: http://www.wellweb.com/ BREAST/JanetJoy.htm.

Jozwik, M., Rouanet, P., Sobierajski, J., & Pujol, H. (1995). Immediate breast reconstruction revisited. *Annales Chirurgiae-et-Gynaecologiae, 84,* 11-16.

Kagan, A. R., Levitt, P. M., Arnold, T. M., & Hattem, J. (1984). Honesty is the best policy: A radiation therapist's perspective on caring for terminal cancer patients. *American Journal of Clinical Oncology, 7,* 381-383.

Kahane, D. H. (1990). *No less a woman.* New York: Prentice Hall.

Kaplan, H. S. (1992). A neglected issue: The sexual side effects of current treatments for breast cancer. *Journal of Sex and Marital Therapy, 18,* 3-19.

Kaplan, K. M., Weinberg, G. B., Small, A., & Herndon, J. L. (1991). Breast cancer screening among relatives of women with breast cancer. *American Journal of Public Health, 8,* 1174-1179.

Kash, K., Holland, J., Halper, M., & Miller, D. (1992). Psychological distress and surveillance behaviors of women with a family history of breast cancer. *Journal of the National Cancer Institute, 84,* 24-30.

Kass, S. (1999, October). Breast-cancer intervention group aids physical healing, research finds. *APA Monitor* [On-line], *30*(9). Available: http://www.apa.org/monitor/oct99/ nb4.html.

Katzenstein, L. (1994, September). Smoking and breast cancer. *American Health, 13*(7), 13-14.

Kaye, J. M., Lawton, M. P., Gitlin, L. N., Kleban, M. H., Windsor, L. A., & Kaye, D. (1988). Older people's performance on the Pofile of Mood States (POMS). *Clinical Gerontologist, 7*(3/4), 35-56.

Keitel, M., Zevon, M., Rounds, J., Petrelli, N., & Karakousis, C. (1990). Spouse adjustment to cancer surgery: Distress and coping responses. *Journal of Surgical Oncology, 43,* 148-153.

Keitel, M. A., Zevon, M., Rounds, J., & Schroder, M. (1990, August). *Coping, distress, and marital satisfaction: Cancer surgery patients and their spouses.* Poster session presented at the annual meeting of the American Psychological Association, Boston, MA.

Kiebert, G. M., de Haes, J. C. J. M., & van de Velde, C. J. H. (1991). The impact of breast-conserving treatment and mastectomy on the quality-of-life of early-stage breast cancer patients: A review. *Journal of Clinical Oncology, 9,* 1059-1070.

Kiecolt-Glaser, J., Glaser, R., Dyer, C., Shuttleworth, E., Ogrocki, P., & Speicher, C. (1987). Chronic stress and immunity in family caregivers of Alzheimer's disease victims. *Psychosomatic Medicine, 49,* 523-535.

Kolata, G. (1997, June 22). Women want control, just not all of the time. *New York Times,* Section 14, "Women's Desk," p. 3.

Krieger, N. (1990). Social class and the black/white crossover in the age-specific incidence of breast cancer: A study linking census-derived data to population-based registry records. *American Journal of Epidemiology, 131,* 804-814.

Kushner, H. S. (1981). *When bad things happen to good people.* New York: Avon.

Lair, G. S. (1996). *Counseling the terminally ill: Sharing the journey.* Washington, DC: Taylor & Francis.

Lake-Lewin, D., Kunzweiler, J., & Kunick, J. (1990). Variations of immune parameters and breast tumor biology in minority patients with cancer. *Proceedings of the 81st Annual Meeting of the American Association of Cancer Research, 30,* A1264.

Lange, D. (1997, June 22). Making sense of breast cancer treatments. *New York Times,* Section 14, "Women's Desk," p. 13.

Larson, D. G. (1993). *The helper's journey: Working with people facing grief, loss, and life-threatening illness.* Champaign, IL: Research Press.

Lauver, D. (1994). Care-seeking behavior with breast cancer symptoms in Caucasian and African-American women. *Research in Nursing and Health, 17,* 421-431.

Lauver, D., & Ho, C. (1993). Explaining delay in care seeking for breast cancer symptoms. *Journal of Applied Social Psychology, 23,* 1806-1825.

Laya, M. B., Larsen, E. B., Taplin, S. H., & White, E. (1996). Effect of estrogen replacement therapy on the specificity and sensitivity of screening mammography. *Journal of the National Cancer Institute, 88,* 643-649.

Lazarus, A. A. (1989). *The practice of multimodal therapy.* Baltimore: Johns Hopkins University Press.

Lazarus, R. S., & Folkman, S. (1984). *Stress, appraisal, and coping.* New York: Springer.

Lerman, C., & Croyle, R. T. (1996). Emotional and behavioral responses to genetic testing for susceptibility to cancer. *Oncology, 10,* 191-199.

Lerman, C., Daly, M., Miller, S., Sands, C., Balshem, A., Lustbader, E., Heggan, T., Goldstein, L., James, J., & Engstrom, P. (1993). Mammography adherence and psychological distress among women at risk for breast cancer. *Journal of the National Cancer Institute, 85,* 1074-1080.

Lerman, C., Lustbader, E., Rimer, B., Daly, M., Miller, S., Sands, C., & Balshem, A. (1995). Effects of individualized breast cancer risk counseling: A randomized trial. *Journal of the National Cancer Institute, 87,* 286-292.

Lerman, C., Schwartz, M., Miller, S., Daly, M., Sands, C., & Rimer, B. (1996). A randomized trial of breast cancer risk counseling: Interactive effects of counseling, educational level, and coping style. *Health Psychology, 15,* 75-83.

Lichtman, R. R. (1982). *Close relationships after breast cancer.* Unpublished doctoral dissertation, University of California, Los Angeles.

Lichtman, R. R., & Taylor, S. E. (1986). Close relationships and the female cancer patient. In B. L. Anderson (Ed.), *Women with cancer: Psychological perspectives.* (pp. 233-256). New York: Springer.

Lichtman, R. R., Taylor, S. E., & Woods, J. (1987). Social support and marital adjustment after breast cancer. *Journal of Psychosocial Oncology, 5*(3), 47-74.

Long, E. (1993). Breast cancer in African-American women: Review of the literature. *Cancer Nursing, 16,* 124.

Lopez, M. J., & Porter, K. A. (1996). The current role of prophylactic mastectomy. *Surgical Clinics of North America, 76,* 231-242.

Love, S. M. (1995). *Dr. Susan Love's breast book.* New York: Addison-Wesley.

Lowery, B., Jacobsen, B., & DuCette, J. (1993). Causal attribution, control, and adjustment to breast cancer. *Journal of Psychosocial Oncology, 10*(4), 37-53.

Lucas, V. A. (1992). An investigation of the health care preferences of the lesbian population. *Health Care for Women International, 13,* 221-228.

Lyles, J. N., Burish, T. G., Krozely, M. G., & Oldham, R. K. (1982). Efficacy of relaxation training and guided imagery in reducing the aversiveness of cancer chemotherapy. *Journal of Consulting and Clinical Psychology, 50,* 509-521.

Maguire, P. M. (1989). Breast conservation versus mastectomy: Psychological considerations. *Seminars in Surgical Oncology, 5,* 137-144.

Marwill, S. L., Freund, K. M., & Barry, P. B. (1996). Patient factors associated with breast cancer screening among older women. *Journal of the American Geriatrics Society, 44,* 1210-1214.

Mathews, H. F., Lannin, D. R., & Mitchell, J. P. (1994). Coming to terms with advanced breast cancer: Black women's narratives from Eastern North Carolina. *Social Science and Medicine, 38,* 789-800.

McCaul, K. D., Branstetter, A. D., Schroeder, D. M., & Glasgow, R. E. (1996). What is the relationship between breast cancer risk and mammography screening? A meta-analytic review. *Health Psychology, 15,* 423-429.

McCaul, K. D., Schroeder, D. M., & Reid, P. A. (1996). Breast cancer worry and screening: Some prospective data. *Health Psychology, 15,* 430-433.

McKenna, M. C., Zevon, M. A., Corn, B., & Rounds, J. (1999). Psychosocial factors and the development of breast cancer: A meta-analysis. *Health Psychology, 18,* 520-531.

McPhail, G. (1999). Menopause as an issue for women with breast cancer. *Cancer Nursing, 22,* 164-171.

Melzack, R. (1987). The Short-Form McGill Pain Questionnaire. *Pain, 30,* 191-197.

Meyerowitz, B. E. (1980). Psychosocial correlates of breast cancer and its treatments. *Psychological Bulletin, 87,* 108-131.

Mickley, J. R., Soeken, K., & Belcher, A. (1992). Spiritual well-being, religiousness, and hope among women with breast cancer. *Journal of Nursing Scholarship, 24,* 267-272.

Millar, M. G., & Millar, K. U. (1992). Feelings and beliefs about breast cancer and breast self examination among women in three age groups. *Family and Community Health, 15*(3), 30-37.

Miller, K. D., & Sledge, G. W., Jr. (1999). Taxanes in the treatment of breast cancer. *Seminars in Oncology, 25*(5, Suppl. 12), 12-17.

Monson, M. A., & Harwood, K. V. (1998). Helping women select primary breast cancer treatment. *American Journal of Nursing* (Suppl.), 3-7.

Morris, J., & Ingham, R. (1988). Choice of surgery for early breast cancer: Psychosocial considerations. *Social Science and Medicine, 27,* 1257-1262.

Morris, J., & Royle, G. T. (1988). Offering patients a choice of surgery for early breast cancer: A reduction in anxiety and depression in patients and their husbands. *Social Science and Medicine, 26,* 583-585.

Morrison, C. (1996). Determining crucial correlates of breast self examination in older women with low incomes. *Oncology Nursing Forum, 23,* 83-93.

Morrow, G. R. (1986). Effect of the cognitive hierarchy in the systematic desensitization treatment of anticipatory nausea in cancer patients: A component comparison with relaxation only, counseling, and no treatment. *Cognitive Therapy and Research, 10,* 421-446.

Morrow, G. R., & Dobkin, P. L. (1988). Anticipatory nausea and vomiting in cancer patients undergoing chemotherapy treatment: Prevalence etiology and behavioral interventions. *Clinical Psychology Review, 8,* 517-556.

Morrow, G. R., & Morrell, C. (1982). Behavioral treatment for the anticipatory nausea and vomiting induced by cancer chemotherapy. *New England Journal of Medicine, 307,* 1476-1480.

Mouton, C. P., Harris, S., Rovi, S., Solorzano, P., & Johnson, M. S. (1997). Barriers to black women's participation in cancer clinical trials. *Journal of the National Medical Association, 89,* 721-727.

Moyer, A. (1997). Psychosocial outcomes of breast-conserving surgery versus mastectomy: A meta-analytic review. *Health Psychology, 16,* 284-298.

Munkes, A., Oberst, M., & Hughes, S. (1992). Appraisal of illness, symptom distress, and mood states in patients receiving chemotherapy for initial and recurrent disease. *Oncology Nursing Forum, 19,* 1201-1209.

Muschel, I. J. (1984, October). Pet therapy with terminal cancer patients. *Social Casework, 65,* 451-458.

National Institutes of Health, National Cancer Institute. (1996). *Understanding breast changes: A health guide for all women.* (NIH Publication No. 96-3536). Bethesda, MD: Author.

Nelson, D. V., Friedman, L. C., Baer, P. E., Lane, M., & Smith, F. E. (1994). Attitude to cancer: Psychometric properties of fighting spirit and denial. *Journal of Behavioral Medicine, 12,* 341-355.

Nezu, A. M., Nezu, C., & Houts, P. S. (1999). *Helping cancer patients cope: A problem solving approach.* Washington, DC: American Psychological Association.

Northouse, L. L. (1988). Social support in patients' and husbands' adjustment to breast cancer. *Nursing Research, 37,* 91-95.

Northouse, L. L. (1989). A longitudinal study of the adjustment of patients and husbands to breast cancer. *Oncology Nursing Forum, 16,* 511-516.

Northouse, L. L., Dorris, G., & Charron-Moore, C. (1995). Factors affecting couples' adjustment to recurrent breast cancer. *Social Science and Medicine, 41,* 69-76.

Northouse, L., & Swain, M. (1987). Adjustment of patients and husbands to the initial breast cancer. *Nursing Research, 36,* 221-225.

Oberst, M. T., & James, R. H. (1985). Going home: Patient and spouse adjustment following cancer surgery. *Topics in Clinical Nursing, 7,* 46-57.

Offit, K., Gilewski, T., McGuire, P., Schluger, A., Hampel, H., Brown, K., Swensen, J., Neuhausen, S., Skolnick, M., Norton, L., & Goldgar, D. (1996). Germline BRCA1 185delAG mutations in Jewish women with breast cancer. *Lancet, 347,* 1643-1645.

Oktay, J. S., & Walter, C. A. (1991). *Breast cancer in the life course: Women's experiences.* New York: Springer.

Okun, B. (1996). *Understanding diverse families.* New York: Guilford Press.

Owens, R. G., Ashcroft, J. J., Leinster, S. J., & Slade, P. D. (1987). Informal decision analysis with breast cancer patients: An aid to psychological preparation for surgery. *Journal of Psychosocial Oncology, 5*(2), 23-33.

Paniagua, F. A. (1994). *Assessing and treating culturally diverse clients.* Thousand Oaks, CA: Sage.

Pargament, K. I., (1997). *The psychology of religion and coping.* New York: Guilford Press.

Parker, D. F., Levinson, W., Mullooly, J. P., & Frymark, S. L. (1989). Using the quality of life index in a cancer rehabilitation program. *Journal of Psychosocial Oncology, 7*(3), 47-62.

Pattison, E. M. (1977). *The experience of dying.* Englewood Cliffs, NJ: Prentice Hall.

Pattison, E. M. (1978). The living-dying process. In C. A. Garfield (Ed.), *Psychosocial care of the dying patient.* New York: McGraw-Hill.

Payne, D. K., Sullivan, M. D., & Massie, M. J. (1996). Women's psychological reactions to breast cancer. *Seminars in Oncology, 23*(1, Suppl. 2), 89-97.

Penman, D. T., Bloom, J. R., Fotopoulos, S., Cook, M. R., Holland, J. C., Gates, C., Flamer, D., Murawski, B., Ross, R., Brandt, U., Muenz, L. R., & Pee, D. (1987). The impact of mastectomy on self-concept and social function: A combined cross-section and longitudinal study with comparison groups. In S. D. Stellman (Ed.), *Women and cancer* (pp. 101-130). New York: Haworth.

Pennebaker, J. W. (Ed.). (1995). *Emotion, disclosure, and health.* Washington, DC: American Psychological Association.

Perez, D. J., Allan, S. G., Humm, G. P., & Wynne, C. J. (1995). The information needs of patients with breast cancer. *Australian and New Zealand Journal of Medicine, 25,* 521-522.

Peters-Golden, H. (1982). Breast cancer: Varied perception of social support in the illness experience. *Social Science and Medicine, 16,* 483-491.

Peterson, K., & Bricker-Jenkins, M. (1996). Lesbians and the health care system. In J. K. Peterson (Ed.), *Health care for lesbians and gay men: Confronting homophobia and heterosexism* (pp. 33-47). New York: Harrington Park Press/Haworth Press.

Pierce, P. F. (1993). Deciding on breast cancer treatment: A description of decision behavior. *Nursing Research, 42,* 22-28.

Pfefferbaum, B., Pasnau, R. O., Jamison, K., & Wellisch, D. K. (1977-78). A comprehensive program of psychological care for mastectomy patients. *International Jounral of Psychiatry in Medicine, 8,* 63-72.

Polinsky, M. L. (1990). *Breast cancer survivorship: A study of Reach to Recovery volunteers in Southern California.* Unpublished doctoral dissertation, University of Southern California, Los Angeles.

Ptacek, J. T., Ptacek, J. G., & Dodge, K. L. (1994). Coping with breast cancer from the perspectives of husbands and wives. *Journal of Psychosocial Oncology, 12*(3), 47-72.

Rando, T. A. (1984). *Grief, dying and death: Clinical interventions for caregivers.* Champaign, IL: Research Press.

Ravdin, P. M. (1999). Emerging role of docetaxel (Taxotere) in the adjuvant therapy of breast cancer. *Seminars in Oncology, 26*(3, Suppl. 9), 20-30.

Reaby, L. L., & Hort, L. K. (1995). Postmastectomy attitudes in women who wear external breast prostheses compared to those who have undergone breast reconstructions. *Journal of Behavioral Medicine, 18,* 55-67.

Rebbeck, T. R., Levin, A. M., Eisen, A., Synder, C., Watson, P., Cannon-Albright, L., Isaacs, C., Olofunmilayo, O., Neuhausen, S. L., Lynch, H. T., & Weber, B. L. (1999). Breast cancer risk after bilateral prophylactic oophorectomy in BRCA1 mutation carriers. *Journal of the National Cancer Institute, 91,* 1475-1479.

Redd, W. H., Andersen, G. V., & Minagawa, R. Y. (1982). Hypnotic control of anticipatory emesis in patients receiving cancer chemotherapy. *Journal of Consulting and Clinical Psychology, 50,* 14-19.

Redd, W. H., Jacobsen, P. B., Die-Trill, M., Dermatis, H., McEvoy, M., & Holland, J. C. (1987). Cognitive/attentional distraction in the control of conditioned nausea in pediatric cancer patients receiving chemotherapy. *Journal of Consulting and Clinical Psychology, 55,* 391-395.

Rimer, B. K., Keintz, M. K., Kessler, H. B., Engstrom, P. F., & Rosan, J. R. (1989). Why women resist screening mammography: Patient-related barriers. *Radiology, 172,* 243-246.

Roberts, C. S., Elkins, N. W., Baile, W. F., Jr., & Cox, C. E. (1989). Integrating research with practice: The psychosocial impact of breast cancer. *Health and Social Work, 14,* 261-268.

Roberts, F. D., Newcomb, P. A., Trentham-Dietz, A., & Storer, B. E. (1996). Self-reported stress and breast cancer. *Cancer, 77,* 1089-1093.

Rolland, J. S. (1994). *Families, illness, and disability: An integrative treatment model.* New York: Basic Books.

Rosenfeld, I. (1996). *Doctor Rosenfeld's guide to alternative medicine.* New York: Random House.

Rothman, A. J., Salovey, P., Turvy, C., & Fishkin, S. A. (1993). Attributions of responsibility and persuasion: Increasing mammography utilization among women over 40 with an internally oriented message. *Health Psychology, 12,* 39-47.

Sabo, D., Brown, J., & Smith, C. (1986). The male role and mastectomy: Support groups and men's adjustment. *Journal of Psychosocial Oncology, 4*(1-2), 19-31.

Sales, E., Schultz, R., & Biegel, D. (1992). Predictors of strain in families of cancer patients: A review of the literature. *Journal of Psychosocial Oncology, 10*(2), 1-26.

Satariano, W. A., Belle, A. G., & Swanson, G. M. (1986). The severity of breast cancer at diagnosis: A comparison of age and extent of disease in black and white women. *American Journal of Public Health, 76,* 779-782.

Schag, C. A. C., Ganz, P. A., Polinsky, M. L., Fred, C., Hirji, K., & Petersen, L. (1993). Characteristics of women at risk for psychosocial distress in the year after breast cancer. *Journal of Clinical Oncology, 11,* 783-793.

Schag, C. A., Heinrich, R. L., Aadland, R. L., & Ganz, P. A. (1990). Assessing problems of cancer patients: Psychometric properties of the Cancer Inventory of Problem Situations. *Health Psychology, 9,* 83-102.

Scheier, M. F., & Carver, C. S. (1985). Optimisim, coping, and health: Assessment and implications of generalized outcome expectancies. *Health Psychology, 4,* 219-247.

Scheier, M. F., & Carver, C. S. (1987). Dispositional optimism and physical well-being: The influence of generalized outcome expectancies on health. *Journal of Personality, 55,* 169-210.

Schwartz, M., Taylor, K., Willard, K., Siegel, J., Lamdan, R., & Moran, K. (1999). Distress, personality, and mammography utilization among women with a family history of breast cancer. *Health Psychology, 18,* 327-332.

Seligman, L. (1996). *Promoting a fighting spirit.* San Francisco: Jossey-Bass.

Shapiro, D. E., Boggs, S. R., Melamed, B. G., & Graham-Pole, J. (1992). The effect of varied physician affect on recall, anxiety, and perceptions in women at risk for breast cancer: An analogue study. *Health Psychology, 11,* 61-66.

Siegel, L. J. (1993). Psychotherapy with medically at-risk children. In T. R. Kratochwill & R. J. Morris (Eds.), *Handbook of psychotherapy with children and adolescents* (pp. 472-501). Boston: Allyn & Bacon.

Silberfarb, P. M., Maurer, H., & Crouthamel, C. (1980). Psychosocial aspects of neoplastic disease: I. Functional status of breast cancer patients during different treatment regimens. *American Journal of Psychiatry, 137,* 450-455.

Simkin, R. J. (1991). Lesbians face unique health care problems. *Canadian Medical Association Journal, 145,* 1620-1623.

Simonton, S., Simonton, O. C., & Creighton, J. L. (1978). *Getting well again.* New York: Bantam Books.

Snow, I. F. (1983). Cross-cultural medicine: Traditional health beliefs and practices among lower class Black Americans. *Western Journal of Medicine, 139,* 820-829.

Solomon, S., Greenberg, J., & Pyszczynski, T. (1991). Terror management theory of self-esteem. In C. R. Snyder & D. R. Forsyth (Eds.), *Handbook of social and clinical psychology: The health perspective* (pp. 21-40). New York: Pergamon.

Spiegel, D. (1985). The use of hypnosis in controlling cancer pain. *Cancer: A Cancer Journal for Clinicians, 35,* 221-231.

Spiegel, D. (1998, August). Supportive-expressive group treatment for women with breast cancer. Paper presented at the Counseling Health Psychology Conference at Stanford, Palo Alto, CA.

Spiegel, D., & Bloom, J. R. (1983). Group therapy and hypnosis reduce metastatic breast carcinoma pain. *Psychosomatic Medicine, 45,* 333-339.

Spiegel, D., Bloom, J., & Gottheil, E. (1983). Family environment as a predictor of adjustment to metastatic breast carcinoma. *Journal of Psychosocial Oncology, 1*(1), 33-44.

Spiegel, D., Bloom, J. R., Kraemer, H. C., & Gottheil, E. (1989). Effect of psychosocial treatment on the survival of patients with metastatic breast cancer. *Lancet, 8668,* 888-891.

Spiegel, D., Bloom, J. R., & Yalom, I. (1981). Group support for patients with metastatic cancer: A randomized prospective outcome study. *Archives of General Psychiatry, 38,* 527-533.

Spiegel, D., & Spira, J. (1991). *Supportive-expressive group therapy: A treatment manual of psychosocial intervention for women with recurrent breast cancer.* Palo Alto, CA: Psychosocial Treatment Laboratory, Stanford University School of Medicine.

Spiegel, D., & Yalom, I. D. (1978). A support group for dying patients. *International Journal of Group Psychotherapy, 28,* 233-245.

Spiegel, H., & Spiegel, D. (1978). *Trance and treatment.* New York: Basic Books.

Stanton, A. L., & Snider, P. R. (1993). Coping with a breast cancer diagnosis: A prospective study. *Health Psychology, 12,* 16-23.

Stefanek, M. E., Helzlsouer, K. J., Wilcox, P. M., & Houn, F. (1995). Predictors of and satisfaction with bilateral prophylactic mastectomy. *Preventive Medicine, 24,* 412-419.

Steginga, S., Occhipinti, S., Wilson, K., & Dunn, J. (1998). Domains of distress: The experience of breast cancer in Australia. *Oncology Nursing Forum, 25,* 1063-1070.

Stevens, P. E., & Hall, J. M. (1988). Stigma, health beliefs and experiences with health care in lesbian women. *Image—The Journal of Nursing Scholarship, 20*(2), 69-73.

Suinn, R. S. (1997). Working with cancer patients. *The Health Psychologist, 18*(4), 6, 17, 22.

Taylor, S., Lichtman, R., & Wood, J. (1984). Attributions, beliefs about control, and adjustment to breast cancer. *Journal of Personality and Social Psychology, 46,* 489-502.

Telch, C. F., & Telch, M. J. (1986). Group coping skills instruction and supportive group therapy for cancer patients: A comparison of strategies. *Journal of Consulting and Clinical Psychology, 54,* 802-808.

Tomoyasu, N., Bovbjerg, D. H., & Jacobsen, P. B. (1996). Conditioned reactions to cancer chemotherapy: Percent reinforcement predicts anticipatory nausea. *Physiology and Behavior, 59,* 273-276.

Trippet, S. E., & Bain, J. (1992). Reasons American lesbians fail to seek traditional health care. *Health Care for Women International, 13,* 145-153.

Turk, D. C., Meichenbaum, D., & Genest, M. (1983). *Pain and behavioral medicine: A cognitive-behavioral perspective.* New York: Guilford.

United States Department of Health and Human Services. (1998, October 29). *HHS NEWS* [On-line]. Available: www.fda.gov/bbs/topics/NEWS/NEW00662.html.

Vess, J. D., Moreland, J. R., Schwebel, A. J., & Kraut, E. (1989). Psychosocial needs of cancer patients: Learning from patients and their spouses. *Journal of Psychosocial Oncology, 6,* 31-51.

Vinokur, A. D., Threatt, B. A., Caplan, R. D., & Zimmerman, B. L. (1989). Physical and psychosocial functioning and adjustment to breast cancer: Long-term follow-up of a screening population. *Cancer, 63,* 394-405.

Vugia, H. D. (1991). Support groups in oncology: Building hope through the human bond. *Journal of Psychosocial Oncology, 9*(3), 89-107.

Wagner, B. M., & Compas, B. E. (1990). Gender, instrumentality, and expressivity: Moderators of the relation between stress and psychological symptoms during adolescence. *American Journal of Community Psychology, 18,* 383-406.

Wallston, K. A., Wallston, B. S., & DeVellis, R. (1978). Develoment of the Multidimensional Health Locus of Control (MHLOC) Scale. *Health Education Monographs, 6,* 160-170.

Ward, S., Leventhal, H., Easterling, D., Luchterhand, C., & Love, R. (1991). Social support, self-esteem, and communication in patients receiving chemotherapy. *Journal of Psychosocial Oncology, 9*(1), 95-116.

Ward, S. E., Viergutz, G., Tormey, D., DeMuth, J., Paulen, A. (1992). Patients' reactions to completion of adjuvant breast cancer therapy. *Nursing Research, 41,* 362-366.

Watson, M., Greer, S., Young, J., Inayat, Q., Burgess, C., & Robertson, B. (1988). Development of a questionnaire measure of adjustment to cancer: The AC scale. *Psychological Medicine, 18,* 203-209.

Waxler-Morrison, N., Hislop, T. G., Mears, B., & Kan, L. (1991). Effects of social relationships on survival for women with breast cancer: A prospective study. *Social Science and Medicine, 33,* 177-183.

Weisman, A. D., & Worden, J. W. (1976). The existential plight in cancer: Significance of the first 100 days. *International Journal of Psychiatry in Medicine, 7,* 1-15.

Wickman, M., Jurell, G., & Sandelin, K. (1995). Immediate breast reconstruction: Short-term experience in 75 consecutive cases. *Scandinavian Journal of Plastic and Reconstructive Surgery and Hand Surgery, 29,* 153-159.

Worden, J. W. (1989). The experience of breast cancer. *CA—A Cancer Journal for Clinicians, 39,* 305-310.

Wortman, C. B., & Dunkel-Schetter, C. (1979). Interpersonal relationships and cancer: A theoretical analysis. *Journal of Social Issues, 35,* 120-155.

Yalom, I. (1985). *The theory and practice of group psychotherapy* (3rd ed.). New York: Basic Books.

Yalom, I., & Greaves, C. (1977). Group therapy with the terminally ill. *American Journal of Psychiatry, 134,* 396-400.

Zahlis, E. H., & Shands, M. E. (1991). Breast cancer: Demands of the illness on the patient's partner. *Journal of Psychosocial Oncology, 9*(1), 75-93.

Zujewski, J., Nelson, A., & Abrams, J. (1998). Much ado about not enough data: High-dose chemotherapy with autologous stem cell rescue for breast cancer. *Journal of the National Cancer Institute, 90,* 200-209.

Index

About the Authors

Merle A. Keitel, Ph.D., is Associate Professor at Fordham University in the Graduate School of Education. She is currently serving as Director of Training of the Counseling Psychology doctoral program and as Coordinator of the Master's and Professional Diploma programs in Counseling and Personnel Services. She has taught counselors- and psychologists-in-training for over 13 years. She has also worked as a clinical and research associate at Roswell Park Memorial Institute in Buffalo, New York, a comprehensive cancer hospital and research center, and in private practice. She has written numerous book chapters and articles and has presented at national conferences primarily in the areas of health psychology, stress and coping, and women's issues.

Mary Kopala, Ph.D., is Associate Professor at Hunter College, City University of New York, in the School of Education. A counseling psychologist, she has taught graduate students in counseling for over 11 years. She has also worked as a clinician in private practice, where her client load consisted primarily of individuals who were confronting health issues. She has written numerous book chapters and articles and has presented at national and regional conferences. She has recently coedited a book on the use of qualitative research methods in psychology.